M000276977

"Fifty years ago Klaus Schwab first proposed his theory that businesses are not only responsible to their shareholders, but also to all their stakeholders. With a global economic system generating deep divisions and inequalities, Klaus renews his call for a form of capitalism that works for everyone and where businesses don't just take from society but truly give back and have a positive impact. *Stakeholder Capitalism* is an urgent call to action."

—Marc Benioff, Chair and CEO, Salesforce

"If you think this is just another pre-COVID/post-COVID book, think again. Klaus Schwab draws on his vast experience to take us on a roller-coaster ride past the highs and lows of post-war capitalism. His knack for economic storytelling gives you a real and deep insight into where we are headed and what we should be aiming for."

—Alexander De Croo, Prime Minister of Belgium

"We can no longer think short term. Companies need to answer to more than their shareholders; they need to be accountable to higher morals. Now, in the middle of the COVID-19 crisis, Klaus Schwab shows us that we cannot go back to business as usual. He inspires us to look at the current response of global solidarity between people, companies, and governments to this health crisis and see it as the unequivocal way to a new paradigm to tackle the climate crisis and the scandal of rising inequality in the world."

—Angélique Kidjo, Musician and UNICEF Goodwill Ambassador

"For a half-century, Klaus Schwab has been consistent in his belief that public companies can drive great returns for their shareholders AND address society's most important priorities. The world now understands that the system he envisioned—what we call Stakeholder Capitalism—can align capital to those outcomes better than any other."

—Brian Moynihan, CEO, Bank of America

"*Stakeholder Capitalism* offers a timely analysis that shows how the neoliberal economic system privileges billionaires and extractive corporations over the dignity of billions of people and the protection of our planet. As COVID-19 has deepened despair and economic, gender and racial inequalities, governments must—with stakeholders—act decisively to depart from shareholder-first capitalism and instead put human rights at the heart of our economy."
—**Gabriela Bucher, Executive Director, Oxfam International**

"Professor Schwab's new book offers us insightful perspectives on the world's economic history and the thinking that has led us towards the greatest challenges we face today – none larger than climate change. More importantly, it offers a blueprint for the future, inviting us to build a more inclusive, prosperous, healthier and greener world by embracing Stakeholder Capitalism at scale."
—**N. Chandrasekaran, Executive Chairman, Tata Sons**

"In *Stakeholder Capitalism* my good friend Professor Schwab outlines an inspiring way forward in making the global economy more equitable, sustainable and future-proof. A vision that fits in perfectly with all his efforts over the years to build a better world. Once again, Professor Schwab gives us food for thought and reflection with this fascinating book."
—**Mark Rutte, Prime Minister of the Netherlands**

STAKEHOLDER
CAPITALISM

STAKEHOLDER CAPITALISM

A GLOBAL ECONOMY THAT WORKS FOR PROGRESS, PEOPLE AND PLANET

KLAUS SCHWAB

with Peter Vanham

WILEY

Copyright © 2021 by World Economic Forum. All rights reserved.

Published by John Wiley & Sons, Inc., Hoboken, New Jersey.

Published simultaneously in Canada.

No part of this publication may be reproduced, stored in a retrieval system, or transmitted in any form or by any means, electronic, mechanical, photocopying, recording, scanning, or otherwise, except as permitted under Section 107 or 108 of the 1976 United States Copyright Act, without either the prior written permission of the Publisher, or authorization through payment of the appropriate per-copy fee to the Copyright Clearance Center, Inc., 222 Rosewood Drive, Danvers, MA 01923, (978) 750-8400, fax (978) 646-8600, or on the Web at www.copyright.com. Requests to the Publisher for permission should be addressed to the Permissions Department, John Wiley & Sons, Inc., 111 River Street, Hoboken, NJ 07030, (201) 748-6011, fax (201) 748-6008, or online at http://www.wiley.com/go/permissions.

Limit of Liability/Disclaimer of Warranty: While the publisher and author have used their best efforts in preparing this book, they make no representations or warranties with respect to the accuracy or completeness of the contents of this book and specifically disclaim any implied warranties of merchantability or fitness for a particular purpose. No warranty may be created or extended by sales representatives or written sales materials. The advice and strategies contained herein may not be suitable for your situation. You should consult with a professional where appropriate. Neither the publisher nor author shall be liable for any loss of profit or any other commercial damages, including but not limited to special, incidental, consequential, or other damages.

If the book title or subtitle includes trademarks/registered trademarks (Microsoft, for example) that require a statement on the copyright page, please add here.

For general information on our other products and services or for technical support, please contact our Customer Care Department within the United States at (800) 762-2974, outside the United States at (317) 572-3993 or fax (317) 572-4002.

Wiley publishes in a variety of print and electronic formats and by print-on-demand. Some material included with standard print versions of this book may not be included in e-books or in print-on-demand. If this book refers to media such as a CD or DVD that is not included in the version you purchased, you may download this material at http://booksupport.wiley.com. For more information about Wiley products, visit www.wiley.com.

Library of Congress Cataloging-in-Publication Data is Available:
ISBN 9781119756132 (Hardcover)
ISBN 9781119756156 (ePDF)
ISBN 9781119756149 (ePub)

COVER ART & DESIGN: PAUL MCCARTHY

10 9 8 7 6 5 4 3 2 1

Printed and bound by CPI Group (UK) Ltd, Croydon, CR0 4YY

*To my parents, Eugen Wilhelm Schwab (†) and Erika Epprecht (†),
who taught me firsthand the value of education, collaboration,
and the stakeholder principle*

Contents

About the Authors

Professor **Klaus Schwab** is the founder and executive chairman of the World Economic Forum. In 1971, he first published *Modern Enterprise Management in Mechanical Engineering*. In the book, he argues that a company must serve not only shareholders but all stakeholders to achieve long-term growth and prosperity. To promote the stakeholder concept, he founded the World Economic Forum the same year.

Since his first publication, Schwab has authored and co-authored various books and reports, including the yearly World Economic Forum *Global Competitiveness Report* (1979–present), *The Fourth Industrial Revolution* (2016), a worldwide best seller translated into 30 languages, *Shaping the Future of the Fourth Industrial Revolution* (2018, with Nicholas Davis), and *COVID-19: The Great Reset* (2020, with Thierry Malleret). Alongside his leadership of the World Economic Forum, Schwab also started the Schwab Foundation for Social Entrepreneurship with his wife, Hilde (1998), The Forum of Young Global Leaders (2006), and the Global Shapers Community (2011).

Professor Schwab holds doctorates and master's degrees in economics (University of Fribourg) and in engineering (Swiss Federal Institute of Technology) and obtained a master's degree in public administration (MPA) from the Kennedy School of Government at Harvard University. In 1972, he became a professor at the University of Geneva, where he is now honorary professor. Throughout his career, Schwab has received 17 honorary doctorates. Schwab was knighted in France (Knight of the *Légion d'Honneur*, 1997), in England (by Queen Elisabeth II, Knight

Commander of the Order of St Michael and St George, 2006), and Germany (Knight Commanders Cross, 2012). He also received the Grand Cordon of the Rising Sun of Japan (2013), among many other national distinctions. He lives in Geneva with his wife, Hilde.

Peter Vanham is the head of Chairman's Communications and the International Media Council at the World Economic Forum. He previously led the Forum's US media relations from New York, and worked as a journalist in Philadelphia, London, Zurich, and Berlin. Vanham is the author of *Before I Was CEO* (2016), recounting the life and career lessons from CEOs before they made it to the top, and has contributed stories on emerging markets and business leadership to *The Financial Times*, *Business Insider*, *Harvard Business Review*, and many other media. He holds master's degrees in business and economics journalism (Columbia University) and commercial engineering (KU Leuven). He lives in Geneva with his wife, Valeria.

Preface

In early February 2020 I sat down in Geneva to discuss this book with a colleague, when the phone rang in my office. It turned out to be what you could call an *AC/BC* moment, when attention shifted from the time *before COVID-19* to the reality that set in *after COVID-19*.

Before that call, me and my colleagues had been preoccupied with the long-term challenges of the world economy, including climate change and inequality. I had reflected in depth on the global economic system built in the 75 years since the end of the Second World War, and the 50 years since the creation of the World Economic Forum. I examined the various elements of our globalized world today, including the benefits, trade-offs, and dangers. Then I considered what changes to the system were needed in the next 50 or 75 years, to make sure it would be more equitable, sustainable, and resilient for future generations.

But in one call, that long-term agenda was upended. My focus moved to the immediate crisis that was about to be faced by all of us, in every country on the planet.

On the other end of the line was the head of our Beijing representative office in China. Usually, these kinds of calls cover routine matters, providing a chance to catch up on established initiatives and programs. But this one was different. The director had called to update me on the epidemic that had hit China hard earlier that winter: COVID-19. Initially confined to the city of Wuhan, this novel coronavirus, which often causes a severe respiratory disease, was rapidly becoming a primary public health concern across the country. Our colleague explained that much of Beijing's population had travelled beyond the city to attend Lunar New Year celebrations and, as they returned, they carried the novel coronavirus with them, causing an outbreak and subsequent lockdown in the capital.

My colleague kept his cool, providing objective facts on what the lockdown meant for our employees and operations. But from his voice, I could tell that he was very worried. His family, and everyone in his life, was affected, facing the dangers of infection and the lockdown in place. The measures taken by authorities were drastic. Employees would be forced to work from home indefinitely, only being allowed to leave their apartments under very strict conditions. If anyone showed symptoms, they'd be tested and quarantined immediately. But even with these draconian measures, it wasn't certain that the health threat would be kept in check. The epidemic was spreading so rapidly that, even as people were locked inside, they were terrified of contracting the virus. Meanwhile, news from the hospitals was that the disease was very aggressive, hard to treat, and overwhelming the health system.

Back in Switzerland, we had known about SARS-CoV-2, the virus that causes COVID-19, since our Annual Meeting in late January 2020. It had been a topic of conversation in public health discussions, among participants from or with major operations in Asia. But until that phone conversation, I had hoped the outbreak would be limited in its duration and geographic spread, similar to how the coronaviruses SARS and MERS had been contained. I hoped it would not personally affect so many of my own colleagues, friends, and family.

During the phone call, my understanding of the global public health threat changed. In the days and weeks following, I halted the work on this book, and the World Economic Forum went into crisis mode. We set up a special task force, asked all employees to work from home, and focused all our efforts on aiding the international emergency response. It was not a moment too soon. A week later, the virus forced a lockdown in much of Europe, and a few weeks after that, much of the world was facing a similar situation, including the United States. In the following months, several million people died or were hospitalized, hundreds of millions of people lost their jobs or income, and countless businesses and governments went physically or virtually bankrupt.

As I write this preface in the fall of 2020, the global state of emergency caused by the first wave of COVID-19 has mostly receded, but a new wave of infections is putting the world once more on high alert. Countries around the world cautiously resumed social and economic life, but the economic recovery is very uneven. China was among the first major countries to end its lockdowns and reopen businesses, and is even expected to see economic growth over the full year 2020.

In Geneva, New York, San Francisco, and Tokyo, our other permanent bases, by contrast, parts of public life have resumed also, but in a much more fragile way. And all around the world, many lives and livelihoods were lost; billions were spent to keep people, businesses, and governments afloat; existing social divisions deepened and new ones emerged.

By now, we have some distance from the initial crisis, and many of us—including myself—have come to realize the pandemic and its effects are deeply linked to problems we had already identified with the existing global economic system. This perspective brought me back to the discussion I had been having in February 2020 on the date of that fateful phone call from Beijing. Many of the analyses we had previously been working on were more true than ever. You will be able to read about them in this book. I will present in what follows my observations on rising inequality, slowing growth, sputtering productivity, unsustainable levels of debt, accelerating climate change, deepening societal problems, and the lack of global cooperation on some of the world's most pressing challenges. And as I hope you will agree, these observations are as valid after COVID-19 as they were before.

However, one thing has changed in the interim period between "BC" and "AC": there is, I notice, a greater understanding among the population, business leaders, and government that creating a better world would require working together. The idea that we need to rebuild differently post-COVID is widely shared. The sudden and all-encompassing impact of COVID-19 made us understand, much more than the gradual effects of climate change or increasing inequality, that an economic system driven by selfish and short-term interests is not sustainable. It is unbalanced, fragile, and increases the chance of societal, environmental, and public health disasters. As COVID-19 demonstrates, when disasters strike, they put an unbearable strain on public systems.

In this book, I will argue that we can't continue with an economic system driven by selfish values, such as short-term profit maximization, the avoidance of tax and regulation, or the externalizing of environmental harm. Instead, we need a society, economy, and international community that is designed to care for all people and the entire planet. Concretely, from a system of "shareholder capitalism," which prevailed in the West in the past 50 years, and a system of "state capitalism," that gained prominence in Asia, and is centered on the primacy of the state, we should move to a system of "stakeholder capitalism." That is the core message of this book. In what follows, I show how such a system can be built, and why it is so necessary to do so now.

Part I (Chapters 1 through 4) provides an overview of global economic history since 1945, both in the West and Asia. It explores the major achievements and shortcomings of the economic system we live in, including increased economic growth, and also inequality, environmental degradation, and debts for future generations. It also looks at how societal trends, such as increased political polarization, are related to the state of the economy and our governance systems. Part II (Chapters 5 through 7) digs deeper in the possible causes and consequences of our economies' problems and progress. It looks at the role played by technological innovation, globalization, and trade, and the use of natural resources. Finally, Part III (Chapter 8 through 11) looks at possible changes to our global economic system. It provides a definition of *stakeholder capitalism*, and shows what it can mean in practice for businesses, governments, international organizations, and civil society.

Throughout the book, I have tried to be fair and even-handed, whether in presenting the global problems we are facing, their possible causes and consequences, and the solutions I see to create a better world going forward. But I should immediately add that the views I present here are my own, and inevitably colored by my personal life experiences. I talk about some of those formative experiences as a child, student, and young professional in the first chapter of this book. I hope they help you as a reader to understand my world view, which is based on the belief that the best outcomes in a society and economy result from cooperation, whether between the public and the private sector, or peoples and nations from around the world.

I hope this book inspires you, whoever you are, to help build such a system. By working together to build an economic system built on inclusivity, sustainability, and equality, we can change COVID-19's legacy. While it inevitably includes death and ruined lives and livelihoods, it can perhaps help us orient ourselves toward a more resilient world. In that way, I hope the post-pandemic world could be to our generation what the post–World War II era was to my parents' generations: a moment of unity, where the recent past is a stark reminder of a world that nobody wants, and the present and future are an opportunity to create a world where everyone can thrive.

In the decades after the war, we did so by building a social compact at home—including a social market economy in Europe, and a "Great Society" in the US. We also created a multilateral system aimed at preserving peace, fostering collaboration, and creating financial home—including institutions such as the World Bank, International Monetary Fund, and the UN.

Now, I hope we will use the post-COVID recovery to enact stakeholder capitalism at home, and a more sustainable global economic system all around the world.

Thank you for reading,

Klaus Schwab
Geneva, December 2020

PART I
THE WORLD I GREW UP IN

1

75 Years
of Global Growth
and Development

In the 75 years since the end of World War II, there has been a surge of global economic development. But despite this, the world is living a tale of two realities.

On the one hand, we have rarely been as well off as we are today. We live in a time of relative peace and absolute wealth. Compared with previous generations, many of us live long and mostly healthy lives. Our children get to go to school, even often college, and computers, smartphones, and other tech devices connect us to the world. Even a generation or two ago, our parents and grandparents could only dream of the lifestyle many of us have today and the luxuries that come with abundant energy, advances in technology, and global trade.

On the other hand, our world and civil society are plagued by maddening inequality and dangerous unsustainability. The COVID-19 public health crisis is just one event that demonstrates that not everyone gets the same chances in life. Those with more money, better connections, or more impressive ZIP codes were affected by COVID at far lower rates; they were more likely to be able to work from home, leave densely populated areas, and get better medical care if they did get infected.

3

This is a continuation of a pattern that has become all too familiar in many societies. The poor are consistently affected by global crises, while the wealthy can easily weather the storm.

To understand how we got here—and how we can get out of this situation—we must go back in time, to the origins of our global economic system. We must play back the picture of post-war economic development and look at its milestones. The logical starting point for this is "Year Zero" for the modern world economy: 1945. And there is perhaps no better place from where to tell this story than Germany, for which that year was truly a new beginning.

Foundations of the Post-War Global Economic Order

Children like me, who started primary school in Germany in 1945, were too young to understand why the country they lived in had been at war before or why the next years would change so markedly. But we understood all too well that future conflict was to be avoided at all costs. As in the years following the First World War, "Nie Wieder Krieg," or "Never Again War," became a rallying cry all over Germany. People had had enough of conflict. They wanted to rebuild their lives in peace and work together toward a better quality of life.

This would not come easily, in Germany or elsewhere. As World War II came to an end, the country lay in ruins. Barely a fifth of the historic buildings in Germany's main cities still stood. Millions of homes had been wiped out. Swabia, the region in southern Germany where I grew up, was no exception. In its most industrialized city, Friedrichshafen, almost every factory was razed to the ground. This included those of Maybach and Zeppelin, two legendary manufacturers of cars and aircraft whose production capacity had been used by the Nazi government for military purposes during the war.

It is one of my earliest memories, how on the roof of my parents' house, just 18 kilometers away from Friedrichshafen, we watched the fires that led to Friedrichshafen's destruction. We prayed that the raid would not also hit our hometown, and luckily it didn't, but 700 people died in the last raid of Friedrichshafen alone. I remember how my parents cried when they heard the news, knowing many people personally in this neighboring city. By the war's end, only a quarter of the 28,000 original inhabitants of Friedrichshafen remained.[1] The rest had fled, disappeared, or died.

Ravensburg, where I lived, was one of the rare towns spared by Allied bombardment, a fate likely due to its lack of military-industrial capacity. But the consequences of war were all around us. By the end of the war, as the French Allied army moved in, Ravensburg had become a vast shelter for internal refugees, forced laborers, prisoners of war, and wounded soldiers.[2] The chaos in the city was complete. The only silver lining at midnight on May 8, 1945, was that the war had truly ended. In Germany, we came to mark this moment as the "Stunde Null," or "Zero Hour." Historians such as Ian Buruma later referred to the year that followed as "Year Zero."[3] Germany's economy was a wasteland, and it could only hope to be allowed to begin again, with a clean slate.

The other Axis powers, Italy and Japan, faced similar challenges. The Axis nations' productive capacity had been decimated. Turin, Milan, Genoa, and other Italian cities had suffered extensive bombings, and Hiroshima and Nagasaki saw unparalleled devastation by atomic bombs. other European countries were also shell-shocked and went through an initial period of chaos. Further east, China and much of Southeast Asia were mired in internal conflicts. Economies in Africa, the Middle East, and South Asia were still shackled by colonial rule. The Soviet Union had suffered enormous losses during World War II. Only the economies of the Americas, led by the United States, had come through the war largely unscathed.

It was thus up to Washington and Moscow to lead the post-war era, each in its sphere of influence. In Swabia, then part of Allied-occupied Germany, the future depended in large part on the choices the United States would make.

America faced a difficult balancing act. It was determined not to repeat the mistakes from the Treaty of Versailles, which ended World War I. Signed in 1919, the Treaty of Versailles saddled the defeated Central Powers (Germany, Austria-Hungary, the Ottoman Empire, and Bulgaria)

---

[1] 70 Jahre Kriegsende, Schwabische Zeitung, Anton Fuchsloch, May 2015, (in German) http://stories.schwaebische.de/kriegsende#10309.

[2] Wie der Krieg in Ravensburg aufhort, Schwabische Zeitung, Anton Fuchsloch, May 2015, (in German) http://stories.schwaebische.de/kriegsende#11261.

[3] *Year Zero, A History of 1945*, Ian Buruma, Penguin Press, 2013, https://www.penguinrandom house.com/books/307956/year-zero-by-ian-buruma/.

with an unbearable debt load. This curtailed their economic development and led to an erratic economic recovery, which planted the seeds
for the Second World War.

After World War II, Washington took another approach. It wanted to
revive the European economies that lay within its sphere of influence,
including the parts of Germany under British, French, and American
occupation. The United States wanted to promote trade, integration, and
political cooperation. As early as 1944, America and its allies had created
economic institutions such as the International Monetary Fund and the
International Bank for Reconstruction and Development (now part of
the World Bank).[4] Over the decades that followed, they continued their
efforts to develop a stable, growing economic system in West Germany
and throughout Western Europe.

From 1948 onward, the United States and Canada also provided
specific regional aid. Through the Marshall Plan, named after then–US
Secretary of State George Marshall, the United States helped Western
European countries purchase American goods and rebuild their industries, including Germany and Italy. Providing aid to former Axis powers
was a contentious decision, but it was deemed necessary because without the German industrial motor, there could be no strong, industrial
Europe. (The Organisation for European Economic Cooperation and
Development (OEEC), the forerunner of the OECD, was an important
administrator of the program.)

America did not limit its efforts to aid. It also encouraged trade
by setting up European markets for coal, steel, and other commodities.
That led to the creation of the European Coal and Steel Community,
the embryonic form of what is now the European Union. In Asia, too,
the United States provided aid and credit to countries including Japan,
China, the Republic of Korea, and the Philippines. Elsewhere, the Soviet
Union expanded its sphere of influence, promoting an economic model
based on centralized planning and state ownership of production.

Local governments, industries, and workers also played a role in
the reconstruction effort. For example, in 1947, the Zeppelin Foundation transferred almost all its assets to the city of Friedrichshafen[5] in the
hopes of reigniting a prosperous future for the Zeppelin companies and

---

[4]Organisation for Economic Co-operation and Development (OECD), Eurostat, https://
ec.europa.eu/eurostat/statistics-explained/pdfscache/1488.pdf.

[5]Friedrichshafen, History of the Zeppelin Foundation, https://en.friedrichshafen.de/citizen-
city/zeppelin-foundation/history-of-the-zeppelin-foundation/.

their workers. At the same time, Friedrichshafen's citizens worked long days to rebuild their homes. Women played a special role in this rebuilding and in much of the initial work of reconstruction. German magazine *Der Spiegel* later recalled: "With so many men killed in the war, the Allies relied on women to do the hard work of clean-up."[6]

Just as a jigsaw puzzle requires every piece to be placed correctly to create a complete picture, the work of reconstruction required every resource to be deployed and every human effort to be mobilized. It was a task that the entire society took to heart. One of the biggest, most successful manufacturers in Ravensburg was a family enterprise that eventually renamed itself Ravensburger.[7] It resumed its production of puzzles and children's books, a business that continues to this day. And in Friedrichshafen, ZF, a subsidiary of the Zeppelin Foundation, re-emerged as a manufacturer of car parts. Companies like these, often from Germany's famous *Mittelstand*, i.e., the small and mid-sized businesses that form the backbone of the German economy, played a critical part in the post-war economic transformation.

The Glorious Thirty Years in the West

For many people living in Europe—myself included—the relief of the end of the war soon made way for the fear of another one. The free market approach in US-occupied West Germany and the rest of Western Europe clashed with the centrally planned economic model of the Soviet Union, which held sway over East Germany and the rest of Eastern Europe. Which would prevail? Was peaceful coexistence possible, or did things have to end in a head-on conflict? Only time would give us the answers.

At the time, the results were not clear to us or anyone else. This was a battle of ideologies, economic systems, and geopolitical hegemony. For decades, both powers entrenched their positions and their competing systems. Asia, Africa, and Latin America saw the same ideological battle between capitalism and communism play out.

With the benefit of hindsight, we know that the economic institutions the United States created, based on capitalism and free markets,

---

[6]Der Spiegel, A Century-Long Project, October 2010, https://www.spiegel.de/fotostrecke/ photo-gallery-a-century-long-project-fotostrecke-56372-5.html.

[7]The company was founded as the Otto Maier Verlag and later changed its name to Ravensburger.

were building blocks for an era of unparalleled shared economic prosperity. Combined with the will of many people to rebuild, they laid the groundwork for decades of economic progress and economic dominance of the West over the "rest." The Soviet model of centralized planning initially bore fruit, too, allowing it to prosper at first, but it would later collapse.

Beyond the economic shifts, other factors shaped our modern era. Many parts of the world, including the United States and Europe, had a baby boom. Workers were drawn away from the nihilistic demands of wartime production to the socially productive work during peacetime. Education and industrial activity expanded. The leadership provided by heads of government, such as Konrad Adenauer in Germany or Yoshida Shigeru in Japan, was a crucial piece of the puzzle too. They committed themselves and their governments to reconstructing their economies and societies in an inclusive way and to developing strong relations with the Allies aimed at a sustained peace, rather than give in to the quest for revenge that had dominated after the First World War. Given the national focus on community and economic reconstruction, there was an increase in societal cohesion (which is more deeply discussed in Chapter 4).

Between 1945 and the early 1970s, these factors came together to drive a Wirtschaftswunder, or economic miracle, in Germany and the rest of Europe. A similar boom got underway in the United States, Japan, and South Korea (and, initially, in the Soviet Union). The West entered its golden age of capitalism, and the innovations of the Second Industrial Revolution were widely implemented: highways for car and truck transport were built en masse, the age of commercial flying arrived, and container ships filled the sea lanes of the world.

In Swabia, too, new technologies were implemented on the back of this economic miracle. At Ravensburger, for example, sales tripled in the 1950s, kicking off the phase of mass industrial production that began in 1962. Family board games like Rheinreise (which literally translates as "Journey on the Rhine") became extremely popular[8] as the children of the baby boom came of age. Ravensburger expanded further in the 1960s,[9] when the company introduced puzzles to its product line. (The brand's logo, a blue triangle on the corner of its boxes, became iconic.) Around the same time, ZF Friedrichshafen resurfaced in the 1950s as a

---

[8]Company interview with Heinrich Huentelmann and Tristan Schwennsen, August 2019.

[9]Ravensburger, About Ravensburger, https://www.ravensburger-gruppe.de/en/about-ravensburger/company-history/index.html#1952-1979.

manufacturer for automotive transmissions, complementing its assortment with automatic transmissions by the mid-1960s.[10] It helped propel German car manufacturers such as BMW, Audi, Mercedes, and Porsche to the top, at a time when the European car industry was booming. (ZF's success lasts until this day, as the company in 2019 posted global revenues in excess of $40 billion, had almost 150,000 employees worldwide, and operations in over 40 countries around the world.)

Looking at economic indicators in the leading economies of the world, it seemed as though everyone was winning. Annual economic growth averaged up to 5, 6, and even 7 percent. Gross domestic product (GDP) is the monetary value of the goods and services produced in a given economy. Often used to measure economic activity in a country, it doubled, tripled, and even quadrupled in some western economies over the next decade or two. More people went to high school and into middle-class jobs, and many baby boomers became the first in their families to go to college and climb up the socioeconomic ladder.

For women, climbing up that ladder had an extra dimension. At first slowly, then steadily, emancipation advanced in the West. More women went to college, entered and stayed in the workforce, and made more conscious decisions about their work-life balance. The booming economy had plenty of room for them, but they were also supported by advancements in medical contraception, the increased accessibility of household appliances, and, of course, the emancipation movement. In the United States, for example, female labor-force participation jumped by 15 percent between 1950 and 1970,.from about 28 to 43 percent.[11] In Germany, the percent of female students at university rose from 12 percent in 1948 to 32 percent in 1972.[12]

At the Ravensburger company, women came to the forefront, too. Starting in 1952, Dorothee Hess-Maier, a granddaughter of the company's founder, became the first woman at the helm of the company, alongside her cousin Otto Julius. It was exemplary of a broader trend. Women's liberation in Western societies continued for the remainder of the century and into the 21st. Anno 2021, there are more women than

---

[10]Heritage, ZF, https://www.zf.com/mobile/en/company/heritage_zf/heritage.html.

[11]Our World in Data, Working women: Key facts and trends in female labour force participation, https://ourworldindata.org/female-labor-force-participation-key-facts.

[12]Kompetenzzentrum Frauen in Wissenschaft und Forschung, Entwicklung des Studentinnenanteils in Deutschland seit 1908, https://www.gesis.org/cews/unser-angebot/informationsangebote/statistiken/thematische-suche/detailanzeige/article/entwicklung-des-studentinnenanteils-in-deutschland-seit-1908/.

men enrolled in university in many countries around the world, including the US and Saudi Arabia[13](!), and women form close to half of the workforce in many countries. Despite this, inequalities related to pay and other factors remain.[14]

Over the course of those early post-war decades, many countries used their economic windfall to build the foundations of a social market economy. In Western Europe, notably, the state offered unemployment benefits, child and education support, universal health care, and pensions. In the United States, pro-social policies were less *en vogue* than in Europe, but thanks to the rapid economic growth, more people than ever did ascend to the middle class, and social security programs did grow both in the number of beneficiaries and the overall funds allocated to them, especially in the two decades between 1950 and 1970.[15] Median wages rose sharply, and poverty fell.

France, Germany, the Benelux countries, and the Scandinavian countries also promoted collective bargaining. In most German companies, for example, the Works Council Act of 1952 determined that one-third of the members of the supervisory board had to be selected by workers. An exception was made for family-owned companies, as ties between the community and management there were typically strong, and social conflict was rarer.

As I grew up in that golden era, I developed a keen appreciation for the enlightened role the United States had played in my country and the rest of Europe. I became convinced that economic cooperation and political integration were key to building peaceful and prosperous societies. I studied in both Germany and Switzerland and came to believe the borders between European nations would one day disappear. In the 1960s, I even had the opportunity to study one year in the United States and learn more about its economic and management models. It was a foundational experience.

Like so many of my generation, I was also a beneficiary of the middle-class, solidarity society European countries had developed. Early on, I became very intrigued by the complementary roles business and

[13]School Enrollment, Tertiary, Saudi Arabia, World Bank, 2018, https://data.worldbank.org/indicator/SE.TER.ENRR?locations=SA.

[14]Global Gender Gap report 2018, http://reports.weforum.org/global-gender-gap-report-2018/key-findings/.

[15]"Historical Background and Development Of Social Security," Social Security Administration, https://www.ssa.gov/history/briefhistory3.html.

government played in shaping the future of a country. For this reason, it was natural to write one of my theses about the right balance between private and public investments. Having worked during more than a year on the shop floor of companies, experiencing real blue-collar work, I also developed a special respect for the contribution of workers in developing economic wealth. My belief was that business, like other stakeholders in society, had a role to play in creating and sustaining shared prosperity. The best way to do so, I came to think, was for companies to adopt a stakeholder model, in which they served society in addition to their shareholders.

I decided to turn that idea into action by organizing a management forum where business leaders, government representatives, and academics could meet. Davos, a Swiss mountain town that in Victorian times had become famous for its sanatorium treatment of tuberculosis (before antibiotics such as isoniazid and rifampin[16] were invented), offered an optimal setting for a sort of global village,[17] I thought. High up in the mountains, in this picturesque town known for its clean air, participants could exchange best practices and new ideas and inform each other of pressing global social, economic, and environmental issues. And so, in 1971, I organized the first meeting of the European Management Forum (the forerunner of the World Economic Forum) there, with guests such as Harvard Business School Dean George Pierce Baker, Columbia University Professor Barbara Ward, IBM President Jacques Maisonrouge, and several members of the European Commission.[18]

The Tumultuous 1970s and 1980s

But just then, in the beginning of the 1970s, it became clear the economic miracle wasn't to last. As we gathered in Davos, cracks in the system had already come to the surface. The post-war boom had plateaued, and social, economic, and environmental issues were emerging. My hope though, was that by more actively learning about successful American management practices, European businesspeople, politicians, and academics could continue to spur prosperity on the continent.

---

[16]Tuberculosis Treatment, Mayo Clinic, https://www.mayoclinic.org/diseases-conditions/tuberculosis/diagnosis-treatment/drc-20351256.

[17]The term "global village" was coined by Canadian thinker Marshall McLuhan in the 1960s.

[18]"The World Economic Forum, a Partner in Shaping History, 1971–2020," p.16 http://www3.weforum.org/docs/WEF_A_Partner_in_Shaping_History.pdf.

Many European companies did in fact make the step toward neighboring international markets. The European Coal and Steel Community (ECSC), which as the name implied focused on a common market for a few key resources, had in the preceding years evolved to become the more all-encompassing European Economic Community (EEC). It allowed for a freer trade of goods and services across the continent. Many *Mittelstand* companies used that opening to set up subsidiaries and start sales in neighboring EEC countries. It was thanks in part to this increase in intra-regional trade that growth could continue in the 1970s.

But some economic variables with a critical effect on growth, employment, and inflation, such as the price of energy, were not favorable. Oil, which alongside coal had fueled the post-war boom, brought a first shock to the system. The price of the world's most important energy source rose fourfold in 1973 and then doubled in 1979, as the major oil-producing and -exporting countries (OPEC)—many of them former Middle Eastern and Arabian colonies of the European powers—flexed their muscles. Controlling the vast majority of the global oil supply at the time, the OPEC countries decided to implement an oil embargo in response to the Yom Kippur War. During that war, many of OPEC's Arab members opposed Israel, which during and after the armed conflict expanded its territory in the region. The embargo, targeted mainly against Israel's western allies including the US and the UK, was very effective.

It was no wonder perhaps, that the OPEC countries used their newly gained market power. In the preceding two decades, many of its members—often former European colonies in Asia, the Middle East, and Africa—had finally gained their independence. But unlike most Western countries in that era, these developing countries were often consumed by political and social turmoil. The economic boom in Europe and the United States remained out of reach for many newly independent countries in Asia, the Middle East, and Africa. The OPEC nations were among the few exceptions, as their most important resource, oil, fueled the world economy.

As economic and industrial progress had been so great in the West over the three previous decades, some people also warned that the expansion was unsustainable and that a new economic system would be needed that is more sustainable for the planet, its limited natural resources, and eventually, humans themselves. Among these voices were European scientists and industrialists of the Club of Rome, who had come to believe that the state of the world, and notably the environmental degradation of the planet, was a major problem for human society. Indeed there were great warning signs for anyone who would take heed, and at the Forum's meetings in Davos, we paid close attention. In 1973, Aurelio Peccei, the club's president, gave a keynote speech at Davos about his organization's findings, warning of an impending end to growth.

Still, after surviving multiple recessions and introducing some energy-saving measures such as daylight savings time and car-free Sundays, the world eventually returned to its familiar growth path in the 1980s. The days of 5 and 6 percent GDP growth were over (at least in the West), but growth levels of 3 to 4 percent there were not at all out of the ordinary. Other economies, including the Asian Tigers (South Korea, Taiwan, Hong Kong, and Singapore) helped to make up for the shortfall.

But beginning in the 1980s, a fundamental change in perspective started to emerge about what had enabled post-war economic growth. During the immediate post-war years, it was believed that increased economic prosperity was something that everyone had contributed to, and so it had to be shared by all. It was an industrial model of progress built on partnership between company owners and their workforces. By contrast, the growth phase of the 1980s was based more on market fundamentalism and individualism and less on state intervention or the building of a social contract.

I think this was a mistake. The stakeholder model requires businesses to think beyond their direct, primary interests and to include the concerns of employees and their communities in their decision-making. In the early years of our Davos gathering, participants had even committed to this in a "Davos Manifesto":[19]

THE 1973 DAVOS MANIFESTO

A. The purpose of professional management is to serve clients, shareholders, workers and employees, as well as societies, and to harmonize the different interests of the stakeholders.

B. 1. The management has to serve its clients. It has to satisfy its clients' needs and give them the best value. Competition among companies is the usual and accepted way of ensuring that clients receive the best value choice. The management's aim is to translate new ideas and technological progress into commercial products and services.

2. The management has to serve its investors by providing a return on its investments, higher than the return on government bonds. This higher

---

[19]The Davos Manifesto, 1973, World Economic Forum, https://www.weforum.org/agenda/2019/12/davos-manifesto-1973-a-code-of-ethics-for-business-leaders/.

return is necessary to integrate a risk premium into capital costs. The management is the shareholders' trustee.

3. *The management has to serve its employees because in a free society leadership must integrate the interests of those who are led. In particular, the management has to ensure the continuity of employees, the improvement of real income and the humanization of the work place.*

4. *The management has to serve society. It must assume the role of a trustee of the material universe for future generations. It has to use the immaterial and material resources at its disposal in an optimal way. It has to continuously expand the frontiers of knowledge in management and technology. It has to guarantee that its enterprise pays appropriate taxes to the community in order to allow the community to fulfil its objectives. The management also has to make its own knowledge and experience available to the community.*

C. *The management can achieve the above objectives through the economic enterprise for which it is responsible. For this reason, it is important to ensure the long-term existence of the enterprise. The long-term existence cannot be ensured without sufficient profitability. Thus, profitability is the necessary means to enable the management to serve its clients, shareholders, employees and society.*

But despite the initial enthusiasm for the Davos Manifesto and the stakeholder-centered approach it advocated, a narrower shareholder-centric paradigm prevailed, particularly in the United States. It was the one put forth by University of Chicago economist and Nobel Prize winner Milton Friedman starting in 1970. He held that the "only social responsibility of business is to increase its profits"[20] and that free markets are what matters above all else. (This is discussed further in Chapter 8.)

The result was unbalanced growth. Economic growth returned in the 1980s, but an ever smaller part of the population benefited from it, and even more harm was done to the planet to achieve it. Union membership started to decline, and collective bargaining became less common (though much of continental Europe, including Germany, France, and Italy clung to it until the 2000s, and some, like Belgium, still do today). Economic policies in two of the West's leading economies—the United Kingdom and the United States—were largely geared toward deregulation, liberalization, and privatization, and a belief that an invisible hand would lead markets to their optimal state. Many other Western

[20]"A Friedman Doctrine—The Social Responsibility of Business Is to Increase Its Profits," Milton Friedman, *The New York Times*, September 1970, https://www.nytimes.com/1970/09/13/archives/a-friedman-doctrine-the-social-responsibility-of-business-is-to.html.

economies later followed their path, in some cases after more left-leaning governments failed to jumpstart economic growth. On a more positive note, new technologies also made their contribution, leading to a Third Industrial Revolution. The personal computer was invented and would become one of the key components of every organization.

Die Wende

These trends did not happen in isolation. As the 1980s progressed, the economies of Eastern Europe started to collapse. Their failure at this industrial transition point showed that the state-led economic model put forth by the Soviet Union was less resilient than the market-based one promoted by the West. In China, the government of new leader Deng Xiaoping started its own Reform and Opening-Up in 1979, gradually introducing capitalist and market-based policies (see Chapter 3).

In 1989, Germany experienced a moment of euphoria, as the Berlin Wall, which separated East from West, fell. Shortly thereafter, political reunification of Germany was at last established. And by 1991, the Soviet Union had officially disintegrated. Many economies that lay in its sphere of influence, including those of East Germany, the Baltics, Poland, Hungary, and Romania, turned toward the West and its capitalist, free-market model. "The end of history," as Francis Fukuyama would call it later,[21] had arrived, it seemed. Europe got another boost, this time leading to even deeper political and economic integration and the establishment of a common market and a monetary union, with the euro currency as its apex.

At Davos, we felt the winds of change as well. Whereas initially the European Management Forum had been primarily a meeting place between European and American academics, policymakers, and businesspeople, over the course of the 1980s it had become global. The 1980s saw the inclusion of representatives from China, India, the Middle East, and other regions and a shared, global agenda. By 1987, a name change had become necessary. We were thenceforth known as the World Economic Forum. It was fitting for the era of globalization that followed.

---

[21] *The New York Times Magazine*, "What Is Fukuyama Saying? And to Whom Is He Saying It?", James Atlas, October 1989, https://www.nytimes.com/1989/10/22/magazine/what-is-fukuyama-saying-and-to-whom-is-he-saying-it.html.

Globalization in the 1990s and 2000s

Indeed, following the Soviet Union's collapse, for more than a decade the world's economies became more intertwined. Countries all over the world started to set up free-trade agreements, and the motors of global growth were more varied than ever. The relative importance of Europe declined, and so-called emerging markets, such as South Korea and Singapore but also larger ones such as Brazil, Russia, India, South Africa, and, of course, China, came to the forefront. (There is no formal definition of emerging markets, as it's a classification made by particular private financial institutions, but one common trait that they share is that they are non-Western economies that often have or had higher-than-average growth rates for a number of years, which could help them gain or regain developed-economy status over time.)

In this way, globalization—a process of growing interdependence between the world's economies, signaled by increasing flows of goods, services, people, and capital—became a dominant economic force. Trade globalization, measured by international trade as a percentage of global GDP, reached its highest level ever—15 percent—in 2001, up from 4 percent at its nadir in the Year Zero of 1945.

Swabia's prominent companies surfed this wave of globalization, too. "China was at the top of ZF's agenda," Siegfried Goll, then a prominent ZF manager, testified in the company's written history.[22] "The development of our business relations began already in the 1980s, initially by means of license contracts. When I retired in 2006, we had no fewer than 20 production locations in China." According to the company's own records, "The first joint venture was established in 1993," and by 1998, "ZF's position in China was so firmly entrenched that the first-ever founding of a fully owned Chinese subsidiary was possible: ZF Drivetech Co. Ltd. in Suzhou."

For some, though, this globalization was too much, too quickly. In 1997, several Asian emerging economies experienced a severe financial crisis, caused in large part by unchecked financial globalization, or the flow of hot money, international investor money that flows easily from one country to another, chasing returns, relaxed capital controls, and bond speculation. At the same time, in the West, an anti-globalization movement took hold, as multinational companies started to have more control over national economies.

---

[22]"Pioneers in China," 1993, ZF Heritage, zf.com/mobile/en/company/heritage_zf/heritage.html.

Even Ravensburger didn't escape the backlash. In 1997, the company management announced that it wished to "introduce a 'pact for the safeguarding of production sites,' as a 'preventive initiative for the maintenance of national and international competitiveness,'" the European Observatory of Working Life wrote in a later case study on the mater.[23] The result was the so-called Ravensburger Pact, in which the company offered its employees job security in exchange for concessions.

Although the pact was accepted by most workers, it also led to a deterioration in employee-employer relations. The industry union argued it went against collective bargaining agreements for the sector and that it was unnecessary, as the company had good economic performance. In the end, the hotly contested pact made all parties reconsider their relationship to each other. The union, which had typically been weak in the family-owned enterprise, grew stronger, and management took on a more constructive approach to its Works Council going forward.

In Germany, similar societal and corporate stresses around economic growth, employment, and the integration of the former East German states ultimately led to a new social pact in the early 2000s, with new laws on co-determination, "mini jobs," and unemployment benefits. But the new equilibrium was for some less beneficial than before, and even though Germany afterward returned to a period of high economic growth, the situation soon got more precarious for many other advanced economies.

A first warning sign came from the dot-com crash in late 2000 and early 2001, when America's technology stocks came crashing down. But the greater shock to US society and the international economic system came later in 2001. In September of that year, the US faced the greatest attack on its soil since the attack on Pearl Harbor in World War II: the 9/11 terrorist attacks. Buildings representing both the economic and the military hearts of America were hit: the Twin Towers in Manhattan and the Pentagon in Washington, DC.

I was in New York that day on a work visit to the UN, and like everyone there, I was devastated. Thousands of people died. The United States came to a standstill. As a sign of solidarity, the following January we organized our Annual Meeting of the World Economic Forum in New York—the first

---

[23]Eurofound, "Pacts for Employment and Competitiveness: Ravensburger AG," Thorsten Schulten, Hartmut Seifert, and Stefan Zagelmeyer, April 2015, https://www.eurofound. europa.eu/es/observatories/eurwork/case-studies/pecs/pacts-for-employment-and-competitiveness-ravensburger-ag-0.

it was held outside Davos. After the dot-com crash and 9/11, the Western economies entered a recession. For a while, the path of economic growth through trade and technology advances hung in the balance.

But the seeds of yet another economic boost had already been planted. As exemplified by ZF's increased presence there, China, the world's largest country by population, had become one of the fastest-growing economies after 20 years of Reform and Opening-Up, and in 2001, it entered the World Trade Organization. What other countries had lost in economic momentum, China gained and surpassed. The country became the "factory of the world," lifted hundreds of millions of its own citizens out of poverty, and at its peak became responsible for more than a third of global economic growth. In its path, commodity producers from Latin America to the Middle East and Africa benefitted as well, as did Western consumers.

Meanwhile, on the ruins of the dot-com crash, surviving and new technology firms started to lay the beginnings of a Fourth Industrial Revolution. Technologies such as the Internet of Things came to the forefront, and machine learning—now dubbed "artificial intelligence"—had a revival and rapidly gained traction. Trade and technology, in other words, were once more back as twin engines of global economic growth. By 2007, globalization and global GDP had reached new peaks. But it was globalization's last hurrah.

The Collapse of a System

From 2007 onward, the global economy started to change for the worse. The world's major economies saw their growth motors sputter. The US went first, with a housing and financial crisis turning into a Great Recession that lasted several quarters. Europe followed next, with a debt crisis that started in 2009 and lasted several years. Most other global economies were caught in the middle, with a global recession in 2009 and real economic growth that hovered around between 2 and 3 percent in the following decade. (Specifically, between a low of 2.5 percent in both 2011 and 2019 and a high of 3.3 percent in 2017, according to the World Bank.[24])

Slow growth now seems the new normal, as the motor of all economic growth, productivity gains, is lacking. Many people in the West

---

[24]GDP Growth, Annual (%), 1961–2019, The World Bank, https://data.worldbank.org/indicator/NY.GDP.MKTP.KD.ZG.

are stuck in low-paying, insecure jobs, with no outlook for progress. Moreover, the IMF had already noted well before the COVID crisis that the world had reached unsustainable debt levels.[25] Anno 2020, public debt, which had previously reached a high in the 1970s crises, was again at or near record levels too in many countries. According to the IMF's 2020 fiscal monitor, public debt in advanced economies reached more than 120 percent of GDP in the wake of the COVID crisis, an increase of over 15 percent in a single year, and in emerging economies shot up to over 60 percent of GDP (from just over 50 percent in 2019).[26]

Finally, more and more people are questioning even how useful it is to pursue growth as an indicator of progress. According to the Global Footprint Network,[27] 1969 was the last time the global economy didn't "overspend" nature's resources for the planet. Fifty years on, our ecological footprint is greater than ever, as we use up more than 1.75 times the resources the world can replenish.

All these macroeconomic, social, and environmental trends are mirrored in the incremental effects of decisions taken by individuals, companies, and governments, both local and national. And it confronts those same societies, which have come so far from the era of wars, poverty, and destruction, with an unpleasant new reality: they grew rich but at the expense of inequality and unsustainability.

■ ■ ■

Swabia in the 21st century, is in many ways as wealthy as it has ever been, with high wages, low unemployment, and many leisurely activities. The beautiful city centers of Ravensburg and Friedrichshafen in no way resemble the sorry state they were in in 1945. Ravensburg still provides a welcome for refugees, but this time the wars are further afield. Even the city's puzzle game manufacturer has adapted to a world of global supply chains and jigsaws disrupted by digital gaming.

---

[25]International Monetary Fund, New Data on Global Debt, https://blogs.imf.org/2019/01/02/new-data-on-global-debt/.

[26]Gross debt position, Fiscal Monitor, April 2020, International Monetary Fund, https://www.imf.org/external/datamapper/datasets/FM.

[27]Global Footprint Network, https://www.footprintnetwork.org/2019/06/26/press-release-june-2019-earth-overshoot-day/.

But the puzzle the people of this region, its drivetrain and jigsaw manufacturers, and other societal stakeholders here and in other parts of the world have to solve is not an easy one. It is a global one, with many complex and interdependent pieces. So before we attempt to solve it, we need to list those pieces. It is this assignment that we will take on in the next chapter. And to guide us, we will get the help of a famous economist.

2

Kuznets' Curse

The Issues of the World Economy Today

There might have been no better person to piece together the puzzle of the world economy today than Simon Kuznets, a Russian-born[1] American economist, who died in 1985.

It may seem odd at first that a man who passed away in the mid-1980s would be so relevant to today's global economic challenges, but I believe the issues we are facing today may not have become so problematic had we better heeded the lessons of this Nobel Prize–winning economist.

Indeed, Kuznets warned more than 80 years ago that gross domestic product (GDP) was a poor tool for economic policymaking. Ironically, he had helped pioneer the very concept of GDP a few years earlier and had a hand in its becoming the holy grail of economic development. He also warned that his own Kuznets curve, which showed that income inequality dropped as an economy developed, was based on "fragile data,"[2] meaning data from a relatively brief period of the post-war Western economic miracle that took place in the 1950s. If the period of

---

[1]Kuznets was born in Pinsk, then part of the Russian Empire. Nowadays, Pinsk is part of Belarus.

[2]"Political Arithmetic: Simon Kuznets and the Empirical Tradition in Economics", Chapter 5: The Scientific Methods of Simon Kuznets, Robert William Fogel, Enid M. Fogel, Mark Guglielmo, Nathaniel Grotte, University of Chicago Press, p. 105, https://www.nber.org/system/files/chapters/c12917/c12917.pdf.

his study turned out to be an anomaly, the theory of this curve would be disproven. Kuznets also never approved of the curve's off-shoot, the so-called environmental Kuznets curve, which asserted countries would also see a drop in the environmental harm they produced as they reached a certain state of development.

Today we live with the consequences of not having been more rigorous in our analyses or having been too dogmatic in our beliefs. GDP growth has become an all-consuming goal, and at the same time, it has stalled. Our economies have never been so developed, yet inequality has rarely been worse. And instead of seeing a drop in environmental pollution, as one might have hoped, we are in the midst of a global environmental crisis.

That we are facing this myriad of economic crises may well be Kuznets' *curse*. It is the ultimate "I told you so" of an oft misunderstood economist and forms the root of the feeling of betrayal people have toward their leaders. But before we get deeper into this curse, let's examine who exactly Simon Kuznets was and find out what people remembered him for.

The Original Kuznets' Curse: GDP as Measure of Progress

Simon Smith Kuznets was born in Pinsk, a city in the Russian Empire in 1901, the son of Jewish parents.[3] As he made his way through school, he showed a talent for mathematics and went on to study economics and statistics at the University of Kharkiv (now in Ukraine). But despite his promising academic results, he would not stay in the country of his birth after reaching adulthood. In 1922, Vladimir Lenin's Red Army won a years-long civil war in Russia. With the Soviet Union in the making, Kuznets, like thousands of others, emigrated to the United States. There, he first got a PhD in economics at Columbia University and then joined the National Bureau of Economic Research (NBER), a well-respected economic think tank. It was here he built his illustrious career.

His timing was impeccable. In the decades after his arrival, the US grew to become the leading world economy. Kuznets was there to help

---

[3]A direct quotation of Kuznets' autobiography for the Nobel Prize committee. The Nobel Prize, "Simon Kuznets Biographical," 1971, https://www.nobelprize.org/prizes/economic-sciences/1971/kuznets/biographical/.

the country make sense of that newly found position. He pioneered key concepts that dominate economic science and policymaking to this day such as national income (a forerunner to GDP) and annual economic growth and became himself one of the world's most prominent economists along the way.

The economic development curve of the United States in those years was a turbulent one. In the 1920s, the country was on an economic high; it came out of the First World War swinging. The US emerged as a political and economic power and put its foot next to that of an already enfeebled British Empire. Britain had dominated the world during the First Industrial Revolution, ruling a third of the world until 1914. America instead became a leader of the Second Industrial Revolution, which really took off after World War I. US manufacturers introduced goods such as the car and the radio to the country's huge domestic market, selling them to a public hungry for modern goods. Aided also by a spirit of free trade and capitalist principles, a positive spiral of investment, innovation, production, consumption, and trade ensued, and America became the world's wealthiest country in GDP per capita terms.

But the heady experience of the "Roaring Twenties" turned into the calamitous Great Depression. By 1929, the booming economy had spiraled out of control. Inequality was sky-high, with a handful of individuals, such as John D. Rockefeller, controlling colossal amounts of wealth and economic assets, while many workers had a much more precarious existence, still often depending on payday jobs and agricultural harvests. Moreover, an ever-rising stock market, not backed by any similar trend in the real economy, meant financial speculation was reaching a fever pitch. In late October 1929, a colossal collapse of the stock market occurred and set in motion a chain reaction all over the world. People defaulted on their obligations, credit markets dried up, unemployment skyrocketed, consumers stopped spending, protectionism mounted, and the world entered a crisis from which it would not recover until after the Second World War.

As US policymakers grappled with how to contain and end the crisis at home, they lacked the answer to a fundamental question: How bad is the situation, really? And how will we know if our policy answers will work? Economic metrics were scarce, and GDP, the measure we use today to value our economy, had not been invented.

Enter Simon Kuznets. An expert in statistics, mathematics, and economics, he developed a standard way of measuring the gross national income (GNI) or gross national product (GNP) of the United States. He was convinced this measure would give a better idea of just how much goods and services were produced by American-owned companies in a given year. A few years later, he also became the intellectual father of the closely linked GDP, presenting the slightly different concept in a 1937 report to US Congress.[4] (GDP takes into account only the domestically produced goods and services, while GNI or GNP include income or products produced abroad by companies owned by a country's citizens.)

It was a stroke of genius. Over the remainder of the 1930s, other economists helped standardize and popularize this measure of economic output to such an extent, that by the time the Bretton Woods conference was held in 1944, GDP was confirmed as the main tool for measuring economies.[5] The definition of GDP that was used then is still valid today: GDP is the sum of the value of all goods produced in a country, adjusted for the country's trade balance. There are various ways of measuring GDP, but the most common is probably the so-called expenditure approach. It calculates total gross domestic production as the sum of consumption that stems from it (adjusting for exports and imports):

Gross Domestic Product
    = Consumption + Government Expenditure + Private Investment
    + Exports − Imports

Since then, GDP has been the metric you will find in World Bank and IMF reports on a country. When GDP is growing, it gives people and companies hope, and when it declines, governments pull out all the policy stops to reverse the trend. Although there were crises and setbacks, the story of the overall global economy was one of growth, so the notion that growth is good reigned supreme.

But there is a painful end to this story, and we could have foreseen it had we better listened to Simon Kuznets himself. In 1934, long before the Bretton Woods Agreement, Kuznets warned US Congress not to focus too narrowly on GNP/GDP: "The welfare of a nation can scarcely

[4] "GDP: A brief history," Elizabeth Dickinson, *Foreign Policy*, January 2011, https://foreignpolicy.com/2011/01/03/gdp-a-brief-history/.
[5] Ibidem.

be inferred from a measure of national income," he said.[6] In this he was right. GDP tells us about consumption, but it does not tell us about well-being. It tells us about production but not pollution or the resource use. It tells us about government expenditure and private investments but not about the quality of life. Oxford economist Diane Coyle told us in an August 2019 interview[7] that, in reality, GDP was "a war-time metric." It tells you what your economy can produce when you're in war, but it does not tell you how you can make people happy when you're at peace.

Despite the warning, no one listened. Policymakers and central banks did everything they could to prop up GDP growth. Now, their efforts are exhausted. GDP does not grow like it used to, and well-being stopped increasing a long time ago. A feeling of permanent crisis has taken hold of societies, and perhaps with good reason. As Kuznets knew, we never should have made GDP growth the singular focus of policy-making. Alas, that is where we are. GDP growth is our key measurement and has permanently slowed.

Low GDP Growth

As we outlined in Chapter 1, the global economy in the last 75 years has known many periods of rapid expansion, as well as some significant recessions. But the global economic expansion that started in 2010 has been tepid. While global growth[8] reached peaks of 6 percent and more per year until the early 1970s and still averaged more than 4 percent in the run up to 2008, it has since fallen back to levels of 3 percent or less[9] (see Figure 2.1).

The number three matters, because it acted for a long time as a pass-or-fail bar of standard economic theory. Indeed, until about a decade ago, the *Wall Street Journal* pointed out, "Past IMF chief economists called global growth lower than either 3% or 2.5%—depending on who was the chief economist—a recession."[10] One explanation came from

[6]"Beyond GDP: Economists Search for New Definition of Well-Being," *Der Spiegel*, September 2009, https://www.spiegel.de/international/business/beyond-gdp-economists-search-for-new-definition-of-well-being-a-650532.html.

[7]Phone interview with Diane Coyle by Peter Vanham, August 18, 2019.

[8]Measured in constant 2010 US dollars.

[9]World Bank, GDP Growth (annual %), 1961–2018, https://data.worldbank.org/indicator/NY.GDP.MKTP.KD.ZG.

[10]"What's a Global Recession," Bob Davis, *The Wall Street Journal*, April 2009, https://blogs.wsj.com/economics/2009/04/22/whats-a-global-recession/.

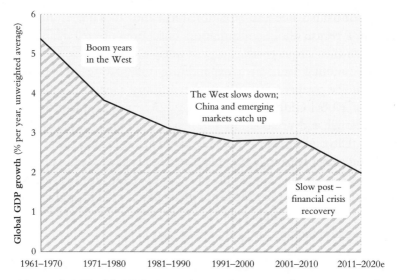

Figure 2.1 World GDP Growth Has Been Trending Downward since the 1960s

Source: Redrawn from World Bank GDP growth (annual %), 1960–2019.

simple math: from the 1950s until the early 1990s, global demographic growth almost consistently lay at 1.5 percent growth per year or higher.[11] A global growth rate that was only slightly over the rate of population growth meant large parts of the world population were in effect experiencing zero or negative economic growth. That type of economic environment is discouraging to both workers, companies, and policymakers because it indicates little opportunity for advancement.

Perhaps in response to slowing economic growth, economists have since changed their definition of what constitutes a global recession. But it does not alter the fact we have seen meager global economic growth ever since. As a matter of fact, economic growth of less than 3 percent per year seems to be the new normal. Even before the COVID crisis, the IMF did not expect global GDP growth to return to above the 3 percent threshold for the next half decade,[12,13,14] and

[11]United States Census Bureau, International Data Base, September 2018, https://www.census.gov/data-tools/demo/idb/informationGateway.php.

[12]"World Economic Outlook," International Monetary Fund, Updated July 2019, https://www.imf.org/en/Publications/WEO/Issues/2019/07/18/WEOupdateJuly2019.

[13]"World Economic Outlook," International Monetary Fund, April 2019, Appendix A https://www.imf.org/~/media/Files/Publications/WEO/2019/April/English/text.ashx?la=en.

[14]This concerns GDP growth based on market exchange rates (see corresponding row on table cited in footnotes 11 and 12).

that outlook has been negatively affected by the worst public health crisis in a century.

From the perspective of conventional economic wisdom, this could lead to systemic fault lines, as people got used to economic growth. There are two reasons for that.

First, global GDP growth is an aggregate measure, which hides several national and regional realities that are often less positive still. In Europe, Latin America, and Northern Africa, for example, real growth is edging closer to zero. For Central or Eastern European countries that still have economic catching up to do with their neighbors to the West or North, such low growth is discouraging. It may accelerate the brain drain, as motivated and educated people seek economic opportunities in higher-income countries, thereby exacerbating the problems of their home countries. The same is true in regions like the Middle East, Northern Africa, and Latin America, where many people still don't have a fully middle-class lifestyle and where jobs that offer financial security are lacking, as are social insurance and pensions.

Second, in regions where growth is higher than the average, like in Sub-Saharan Africa, even top-line growth of 3 percent or more per year isn't enough to allow for rapid per capita income growth, given their equally high rate of population growth. Low- and lower-middle-income countries that have posted relatively high growth levels in recent years include Kenya, Ethiopia, Nigeria, and Ghana.[15] But even if they were to grow consistently at 5 percent per year for the foreseeable future, it could take an entire generation (15–20 years) for their people's incomes to double. (And that is assuming that most of the fruits of economic growth are shared widely, which often is not the case.)

Rapid progress and shared economic growth, like that seen in China in the early 21st century, require real growth rates of 6 to 8 percent in the least developed economies. Lacking this kind of super boost, the great convergence of economic standards of living between North and South, as predicted by some economists, will materialize very slowly, if at all. As Robin Brooks, chief economist at the Institute of International Finance (IIF) told James Wheatley of the *Financial Times* in 2019: "More and more, there is a discussion that the growth story for emerging markets is just over. There is no growth premium to be had any more."[16]

---

[15]"World Bank Country and Lending Groups," World Bank, https://datahelpdesk.world-bank.org/knowledgebase/articles/906519-world-bank-country-and-lending-groups.

[16]"The Great Emerging-Market Growth Story is Unravelling," *The Financial Times*, June 2019, https://www.ft.com/content/ad11f624-8b8c-11e9-a1c1-51bf8f989972.

Looking beyond GDP does not provide more promising prospects. Other economic metrics, notably debt and productivity, are also pointing in the wrong direction.

Rising Debt

Consider first rising debt. Global debt—including public, corporate, and household debt—by mid-2020 stood at some $258 trillion globally, according to the Institute of International Finance,[17] or more than three times global GDP. That number is hard to grasp, because it is so big and because it includes all sorts of debt, going from public debt sold through government bonds to mortgages from private consumers.

But it has been rising fast in recent years, and that certainly is "alarming," as Geoffrey Okamoto of the IMF said in October 2020. Not since World War II were debt levels in advanced economies so high, the *Wall Street Journal* calculated,[18] and unlike in the post-war period, these countries "no longer benefit from rapid economic growth" as a means to decrease their burden in the future.

The COVID pandemic, of course, brought an exceptional acceleration of the debt load in countries around the world, and especially for governments. According to the IMF, by mid-2021, in the span of a mere 18 months, "median debt is expected to be up by 17 percent in advanced economies, 12 percent in emerging economies, and 8 percent in low-income countries"[19] compared to pre-pandemic levels.

But even without the pandemic, debt had been creeping up in the past three decades. As one example: in advanced economies, public debt rose from about 55 percent in 1991, to over 70 percent in 2001, and more than 100 percent in 2011. It is estimated to reach more than 120 percent in 2021.[20]

---

[17]See the IMF estimate of 2019 above. For the IIF estimate of Q1 2020, see https://www.iif.com/Portals/0/Files/content/Research/Global%20Debt%20Monitor_July2020.pdf.

[18]"Coronavirus Lifts Government Debt to WWII Levels—Cutting It Won't Be Easy," *The Wall Street Journal*, August 2020, https://www.wsj.com/articles/coronavirus-lifts-government-debt-to-wwii-levelscutting-it-wont-be-easy-11598191201.

[19]"Resolving Global Debt: An Urgent Collective Action Cause," Geoffrey Okamoto, IMF First Deputy Managing Director, October 2020, https://www.imf.org/en/News/Articles/2020/10/01/sp100120-resolving-global-debt-an-urgent-collective-action-cause.

[20]"Gross Debt Position, % of GDP," Fiscal Monitor, International Monetary Fund, April 2020, https://www.imf.org/external/datamapper/G_XWDG_G01_GDP_PT@FM/ADVEC/FM_EMG/FM_LIDC.

Faced with slowing global growth over the past decades, especially in advanced economies, governments, companies, and households nevertheless increased their debt. Could that have ever been a good idea? Theoretically, yes. When used to invest in productive assets, debt can be a lever of future economic growth and prosperity. But all debt does of course need to be repaid at some point (unless it evaporates because of inflation, but that has been less than 2 percent on average in advanced economies in the past 20 years[21]). The only alternative is to default, but that is akin to playing Russian roulette.

So what kind of debt has been made in recent decades? The debt of governments is often a mix of high-quality and low-quality debt. High-quality debt includes that used for building modern infrastructure or investments in education, for example. High-quality debt is typically paid back over time—and can likely even provide a return on the investment. Such projects should be encouraged. By contrast, low-quality debt, such as deficit spending to boost consumption, generates no returns, even over time. This type of debt should be avoided.

Overall, it is safe to say low-quality debt is on the rise. In part, this is because low interest rates in the West incentivize lending, which discourages borrowers from being careful with their spending. For governments, deficit spending has become the norm in recent decades, rather than the exception. The COVID crisis that erupted in the early months of 2020 hasn't made that picture any rosier. Many governments have effectively used "helicopter money" to sustain the economy: they printed money, creating an even higher debt with their central banks, and handed it to citizens and businesses in the form of one-off subsidies and consumption checks so they could get through the crisis unscathed. In the short term, this approach was necessary to prevent an even worse economic collapse. But in the long run, this debt too will need to be repaid. Overall, it adds to the large amounts of debt in recent years that wasn't used to spur long-term economic growth or to make the switch toward a more sustainable economic system. This debt will thus remain a millstone, hanging around many governments' necks.

One silver lining comes from emerging and developing markets. Before the COVID crisis, they had relatively lower public debt levels

---

[21]"Inflation Rate, Average Consumer Prices, Annual Percent Change, Advanced Economies," World Economic Outlook, International Monetary Fund, April 2020, https://www.imf.org/external/datamapper/PCPIPCH@WEO/ADVEC/OEMDC.

of around 50–55 percent,[22] with much of it invested in infrastructure (though during the COVID crisis, the debt level increased by about 10 percent). Some of these countries can be considered to have a demographic dividend, meaning a population with an average age in the low twenties, that is, heavily skewed toward younger generations. This type of population pyramid could make repaying debt more feasible if the coming surge in their working-age population is complemented by an equally high surge in available jobs. (The latter, however, has proven problematic in some Arab and African economies. Faced with a job shortage, a demographic dividend can rather turn into a ticking time bomb.[23,24])

How some ageing Western countries are supposed to repay their debts in a slowing economy, though, is highly questionable. The economies with the highest government debt load have historically been Japan and Italy. In addition to their debt, they have some of the world's most rapidly shrinking and ageing populations. While private savings of Japanese households can alleviate many of the most acute problems this trend could cause, the country's debt will sooner or later come back to haunt it, as its population shrinks from 127 million to fewer than 100 million over the next three decades, and its ratio of workers to retirees falls even further. It could easily increase the debt burden per head by another quarter or third.[25]

Other European countries such as France, Spain, Belgium, and Portugal, all of which have gross public debt of over 110 percent of GDP[26] (and often much higher than that), could one day find that they are facing a similar fate. In a significant development, the United States joined the 100 percent club in the early 2010s, with its debt rapidly rising further in recent years, to over 130 percent in 2020.[27] The US situation

---

[22]International Monetary Fund, DataMapper, https://www.imf.org/external/datamapper/ GGXWDG_NGDP@WEO/OEMDC/ADVEC/WEOWORLD.

[23]"Youth Dividend or Ticking Time Bomb?" *Africa Renewal*, UN, 2017, https://www. un.org/africarenewal/magazine/special-edition-youth-2017/youth-dividend-or-ticking-time-bomb.

[24]"EM Youth Bulge: A Demographic Dividend or Time Bomb?" Jonathan Wheatley, *Financial Times*, May 2013, https://www.ft.com/content/f08db252-6e84-371d-980a-30ab41650ff2.

[25]National Institute of Population and Social Security Research, Japan, http://www.ipss. go.jp/pp-zenkoku/e/zenkoku_e2017/pp_zenkoku2017e_gaiyou.html#e_zenkoku_II.

[26]"Gross Debt Position, % of GDP," Fiscal Monitor, International Monetary Fund, April 2020, https://www.imf.org/external/datamapper/G_XWDG_G01_GDP_PT@FM/ADVEC/ FM_EMG/FM_LIDC.

[27]Ibidem.

raises a peculiar uncertainty because US government bonds are among the most traded in the world, and the US dollar is the de facto world reserve currency. A US government default is unlikely, given that its Federal Reserve has its hands on the printing press, but if it does happen, the global economic system as we know it might collapse.

It is in the combination of high debt and low growth that things really get problematic, from a financial point of view. In an environment where growth of 3 percent and more can be expected, government debt can quickly evaporate: the relative importance of past debt would decline in comparison to a growing GDP. Even in the recent past, countries like Germany and the Netherlands managed to considerably lower their debt burden on the back of favorable economic growth. But if low growth does remain the new normal, which seems likely, there is no easy mechanism for countries to repay their historical debt. Looking away certainly will not solve this problem.

Low-Interest Rates and Low Inflation

There was one life buoy for low growth and debt until now: low interest rates. Having a low interest on your loan, as many homeowners or student borrowers know, is a blessing. It allows you to pay back your debt without having to worry about the debt load getting larger.

Since the financial crisis, central banks have ushered in an era of low lending rates, giving governments, companies, and consumers low interest rates as a form of relief. The goal is to, ultimately, restore higher growth as people consume more, companies invest more, and governments spend more.

In the United States, the Federal Reserve kept interest rates near zero from 2009 until 2016. It then gradually raised them again to 2.5 percent, half the historical normal rate. But in 2019, the Fed once again cut interest rates[28] several times, and when COVID hit, it crashed back down to 0.25 percent.[29] Given the challenging macroeconomic environment, a return to the era of high interest rates is very unlikely anytime soon. In other advanced economies, rates are even lower. The European Central Bank has kept its key borrowing rate for the eurozone at under 1 percent since 2012, and at zero since 2016. Most other European countries have

---

[28]"U.S. Central Bank Cuts Interest Rate for 1st Time Since 2008," CBC, July 2019, https://www.cbc.ca/news/business/federal-reserve-interest-rate-decision-1.5231891.

[29]"United States Fed Funds Rate, 1971–2020," Trading Economics, https://tradingeconomics.com/united-states/interest-rate.

similar low rates; Japan and Switzerland even charge depositors for buying bonds, in fact meaning they have a negative interest rate.

As indicated, this is a blessing for governments, companies, and individuals alike who are willing and able to take up new loans or for governments who want to refinance their historical debt. Some observers
may even go as far as to suggest the historical debt-to-GDP burden is
not as big a problem as it seems, as it can be perpetually refinanced.

But this view fails to consider that repayment problems can quickly
get out of hand as government funding gaps for other liabilities increase.
Costs related to pensions, health care, and infrastructure are becoming
an ever-growing burden on governments, not to speak of consumption
subsidies, such as governments paying a part of oil and gas prices for
consumers.[30] They produce low-quality debt and are hard to roll back,
given their popularity with voters.

Public health care spending, notably, already rose by 66 percent from
2000 to 2016—long before the COVID-19 crisis hit—according to the
World Health Organization.[31] During the same period, GDP growth in
OECD countries was only 19 percent. In aggregate, public health care
spending in OECD countries now represents close to 7 percent of GDP,
with peaks in the United States and Switzerland at double that rate, and
that percentage can be expected to rise further as populations age and
more viruses or even non-communicable diseases threaten the population. Unless governments can unload these costs to their citizens, many
will increasingly struggle to balance their books.

There are more growing government liabilities. The Global Infrastructure Hub calculated the world faces a $15 trillion infrastructure
funding gap from 2016 to 2040.[32] But infrastructure represents an
investment, on which a return could be earned. The problem posed
by pensions and retirement savings is an order of magnitude larger, and
returns are much lower: unless policies are changed, the World Economic
Forum estimates[33] the pension savings gap will balloon to $400 trillion

---

[30]This practice is common in many oil- and gas-producing countries, such as Iran, Russia,
Saudi Arabia, Iraq, the UAE, Libya, and Kuwait, but also in other emerging markets such as
China, Indonesia, Mexico, and Egypt. See: "Energy Subsidies, Tracking the Impact of Fossil-
Fuel Subsidies," IEA, https://www.iea.org/topics/energy-subsidies.

[31]"Public Spending on Health: A Closer Look at Global Trends," World Health Organization,
https://apps.who.int/iris/bitstream/handle/10665/276728/WHO-HIS-HGF-HF-Working
Paper-18.3-eng.pdf?ua=1.

[32]"Global Infrastructure Outlook," Global Infrastructure Hub, https://outlook.gihub.org/.

[33]"We'll Live to 100—How Can We Afford It?" World Economic Forum, http://www3.
weforum.org/docs/WEF_White_Paper_We_Will_Live_to_100.pdf.

in the eight countries with the world's largest pension systems by 2050, with unsecured public pension promises making up the lion's share of that shortfall.

On top of this debt burden is low inflation. Historically, interest rates and inflation tended to be inversely correlated, and central banks used their power to set interest rates as a tool to either curb inflation or stimulate it. By setting high interest rates, central banks gave people, companies, and governments an incentive to save money rather than spend it, easing upward pressure on prices. By setting low interest rates, they gave people the reverse incentive, namely to spend money and push up prices, since saving it wouldn't yield interest anyway.

Since about a decade, however, this inverse correlation has all but ceased to exist in the West, with the situation particularly dire in Europe and Japan. Despite years of near-zero interest rates, inflation often remained close to zero as well. While this is no problem in the short run, it does take away a long-term lever to ease the debt load. With rising prices, nominal debt tends to become relatively less of a burden. With flat prices, however, historical debt remains as heavy as a burden tomorrow as today.

But the nexus between low growth, low interests, low inflation, and increasing debt has one more ingredient, and it could be the most lethal of them all: slowing productivity growth.

Declining Productivity Growth

Compounding many of the structural issues outlined in this chapter is the fact that productivity gains have been low in recent years. Indeed, it was because of rising productivity, more so perhaps than demographic growth, that the middle class in the West saw their incomes rise quickly during the first decades after the war.

Productivity goes up most often because of innovations in the way things are made or done. Well-known examples of productivity gains are the assembly line Ford introduced in the early 1900s, the introduction of digital computers instead of typewriters in the 1970s and 1980s, or the optimizing of a taxi route thanks to apps such as Waze today. All these innovations enable a given worker to produce the same output, or do the same job, in considerably less time. That in turn allowed companies to increase wages.

In the past, the world knew periods of high productivity gains, which translated into high wage growth. During America's golden age of capitalism in the 1950s and 1960s, for example, the annual productivity growth was almost 3 percent per year.[34] But productivity gains afterward fell to lower levels, and, problematically, even when productivity did rebound, less of it was translated into take-home pay for American workers. Instead, it remained with the businessowners and executives, a phenomenon known as the "decoupling" of wages from productivity.[35]

Since the 2007–2009 financial crisis, US productivity growth has fallen to the meager level of 1.3 percent per year. That is a problem, because it means it is not possible to grow the pie for everyone anymore. The distribution of today's economic gains is a quasi-zero-sum game. Other countries, such as Germany, Denmark, and Japan, have kept up productivity gains better and translated them also in higher wages. But the trendline is unmistakable: productivity gains in the West are experiencing a marked decline.

Taken together, the indicators presented in this chapter—growth, interest rates, debt, and productivity—point to a systemic design error in the Western economic development model. Much of its prosperity model was based on perpetual economic growth and productivity gains. Now, that growth is grinding to a halt, and problems that had been festering under the surface are becoming more acute by the day.

Kuznets' curse is coming back to haunt us. GDP was never a perfect measure for well-being. And now that it is becoming an ever-greater challenge to grow it, we will have to deal with a whole basket of other problems we created while pursuing that higher growth.

The Second Kuznets' Curse: Inequality

While the original Kuznets' curse of our recent past is the result of the blind pursuit of GDP growth, there is a second Kuznets' curse. This one relates more directly to the phenomenon Kuznets became known for in his lifetime: the so-called Kuznets curve.

As Kuznets continued his work as an economist in the 1950s, he started to theorize on an interesting phenomenon. He noticed that US income inequality had started to decline in the post-war period, as the economic boom intensified. That contrasted to the pre-war period, in which America had become a major economic power, but income and

---

[34]"Labor Productivity and Costs," Bureau of Labor Statistics, https://www.bls.gov/lpc/prodybar.htm.

[35]"Decoupling of Wages from Productivity," OECD, Economic Outlook, November 2018, https://www.oecd.org/economy/outlook/Decoupling-of-wages-from-productivity-november-2018-OECD-economic-outlook-chapter.pdf.

wealth were concentrated in the hands of a few. A similar observation, though less extreme, could be made for many other developed countries.

Kuznets theorized about the numbers he found, in a paper for and presidential address to the American Economic Association.[36] He derived a potential game-changing insight for development economics, provided the findings held true over time. Indeed, it implied a sort of economic law. Inequality worsens as a nation begins to develop, but as development continues, inequality subsides. In other words, the price of inequality societies pay for development early on is offset by higher development and lower inequality later.

The theory put forth by Kuznets became a worldwide sensation, especially after Kuznets won the 1971 Nobel Prize for Economics, awarded for his contributions to national income accounting (rather than the theory of the Kuznets curve). Throughout the 1980s, economists built on Kuznets' optimistic theory, plotted graphs that showed

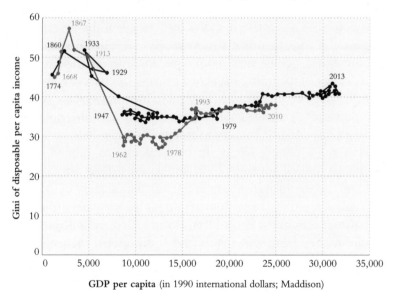

—— The Kuznets relationship for the US, 1774-2013

—— The Kuznets relationship for the United Kingdom/England, 1688-2010

Figure 2.2 Kuznets waves: How income inequality waxes and wanes over the very long run

Source: Redrawn from Lindert, P. H., & Williamson, J. G. (1985). Growth, equality, and history. Explorations in Economic History, 22(4), 341–377..

---

[36]"Some Notes on the Scientific Methods of Simon Kuznets," Robert Fogel, National Bureau of Economic Research, December 1987, https://www.nber.org/papers/w2461.pdf.

how it applied to various countries and periods, and prescribed economic development models because of it.

There was just one problem: over time, the theory no longer held true. Some of the facts we face today reveal this.

Inequality in fact began rising again in highly developed countries. In a 2016 note, economist Branko Milanovic suggested that the current upswing in inequality could be viewed "as a second Kuznets curve", or indeed, as a "Kuznets wave" (Figure 2.2).

Income Inequality

There is a festering wound in our global economic system, and that wound is rising income inequality.

The story starts with an unexpected twist. Global income inequality, measured by plotting incomes of everyone from all over the world, has actually been steadily declining over the last 30 years[37] (see Figure 2.3). This may come as a surprise to many readers, given the perception that the opposite is true in many countries. But the global trend is clear: around the world, people earn more equal incomes, not less.

The decline in inequality happened because of one incredibly powerful force: the huge economic leaps forward in incomes in some of the largest (and previously poorest) countries in the world. China, notably, went from being a low-income country to an upper-middle-income[38] one since its Reform and Opening-Up. By its own calculation, it lifted some 740 million people out of poverty.[39] India, too, knew various periods of rapid growth, and thereby managed to raise the income of many of its people.

The impact of these two countries on global inequality has been all-encompassing: economist Zsolt Darvas of the Bruegel Institute showed that without the changes in China and India, global inequality would have remained exactly where it was, or even gone up quite a bit, depending on the calculation method (see Figure 2.3).

This clarifies the real problem posed by inequality today. Global inequality may have declined, but inequality within nations has drastically worsened.

---

[37]"Global Inequality is Declining—Largely Thanks to China and India," Zsolt Darvas, Bruegel Institute, April 2018, https://bruegel.org/2018/04/global-income-inequality-is-declining-largely-thanks-to-china-and-india/.

[38]"Upper-Middle-Income Countries," World Bank, https://datahelpdesk.worldbank.org/knowledgebase/articles/906519-world-bank-country-and-lending-groups.

[39]"China Lifts 740 Million Rural Poor Out of Poverty Since 1978," Xinhua, September 2018, http://www.xinhuanet.com/english/2018-09/03/c_137441670.htm.

The Gini Index of Income Inequality – globally and in selected countries, 1988-2015 where 0 is perfect equality, and 100 is perfect inequality (i.e., one person has all the income)

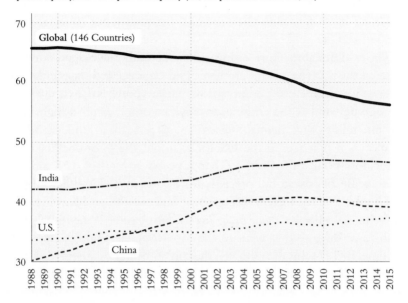

The impact of China and India on global income inequality developments

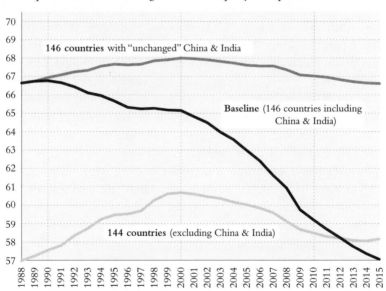

Figure 2.3 The Impact of China and India on Global Income Inequality (Measured in Gini Indices)

Source: Redrawn from Zsolt Darvas, Global income inequality is declining – largely thanks to China and India, April 18, 2018.

In many people's experience, it matters much more how they fare compared to their fellow citizens than to the rest of the world population. In all but a few countries, national inequality has been rising and often rather fast.

The traditional measure of inequality, the Gini coefficient, doesn't do justice to the severity of the problem. The Gini coefficient translates the degree of inequality into a number from 0 (everyone has the same income) to 1 (one person has the entire economy's income). While a higher score over time tells us that inequality has risen, it's difficult to understand what that means in practice. In the US, for example, the Gini coefficient rose from its low point of 0.43 in 1971 to a post-war high of 0.58 today.[40] It is an increase, of course, but precisely how good or bad is either number?

Thomas Piketty, a French economist, laid out the problem in a better way. In his 2013 book *Capital in the Twenty-First Century*,[41] he revealed how the share of income that went to the top 10 percent of earners evolved over time. In 1971, his data showed the top 10 percent earners took home one third of national income. In the early 2010s, they took half of income. This leaves the vast majority of workers—the remaining 90 percent—with only half of the national income to divvy up among themselves.

Later numbers from the World Inequality Report, of which Piketty is a co-author, showed how the trend was even more pronounced for the top 1 percent. Over the same period, 1971 to the early 2010s, their income share doubled[42] and their incomes more than tripled. This means that in the early 2010s, more than 20 percent of the national income went to the top 1 percent of earners. For those at the bottom of the income pyramid, the situation was much bleaker. Many workers saw their real incomes and purchasing power decline since the early 1980s (Figure 2.4). In the UK a similar shift took place.

The social and economic outcomes of this worsening inequality in the US have been highly problematic. There are again many working poor in America, a painful outcome in the wealthiest country the world has ever known. Guy Standing, a British economist, even coined the term *precariat*, to point to "an emerging class, comprising the rapidly

[40]"Minneapolis Fed, "Income and Wealth Inequality in America, 1949–2016," https://www.minneapolisfed.org/institute/working-papers-institute/iwp9.pdf.

[41]"Piketty's Inequality Story in Six Charts," John Cassidy, *The New Yorker*, March 2014, https://www.newyorker.com/news/john-cassidy/pikettys-inequality-story-in-six-charts.

[42]"World Inequality Report, 2018," https://wir2018.wid.world/files/download/wir2018-summary-english.pdf.

growing number of people facing lives of insecurity, moving in and out of jobs that give little meaning to their lives."[43]

Seen from this perspective, it is no wonder that in 2011, a one-page call for action in an activist magazine led to one of the most supported American protest movements of this century. The page in AdBusters read, "17 September. Wall Street. Bring Tent." Protestors did in fact show up in lower Manhattan on that day, they brought tents, and with that, Occupy Wall Street was born. Referencing the extreme inequality in America, the movement's rallying cry became "We are the 99 percent," and the protestors decried the wealth, income, and power accumulated by the 1 percent richest individuals and corporations in America. As you can see from Figure 2.4, this dichotomy between the 1 percent and the rest of income earners was not imaginary.

The same pattern exists in other parts of the world, and in some countries the outrage over these inequalities has erupted with equal force as it has in the English-speaking world. In fact, it was movements in the Mediterranean and Middle East that inspired Occupy Wall Street,

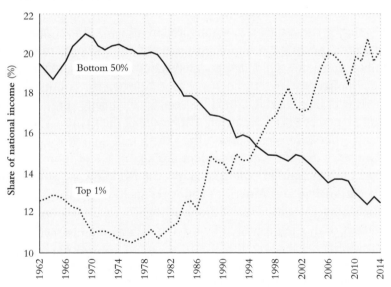

Figure 2.4 In the US, Income Inequality Has Risen Sharply

Source: Redrawn from Piketty, Saez and Zucman (2018), World Inequality Report 2018..

---

[43] *The Precariat: The New Dangerous Class*, Guy Standing, 2011, https://www.bloomsbury.com/uk/the-precariat-9781849664561/.

Kalle Lasn, one of the founders of Occupy, told one of us in a 2012 interview.[44] There, in the early years of this decade, Spanish Indignados took to the streets in protest. A year later, Arab Spring protesters in Tunisia, Egypt, Syria, and other countries took the streets to express their anger over economic inequities within their countries. In Tunisia, they forced a regime change.

"We saw what happened in Tunisia, with the regime change, and started to brainstorm about what that would look like in America," Lasn said. A "soft regime change" in the US, he said, would be to take away power and money from large corporations, which decided "every part of my life. We felt that we had reached a situation—with unemployment of young people, huge student debt, and no good jobs—where if we didn't fight for our future, we wouldn't have a future. That was the core impulse behind Occupy Wall Street."

In other countries, particularly in emerging Asia, the social outrage over rising inequality has been less pronounced. In China, India, and many ASEAN nations, national inequality also rose. However, overall economic growth in that region was much higher, so a rising tide did in fact lift most boats. Still, the specter of class tensions looms over some of these countries as well (see Chapter 3).

As author James Crabtree highlighted in his book *The Billionaire Raj*, India is now one of the most unequal societies in the world, to the point of embodying a new Gilded Age society. Unlike in India, in China, most of the population started on the same footing when the country opened to the world. Despite this, China has seen its inequality surge, too, with the top 10 percent now capturing 41 percent of their nation's income.[45] In many other emerging markets, the situation is even worse. Just as in the United States, the top 10 percent are taking home more than half their nation's income in countries across the Middle East, Sub-Saharan Africa, and many Latin American countries, including Brazil.

Inequality in continental Europe is slightly less pronounced, with 37 percent of income captured by the top 10 percent of earners. While inequality has been rising, it has done so at a considerably slower pace than in most other leading economies. This is partially due to Europe's greater system of check and balances to facilitate income distribution and redistribution.

---

[44]Interview with Kalle Lasn by Peter Vanham, Vancouver, Canada, March 2012.

[45]"World Inequality Report, 2018," https://wir2018.wid.world/files/download/wir2018-summary-english.pdf.

But some uncomfortable realities remain here, too. In much of Southern and Eastern Europe, for example, unemployment remains stuck at high levels, especially for the young. Well-paid jobs there are increasingly hard to get, often to the detriment of both blue-collar workers and university-educated youth. Even Northern European economies, which kept a decent growth pace after the European debt crisis put a strain on Europe-wide growth as of 2010, saw their income inequality levels rise in the past decade. Counterexamples such as Belgium,[46] Estonia, Romania, Slovakia, or the Czech Republic,[47] which experienced declining inequality, remain the exception.

Wealth, Health, and Social Mobility

The Kuznets curve has been disproved when looking at other inequality metrics too. Wealth inequality, which reflects the savings, investments, and other stocks of capital individuals have, is even more lopsided in many countries. And, in lockstep with this wealth disparity, private education and quality health care, which can require large sums of money, are becoming more of a privilege reserved for the upper-middle and upper classes. This is especially the case in countries without proper public alternatives.

This reality is perhaps most keenly felt in the United States, which in this sense looks more like the emerging markets of India and Mexico than the advanced economy it is. Economists Emmanuel Saez and Gabriel Zucman calculated that the wealth held by the one percent richest Americans rose from less than 15 percent in the 1970s to over 40 percent in the early 2010s.[48] As such, wealth inequality is twice as high as income inequality.[49]

---

[46]"How Unequal Is Europe? Evidence from Distributional National Accounts, 1980–2017," Thomas Blanchet, Lucas Chancel, Amory Gethin, World Economic Database, April 2019, https://wid.world/document/bcg2019-full-paper/.

[47]EU income inequality decline: Views from an income shares perspective, Zsolt Darvas, Bruegel Institute, 2018, https://www.bruegel.org/2018/07/eu-income-inequality-decline-views-from-an-income-shares-perspective/.

[48]"Wealth Inequality in the United States since 1913: Evidence from Capitalized Income Tax Data," Emmanuel Saez and Gabriel Zucman, *The Quarterly Journal of Economics*, May 2016, http://gabriel-zucman.eu/files/SaezZucman2016QJE.pdf.

[49]"Share of Total Income going to the Top 1% since 1900, Within-Country Inequality in Rich Countries," Our World in Data, October 2016, https://ourworldindata.org/income-inequality.

These two inequalities—wealth and income—also build on one another and create a vicious cycle.[50] A 2020 *Financial Times* article summarized that by the end of September 2019, a record 56 percent of all US equities was held by the top one percent wealthiest households, amounting to $21.4 trillion. Read that again: the "one percent" does in fact own more than half of all stocks in America. That percentage had steadily gone up in the past three decades, and the rise had been "driven by stagnant wages for many Americans, which held them back from partaking in the stock market's gains of the past decade."

The 0.1 percent made even greater strides. They accumulated well over a fifth of America's wealth by the 2010s, a share almost three times higher as in the mid-1970s. Those at the bottom, on the other hand, saw their wealth share and savings plummet, to the point even of often not being able to cover for health emergencies and education,[51] as has become painfully clear during the 2020 pandemic.

The consequence of this increasing wealth disparity, Nobel Prize–winning economist Joseph Stiglitz asserts, is that US economic mobility is increasingly a thing of the past; even a long or healthy life is out of reach for many. He decried the situation in his 2019 book *People, Power and Profits: Progressive Capitalism for an Age of Discontent*, and a prior *Scientific American* essay. "Families in the bottom 50 percent hardly have the cash reserves to meet an emergency," he wrote. "Newspapers are replete with stories of those for whom the breakdown of a car or an illness starts a downward spiral from which they never recover. In significant part because of high inequality, US life expectancy, exceptionally low to begin with, is experiencing sustained declines."[52]

And indeed, the phenomenon Anne Case and Angus Deaton called "deaths of despair,"[53] is on the rise in America (and increasingly,

---

[50]"How America's 1% Came to Dominate Equity Ownership," Robin Wigglesworth, *Financial Times*, February 2020, https://www.ft.com/content/2501e154-4789-11ea-aeb3-955839e06441.

[51]It is nevertheless interesting to note, as Branko Milanovic has done, that while wealth inequality—driven primarily by stock ownership—is large and growing, there is no longer a true "capitalist" class as Karl Marx alleged in the 19th century. Wealthy households do get a large share of their wealth from "capital," but not all of it: as a matter of fact, most "wealthy" people do also work for a living, having often well-paid positions in finance, legal, or medical industries.

[52]"The American Economy Is Rigged," Joseph Stiglitz, *Scientific American*, November 2018, https://www.scientificamerican.com/article/the-american-economy-is-rigged/.

[53] "Mortality and Morbidity in the 21st Century," Anne Case and Angus Deaton, Brookings Institute, March 2017, https://www.brookings.edu/bpea-articles/mortality-and-morbidity-in-the-21st-century/.

the UK[54]). People are falling off the economic ladder and wither or die because of opioid overdoses, depression, or other health issues associated with their poor economic status.

No phenomenon displays this "wealth and health" nexus in America more than COVID-19, which affected those with fewer means much more than others. New York City provides a striking example. In the early weeks of the pandemic, many of the wealthier Manhattanites could seek shelter in an upstate or out-of-state property, get care in a private hospital, or otherwise protect themselves from the virus. Poorer New Yorkers, by contrast, were much more exposed. They were more likely to work and live in at-risk environments, less likely to have adequate health care coverage, and largely unable to physically move elsewhere. As a result, one early study found, "Coronavirus-related hospitalizations and deaths were highest in the Bronx, which has the highest proportion (38.3%) of African Americans and the lowest annual median household income ($38,467) and proportion (20.7%) of residents with at least a bachelor's degree."[55] That pattern repeated itself elsewhere in the United States—and indeed the world.

But despite the global trend of diseases like COVID hitting poorer communities harder, in other advanced economies, health disparities have so far remained much more constrained, and life expectancy continues to rise. This should hardly come as a major surprise, as outside the US virtually all advanced economies have some form of universal health care. Among the 36 member states of the Organization for Economic Co-operation and Development, for example, only Mexico had a lower percentage of people covered than the US, and most countries achieved a 100 percent coverage rate,[56] either through public or primary private health insurance.

The global record on social and economic mobility are more mixed. The World Economic Forum's 2020 Global Social Mobility index found that "there are only a handful of nations with the right conditions to foster social mobility" and that "most countries underperform in four areas:

---

[54]"Deaths of Despair, Once an American Phenomenon, Now Haunt Britain," *The Economist*, May 2019, https://www.economist.com/britain/2019/05/16/deaths-of-despair-once-an-american-phenomenon-now-haunt-britain.

[55]"Variation in COVID-19 Hospitalizations and Deaths Across New York City Boroughs," *Journal of the American Medical Association*, April 2020, https://jamanetwork.com/journals/jama/fullarticle/2765524.

[56]"Total Public and Primary Private Health Insurance," Organization for Economic Co-operation and Development, https://stats.oecd.org/Index.aspx?DataSetCode=HEALTH_STAT.

fair wages, social protection, working conditions and lifelong learning," even as achieving higher levels of social mobility is an important part of implementing a stakeholder-based model of capitalism. Specifically, the report said:

> Looking at all economies and average income levels, those children who are born into less affluent families typically experience greater barriers to success than their more affluently born counterparts. Furthermore, inequalities are rising even in countries that have experienced rapid growth. In most countries, individuals from certain groups have become historically disadvantaged and poor social mobility perpetuates and exacerbates such inequalities. In turn, these types of inequalities can undermine the cohesiveness of economies and societies.[57]

Other studies found similar dynamics. A 2018 World Bank report showed that only 12 percent of young adults in regions like Africa and South Asia have more education than their parents—often a prerequisite to climb higher up the socioeconomic ladder.[58] Other regions, including East Asia, Latin America, and the Middle East and Northern Africa, did see their average economic mobility improve, according to the report. But it also warned, "While mobility tends to improve as economies get richer, there is nothing inevitable about this process. Rather, as economies develop, mobility is likely to increase if opportunities become more equal, which typically requires higher public investments and better policies."[59] In other words: lacking public investments—an increasingly likely reality for budget-strained governments—economic mobility in many countries could get *worse*, rather than better.

So, what would Simon Kuznets have to say about all these findings, many of which go against his own theory?

We do not need to speculate. According to his colleague at the National Bureau of Economic Research Robert Fogel, Kuznets repeatedly warned that his "allusions to fragmentary data were not evidence but 'pure guesswork.'"[60] Kuznets, in other words, was all too well aware

---

[57]"Global Social Mobility Index 2020: Why Economies Benefit from Fixing Inequality," World Economic Forum, January 2020, https://www.weforum.org/reports/global-social-mobility-index-2020-why-economies-benefit-from-fixing-inequality.

[58]"Fair Progress? Economic Mobility across Generations around the World, 2018," The World Bank, https://www.worldbank.org/en/topic/poverty/publication/fair-progress-economic-mobility-across-generations-around-the-world.

[59]"ibidem".

[60]"Some Notes on the Scientific Methods of Simon Kuznets," Robert Fogel, NBER, December 1987, https://www.nber.org/papers/w2461.pdf.

that his findings in the 1950s may have been only valid in very specific circumstances, which indeed this golden era of capitalism turned out to be. Fogel also noted that even at the time, Kuznets found "factors that arose during the course of growth, and that created pressures both to increase and to reduce inequality."

Branko Milanovic, a former lead economist at the World Bank, recently tried to build a new Kuznets curve in light of these insights. Kuznets notably pointed to technology as a factor that could have a positive or a negative effect on inequality. Milanovic derived from it an inequality curve that seems much more complete, given the evolution we've seen in recent decades. He calls it the Kuznets Wave, and it shows that inequality fluctuates, as waves of technological progress and policy responses to them take hold (see Figure 2.5 below).

In this graph, Milanovic's First Technological Revolution roughly equates to the first two Industrial Revolutions, which saw the implementation of trains and steam power, and the internal combustion engine and electricity, respectively. The second technological revolution equates roughly to the Third and Fourth Industrial Revolutions, which brought us the computer and artificial intelligence, among other innovations. His point is clear: technology has a tendency to increase inequality,

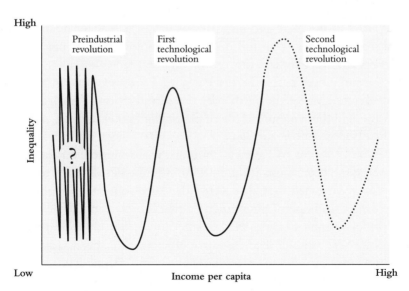

Figure 2.5 Expected Pattern of Changes in Inequality versus Income per Capita, Based on State of Technological Revolution

Source: Redrawn from Piketty, Saez, and Zucman (2018), World Inequality Report 2018..

but as we adapt to it *and take measures to deal with the inequality it creates*, we can achieve a reduction of inequality later. We will come back to this notion in Part II of the book.

But in spite of Kuznets' early warnings and Milanovic's more recent work, policymakers around the world went ahead and implemented policies that favored top-line growth over inclusive development and quick technological deployment over more considered technological governance. That was a mistake, because the current times of rapid technological development have a natural tendency to increase inequality. It has therefore become much more important for policymakers to take countermeasures to slow or halt this trend. That we haven't done so constitutes Kuznets' second curse and implies many people around the world are paying a very high price for the technological progress we have made recently.

The Third Kuznets Curse: The Environment

There is a third and final Kuznets curse, and it has to do with the environment. As the Kuznets curve was gaining traction in the 1960s and 1970s, some people started to worry about externalities caused by the West's high economic growth rates: an increase in pollution, environmental degradation, and depletion of resources. With consumerism taking hold in the West and populations growing quickly globally, one could reasonably ask what toll our socioeconomic system took on our global commons. This was the age of cars and factories laying a thick layer of smoke over cities, the discovery of a growing hole in the protecting ozone layer of the earth's sky, the introduction of nuclear plants and waste, and the widespread use of plastics and other harmful materials such as asbestos in construction.

In a similar vein to Kuznets' temporary observation on inequality, however, some economists thought there was not all too much to worry about: no sooner had they discovered the environmental pollution had been rising than hopeful signs emerged that it too would go down over time. Indeed, as production methods became more sophisticated, they also became cleaner and more resource efficient. On a per-product basis, environmental harm seemed to follow an environmental Kuznets curve. Give it another few years or decades, the thought went, and this problem, like inequality before it, would solve itself. Unfortunately, that isn't how things turned out.

A Degrading Environment

The final reality we must confront, and perhaps the most devastating, is the continued and increasing degradation of the environment caused by our economic system and the life-threatening risks posed by global warming, extreme weather events, and continued overproduction of waste and pollution.

While most reports on the environment today home in on global warming, that is only a subset of a much larger issue. The economic system we have created is utterly unsustainable, notwithstanding the hopeful signs in environmental Kuznets curves. The World Economic Forum first raised awareness on this emerging problem in 1973. Then, Aurelio Peccei, who was the president of the Club of Rome, a think tank, gave a speech in Davos about his famous study on "The Limits to Growth." The publication of this study a year earlier had "caused a sensation for calling into question the sustainability of global economic growth." The authors, who had "examined several scenarios for the global economy," outlined in Davos "the choices that society had to make to reconcile economic development and environmental constraints."[61]

They warned that with the current growth trajectory, there would be a "sudden and serious shortage" of arable land in the next decades.[62] They warned that there was only a limited supply of freshwater on earth and that with increasing demand, competition and conflict would arise over who would get access to it.[63] And they warned that many natural resources, such as oil and gas, were overused and that they led to exponential rates of pollution.[64]

But their warnings were to no avail. The worst of the scenarios the Club of Rome laid out did not come true, so much of the message was forgotten. After a lull in the 1970s, economic production has reached record levels almost every single year since, and left an ever-larger ecological footprint. Despite the Club of Rome's inaccuracies about short-term resource depletion, today we can see just how much

---

[61]These two sentences are adapted from "The World Economic Forum, A Partner in Shaping History, The First 40 Years, 1971-2010," http://www3.weforum.org/docs/WEF_First-40Years_Book_2010.pdf.

[62]*The Limits to Growth*, p. 51, http://www.donellameadows.org/wp-content/userfiles/Limits-to-Growth-digital-scan-version.pdf.

[63]Ibidem, p.53.

[64]Ibidem, p.71.

foresight the Club of Rome had. In 1970, a mere two years before *The Limits to Growth* was published, humanity's global ecological footprint was still below what the earth could regenerate, albeit only by a small margin. If we had continued to produce and consume the way we did then, we may have stayed in equilibrium, keeping the earth habitable and fertile for many generations to come.

But things took another turn as the global population kept rising. Today, the world has about double the number of people it did in the early 1970s. And with standards of living going up as well, the Global Footprint Network (GFN) calculated[65] that by 2020 humanity had used "nature's resource budget" for the entire year by sometime in August, meaning that we overused natural resources during the equivalent of four to five months each year (see Figure 2.6). (The COVID-19 crisis, including the months of mandatory confinement and the halting

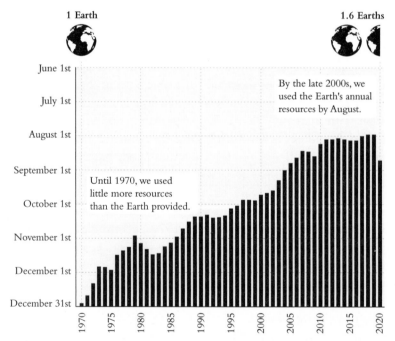

Figure 2.6 "Earth Overshoot Day" Has Been Taking Place on an Earlier Date Almost Each Year since 1970

Source: Redrawn from Global Footprint Network and Biocapacity Accounts 2019, Earth Overshoot Day.

---

[65]"Earth Overshoot Day," Global Footprint Network, https://www.overshootday.org/newsroom/press-release-july-2019-english/.

of many economic activities, did positively affect the "overshoot day,"[66] though it certainly wasn't sustainable.) The caveat, as GFN's chief science officer David Lin told us, is that our "ecological footprint" is of course only an accounting measure: there is no way of saying for sure just how detrimental our economic production and consumption processes really are. But it is clear the world's use of natural resources is unsustainable and is exacerbating many other harmful trends, such as global warming. What exactly is our record on this front?

Consider first fossil fuels, which can regenerate only over millions of years. Even though they can only be used once, coal, oil, and natural gas still account for about 85 percent of the world's primary energy consumption[67] and two thirds of world's electricity production.[68] In fact, their use has nearly doubled about every 20 years in the past century. Despite calls to phase them out, their production even increased in 2018. It is a statistic that unnerved even BP's chief economist Spencer Dale:[69] "At a time when society is increasing its demands for an accelerated transition to a low-carbon energy system," he wrote in his group's 2019 Statistical Review, "the energy data for 2018 paint a worrying picture."

It is not only fossil fuels. More broadly, over the past five decades, the use of natural resources tripled, according to the UN Environment's International Resource Panel.[70] Their extraction and processing have "accelerated" over the last two decades, and "accounts for more than 90 percent of our biodiversity loss and water stress and approximately half of our climate change impacts," the organization warned.

These trends coincided with one of increased pollution of at least three sorts: water, air, and soil.

---

[66]"Delayed Earth Overshoot Day Points to Opportunities to Build Future in Harmony with Our Finite Planet," Global Footprint Network, August 2020, https://www.overshootday. org/newsroom/press-release-august-2020-english/.

[67]"Statistical Review of World Energy 2019, Primary Energy," BP, https://www.bp.com/en/ global/corporate/energy-economics/statistical-review-of-world-energy/primary-energy. html.

[68]"Fossil Fuels, Fossil Fuels in Electricity Production," Our World in Data, https:// ourworldindata.org/fossil-fuels.

[69]"Statistical Review of World Energy 2019, Primary Energy," BP, https://www.bp.com/en/ global/corporate/energy-economics/statistical-review-of-world-energy/primary-energy. html.

[70]"Global Resources Outlook 2019," http://www.resourcepanel.org/reports/global-resources-outlook.

Take first the issue of water. UN Water, the agency coordinating the United Nations work on water and sanitation, estimated that globally 2 billion people live in countries experiencing high water stress,[71] often due to climate change. But even when water is available, it is often heavily polluted. Globally, the agency said,[72] "it is likely that over 80% of wastewater is released to the environment without adequate treatment," with pollution often happening because of "intensive agriculture, industrial production, mining and untreated urban runoff and wastewater." It threatens the access of clean water everywhere from cities to rural areas and poses a great health risk.

Moreover, there is the issue of plastics, whose impact will be felt most dramatically in the coming decades, as the plastic that is currently accumulating in the world's oceans may affect life on land in a myriad of ways. Microplastics have become ubiquitous in the world's water, in part because they take decades to decompose: by current measures, it is estimated we could end up with more plastic than fish in our oceans by 2050.[73] The most famous example in popular imagination is the "Great Pacific Garbage Patch" consisting largely of the debris of microplastics in the Pacific Ocean. But the issue is a global one, affecting all of the world's bodies of water.

Second, almost two-thirds of the world's cities also exceed WHO guidelines on air pollution, according to Greenpeace.[74] Many of the large metropoles of Asia are so polluted it is unhealthy even to walk outside,[75] as many who live or have been there will be able to attest. And third, according to the Food and Agricultural Organization of the UN (FAO),[76] soil pollution is a hidden reality all over the world and a direct threat to human health.

This rapid exploitation and pollution also started to wreak havoc on the world's natural ecosystems and threatened to make global warming spin out of control, with major consequences for people in regions

[71]"Water Scarcity," UN Water, 2018, https://www.unwater.org/water-facts/scarcity/.

[72]"ibidem"

[73]World Economic Forum, 2016: https://www.weforum.org/press/2016/01/more-plastic-than-fish-in-the-ocean-by-2050-report-offers-blueprint-for-change/.

[74]"22 of World's 30 Most Polluted Cities are in India, Greenpeace Says," The Guardian, March 2019.

[75]AirVisual https://www.airvisual.com/world-most-polluted-cities.

[76]"Soil Pollution: A Hidden Reality," Rodríguez-Eugenio, N., McLaughlin, M., and Pennock, D., FAO, 2018, http://www.fao.org/3/I9183EN/i9183en.pdf.

hit hard by climatic change and for future generations. Other data also reveal the human impact on the environment.

The UN-sponsored Intergovernmental Platform on Biodiversity and Ecosystems Services (IPBES) concluded in a 2019 report that "nature is declining globally at rates unprecedented in human history," with species already becoming extinct "at least tens to hundreds of times faster than the average over the past 10 million years."[77] Quoting the research, the *Financial Times* also wrote that "one million of Earth's estimated 8 million plant and animal species are at risk of extinction."[78]

Another specialized UN agency, the Intergovernmental Panel on Climate Change (IPCC), issued a warning late 2018 that the current path of CO_2 emissions would also lead to an unstoppable cycle of global warming—with major disruptions for life on earth—if major reductions weren't achieved by 2030. It said, "Pathways limiting global warming to 1.5°C with no or limited overshoot would require rapid and far-reaching transitions in energy, land, urban and infrastructure (including transport and buildings), and industrial systems."[79] But hopes for even that narrow path to a limited global warming of 1.5°C had all but evaporated two years later. The World Meteorological Organization, another UN-affiliated institution, in July 2020 said that a 1°C warming would already be a reality in the next five years (2020–2024) and believed there was a one in five chance that warming would already reach 1.5°C in that period.[80]

There is no one who hasn't experienced at least some of the realities of a changing climate. As I write this, the past two summers have once again been among the hottest on record.[81] Even high in the Swiss Alpine town of Zermatt, where I go to walk in summer and where temperatures are usually quite moderate, global warming and extreme weather

---

[77]"Extinctions Increasing at Unprecedented Pace, UN Study Warns," *Financial Times*, May 2019, https://www.ft.com/content/a7a54680-6f28-11e9-bf5c-6eeb837566c5.

[78]"ibidem".

[79]UN Intergovernmental Panel on Climate Change, 2018, https://www.ipcc.ch/site/assets/uploads/sites/2/2018/07/sr15_headline_statements.pdf.

[80]"New Climate Predictions Assess Global Temperatures in Coming Five Years," World Meteorological Organization, July 2020, https://public.wmo.int/en/media/press-release/new-climate-predictions-assess-global-temperatures-coming-five-years.

[81]"Here Comes the Bad Season: July 2019 Is Likely to Be the Hottest Month Ever Measured," *The Atlantic*, https://www.theatlantic.com/science/archive/2019/07/july-2019-shaping-be-warmest-month-ever/594229/.

events are hitting home—literally. The Theodul Glacier is retreating further every year, and when I visited in the summer of 2019, the melting glacier caused flooding in the valley, even though not a drop of rain had fallen in days.[82]

Faced with these changes down the ages, people have responded with one simple act: they have started moving. Today, the UN Migration Agency IOM warns that "gradual and sudden environmental changes are already resulting in substantial population movements. The number of storms, droughts, and floods has increased threefold over the last 30 years with devastating effects on vulnerable communities, particularly in the developing world."[83] It expects that the total number of climate migrants alone will by 2050 be as great as the total number of international migrants in the world today, at 200 million people.[84]

Business leaders know environmental risks are rising, as they rank them ever-more prominently in the World Economic Forum's yearly Global Risks report. For the first time in 2020, it said, "Severe threats to our climate account for all of the Global Risks Report's top long-term risks."[85] It pointed to the risks associated with extreme weather events, failure of climate-change mitigation and adaptation, human-made environmental damage, major biodiversity losses, resulting in severely depleted resources, and major natural disasters.

We should not take these risks lightly like we did in the 1970s, especially as the next generation is already looking over our shoulder, wondering what legacy we plan to leave. That would be nothing short of a betrayal of future generations.

Indeed, the dangers posed by global warming have become a major worry for the next generation of youth these past few years, as they start to demand more urgent climate action. Inspired to a large degree by peers such as Swedish school student Greta Thunberg, hundreds of thousands of climate activists have been hitting the streets, giving speeches to whomever would listen and changing their own habits where possible. We understand their concerns and for this reason invited Greta

---

[82]Telebasel, Sich entleerende Gletschertasche lässt Bach in Zermatt hochgehen, https://telebasel.ch/2019/06/11/erneut-ein-rekordheisser-hochsommer-verzeichnet/.

[83]"Migration, Climate Change and the Environment, A Complex Nexus," UN Migration Agency IOM, https://www.iom.int/complex-nexus#estimates.

84"ibidem".

[85]"Burning Planet: Climate Fires and Political Flame Wars Rage," World Economic Forum, January 2020, https://www.weforum.org/press/2020/01/burning-planet-climate-fires-and-political-flame-wars-rage.

Thunberg to speak at our Annual Meeting in 2019. Thunberg's foremost message was that "our house is on fire"[86] and that we should act with an utmost sense of urgency.

We hope we will heed the next generation's call to create a more sustainable economic system with more urgency than in 1973. Since Aurelio Peccei's speech, decades have passed. Since then, we failed to act with sufficient results and have, in doing so, worsened the economic, health, and environmental outlook for future generations—and still left many people behind economically. It was Kuznets' final curse. He had never suggested that our economic system was indefinitely sustainable.

■ ■ ■

We did not listen to Simon Kuznets' cautious warnings: he told us GDP was a poor measure for broad societal progress, as it was more geared toward measuring production capacity than any other signs of prosperity. He wasn't convinced that the declining income inequality during the 1950s would be a permanent feature but rather saw it as a temporary effect of the specific technological advances that favored inclusive growth at the time. And he never subscribed to the notion of any "Environmental Kuznets' Curve," which hypothesized that harm to the environment would decline as an economy developed. We are now paying the price for it.

But before we try to make up for those errors in our economic development though, we must first ask: Is another development path already available? And to what extent can it be found in the East, in the rise of Asia?

---

[86]"Our house is still on fire and you're fuelling the flames, World Economic Forum Agenda, January 2020, https://www.weforum.org/agenda/2020/01/greta-speech-our-house-is-still-on-fire-davos-2020/.

3

The Rise of Asia

The view from the Sham Chun River in Southern China offers a stark contrast. On its southern bank, rice paddies stretch almost as far as the eye can see. On its northern bank, skyscrapers dominate the skyline.

It wasn't always so. Forty years ago, there was almost nothing on either side of the river. The most developed part was on the southern banks, where the city of Hong Kong was a few miles out. Train tracks connected the British-ruled "Northern territories" with the empty Chinese mainland across the river. A lone Chinese guard would inspect the river's crossing point.

Four decades later, the contrast isn't one a visitor from the past might have expected. The rice paddies to the south still belong to Hong Kong, the long-time financial capital of Asia. But the skyscrapers to the north are now part of contemporary China's technology capital, Shenzhen, a city that appeared out of nowhere.

What happened north of the Sham Chun River in those 40 years, represents perhaps the greatest economic miracle ever. In 1979, those living there had an average income of less than a dollar a day. Today, Shenzhen has a per capita GDP of almost US$30,000, about a 100-fold increase over 1979. It is home to tech giants such as Huawei, Tencent, and ZTE,[1] and a "maker movement" of tech start-ups. Hong Kong didn't stand still either, but it now has a formidable twin next door.

---

[1] "Top 5 Tech Giants Who Shape Shenzhen, 'China's Silicon Valley,'" *South China Morning Post*, April 2015, https://www.scmp.com/lifestyle/technology/enterprises/article/1765430/top-5-tech-giants-who-shape-shenzhen-chinas-silicon.

How did this turnaround happen? And what does it tell us about the broader shift of the world economy to the East?

China's Special Economic Zones

I first visited China in April 1979. The country's new leader Deng Xiaoping had only been in power for about a year, and the land I encountered was still deeply impoverished. China had suffered for a long period from foreign invasions, civil war, and policies that had failed to deliver any meaningful economic progress.

That detrimental situation had been 150 years in the making. For much of the past millennia, China had been an economic superpower, alongside India, but things changed during the 19th century. First, there was a so-called Chinese Century of Humiliation from about 1840 onward. During this period, the proud and powerful Chinese civilization was defeated in various Opium Wars with Britain. It also ceded key Chinese ports and cities and territory in Indochina to Britain, France, and Japan, and suffered from Japanese occupation during the Second World War. A key reason for these defeats was that the Industrial Revolution had not spread in China, giving its adversaries economic, military, and technical supremacy.

The turmoil also led to the fall of the established political regime. The Qing Imperial dynasty was overthrown in 1912. After that, various political groups vied for power for several decades, all through the Japanese occupation in the 1930s and 1940s, and until after the end of the Second World War. Initially, the Nationalist Party of Chiang Kai-shek prevailed. He led a national government in China in the first few years after the Japanese occupation had ended. But it was unable to fully gain control over the chaotic situation that resulted after the retreat of Japanese troops and faced strong internal opposition. Instead, the civil war continued, and ultimately, the Nationalists were defeated by Mao's Communist Party.

Under the leadership of Chairman Mao, from 1949 to 1975, the Communist Party of China (CPC) became the lone governing party of the country, ending the political turmoil more decidedly. The CPC founded the People's Republic of China as a single-party state, which brought stability to the regime for the price of democratic freedom.

On the social and economic front, the People's Republic in its early years did not manage to bring about the progress enjoyed in other regions, including the United States, Western Europe, and the Soviet Union.

The country reverted to autarky in terms of food production, central planning for its industrial production, and severe restrictions in terms of political and cultural freedoms. By the late 1970s, when Deng Xiaoping came to power as successor of Mao, the Chinese economy was a shadow of its former self. The Middle Kingdom (as China is sometimes called) had become a developing country, and many of its people lived below the poverty line.

Deng wanted to change that, and in 1978, he visited Singapore. At the time, the island city-state was one of the four so-called Asian Tigers (Hong Kong, Taiwan, Singapore, and South Korea), economies that saw a rapid development in the 1960s and 1970s based on foreign direct investments (FDI), the shielding of key industries from foreign competition, and export-led growth. Having been inspired by the city-state's example, he pursued a new economic development model for China as well: the Reform and Opening-Up, starting in 1979. The kernel of the economic turnaround in this model lay in attracting FDI from some of China's neighbors, including Hong Kong, and allowing these investors to set up businesses in Special Economic Zones (SEZs) on various stretches along the populous Guangdong (Canton) coastline in Southern China. Shenzhen, north of the Sham Chun River, was one of them.

The SEZs were a sandbox for private business to operate in China. Elsewhere in the country, rules on private ownership, incorporation, and profits remained restricted for another number of years. China was a communist country after all. But in the SEZs, foreign investors could set up a business (provided it was aimed at exporting), own or at least lease property, and enjoy special legal and tax treatments.

The goal, researcher Liu Guohong of Shenzhen-based China Development Institute told us in 2019,[2] was to give China a taste of a "market-oriented economy" (Deng would call it "socialism with Chinese characteristics," and his successor Jiang Zemin talked of a "socialist market economy"). But there was virtually no money to develop any economic activity, so having SEZs close to Hong Kong—with its broad pool of money and manufacturing—was the next best option.

The bold plan worked. In 1982, Nanyang Commercial Bank, a Hong Kong–based financial institution started by a Chinese immigrant, set up a branch in Shenzhen, just a few miles north of Hong Kong. It was the first commercial bank in mainland China,[3] and its arrival marked a watershed moment in the development of the country. The Hong Kong

---

[2]Interview with Liu Guohong by Peter Vanham, Shenzhen, China, June 2019.

[3]Nanyang Commercial Bank, https://www.ncb.com.hk/nanyang_bank/eng/html/111.html.

bank set up a cross-border loan to its Chinese affiliate. It allowed the Shenzhen branch to finance long-term leases of land and the opening of factories in Shenzhen.

The Shenzhen authorities also did their part. Previously, land in China was solely state-owned, meaning it could not be accessed by private investors. Now, Shenzhen allowed foreign investors to use land for commercial and industrial purposes. In 1987 the Shenzhen SEZ even organized a public land auction, the first in China since the foundation of the People's Republic in 1949.[4]

During the 1980s, Shenzhen became the kernel from which an entire economy grew. Following the example of Hong Kong and Singapore, Shenzhen at first specialized in low-cost, low-value manufacturing. With incomes starting at under a dollar a day, it wasn't hard to offer competitive salaries, with workers producing goods for export.

The Asian Tigers took notice and were among the first to shift their production. Taiwanese, Hong Kong, Singaporean, and Korean firms moved in, creating wholly foreign enterprises aimed at export or partly owned joint ventures with Chinese investors, which allowed them to sell products within China too.

As a result, people from all over China began flocking to the SEZs, drawn by the jobs and the allure of being part of something new and growing. From some 30,000 residents in the early 1980s, Shenzhen grew to become a fully-fledged Tier 1 city of more than ten million people, alongside Beijing, Shanghai, and Canton's capital to its northwest, Guangzhou. Gone were the days of Shenzhen as a "sleepy fishing village" next to some paddies of rice.

As the Special Economic Zones were a runaway success, the Chinese government created more of them, mostly along China's east coast. Cities such as Dalian, close to Korea and Japan, and Tianjin, the main port city serving Beijing (and both now home to the World Economic Forum's Summer Davos meetings) as well as Fuzhou, home to many Chinese emigrants to Singapore, were added in 1984. In 1990, Shanghai's Pudong district was added, and another few dozen SEZs followed.

The export model functioned as a catalyst. Hundreds of millions of people moved to the coastal SEZs, confident that better salaries in factories, construction firms, or services awaited them there. China's cities exploded, and its rural hinterland emptied. Annual economic growth

---

[4]"First Land Auction Since 1949 Planned in Key China Area," *Los Angeles Times*/Reuters, June 1987, https://www.latimes.com/archives/la-xpm-1987-06-28-mn-374-story.html.

rates reached peaks of 10 percent and more. China grew from a poor country with a GDP of $200 billion in 1980, to a lower-middle-income one, with a GDP six times that size ($1.2 trillion in 2000).

As China embarked on its Reform and Opening-Up economic policies, some inside and outside the country also hoped its political process would change, similar to what happened in the Soviet Union and its sphere of influence, including Poland, Hungary, Czechoslovakia, East Germany, and of course, Russia itself. But while this movement in Europe eventually led to the disintegration of the regime and the birth of new, democratic ones, the Chinese government maintained its central role in political and economic affairs. The 1990s became boom years for China, as many Western companies moved production there, boosting employment, pay, and consumption.

By 2001, China had grown so much and become such an export powerhouse that the time felt right to enter the World Trade Organization (WTO), which fueled yet another wave of export-led growth. Western companies, which had previously been wary or simply unaware of the possibility of manufacturing in China, now also followed suit. American, European, and Japanese companies were among the prime clients of Chinese and Taiwanese manufacturers or creating their own joint ventures.

But China's original star performer didn't stand still. As time went by, the profile of Shenzhen's industrial activities changed. Known for cheap electronics manufacturing and homegrown copycat firms at first, the city became the Silicon Valley of hardware and the home to the "maker movement of technology," as *Wired* put it.[5] Start-up entrepreneurs from all over China, and increasingly the world, started to meet and exchange ideas in Shenzhen, building new and innovative companies along the way.

Today, many foreign companies still have massive manufacturing bases in Shenzhen. The most famous facilities may be those of Foxconn, a Taiwanese electronics company that employs a few hundred thousand employees and produces the bulk of Apple's iPhones (or at least it did so until recently, when geopolitical concerns forced "a quiet and gradual production shift by Apple away from China," including to a newly built Foxconn facility in India[6]). It is just one of many Taiwanese and Hong

---

[5]"The Silicon Valley of Hardware," *Wired*, https://www.wired.co.uk/video/shenzhen-episode-1.

[6]"Exclusive: Apple Supplier Foxconn to Invest $1 Billion in India, Sources Say," Reuters, July 2020, https://www.reuters.com/article/us-foxconn-india-apple-exclusive/exclusive-apple-supplier-foxconn-to-invest-1-billion-in-india-sources-say-idUSKBN24B2GH.

Kong companies that provided the backbone of Shenzhen's early industrial expansion and still have a major footprint there.

But Shenzhen may now be better known for its homegrown technology companies. Huawei, for example, is the single largest manufacturer of telecommunications equipment in the world, making hardware to power entire fifth generation (5G) mobile networks. It also produces smartphones that can be found all over the world (except the US), though the recent trade war between China and the US has put a break on its expansion.

Huawei's success was a long time coming. In 1983, its founder, Ren Zhenfei, was just one of many immigrants trying his luck as a worker in the blossoming Shenzhen electronics industry, after a career in the Chinese army. Four years later, he founded Huawei, a small firm doing contract work for a Hong Kong equipment dealer. The story of the company's rise in the following 30 years in many ways reflects that of China as a whole.

There are many more such examples of Shenzhen start-up success (years of founding in Shenzhen are shown in parentheses):

- **ZTE (1985):** Producer of a variety of telecom equipment, including phones.
- **Ping An Insurance (1988):** China's largest insurance company and a major player in artificial intelligence. It now has 200 million customers, almost 400,000 employees, and posted $160 billion in revenue.[7]
- **BYD (1995):** Short for "Build Your Dreams," BYD is now the world's biggest manufacturer of electric vehicles (EVs), according to Bloomberg, "selling as much as 30,000 pure EVs or plug-in hybrids in China every month."[8]
- **Tencent (1998):** A technology conglomerate that owns the popular Chinese social media app QQ, a large share in e-commerce website JD.com, and the developer of the popular game "League of Legends." It was founded by a group of Shenzhen residents, including current CEO, Pony Ma. It is the world's largest gaming company and one of its biggest social media and e-commerce players.

---

[7]"Global 500: Ping An Insurance," *Fortune*, https://fortune.com/global500/2019/ping-an-insurance.

[8]"The World's Biggest Electric Vehicle Company Looks Nothing Like Tesla," Bloomberg, April 2019, https://www.bloomberg.com/news/features/2019-04-16/the-world-s-biggest-electric-vehicle-company-looks-nothing-like-tesla.

Shenzhen long ago stopped being a cheap manufacturing base, but it is still the southern star for China's development, which has entered an entirely new phase. After an era in which it was the factory of the world, China has turned the page. It is the second-largest economy in the world now, and the magnetic pole for many Asian and other emerging markets' economies.

In this phase, SEZs with their focus on export continue to play a significant part. But they are increasingly eclipsed by new types of pilot zones: those of science parks, start-up incubators, and innovation hubs. There, tech start-ups and innovators are incubating products for China's increasingly tech-savvy and wealthy consumers and businesses. Shenzhen again is a leader in this field, but other locations, including Beijing's Zhongguancun neighborhood in the Haidian district (where ByteDance, the creator of TikTok, was launched), Shanghai's Zhangjiang hi-tech zone, and others are also contenders.

The Price of Progress

If you cross the Sham Chen River today, you enter a concrete jungle, the sprawling metropolis that is Shenzhen. But on a hot day in summer, you will hardly see more people in the street than you might have in the sleepy fishing village that preceded it. In part because of global warming, summer temperatures are now often so high that it's impossible to walk in the city without breaking a sweat. Instead, people have moved underground. They get around through the air-conditioned halls of Link City, an underground commercial street, or they stay in the cooled offices of the city's many skyscrapers. At other times, Shenzhenites suffer from flash floods,[9] another phenomenon that has gotten worse as climate change has intensified. The city has gotten wealthy, but all its wealth could not save it from the forces of nature.

China's rise represents an incredible milestone, but it shouldn't distract us from the even bigger picture. The global trends we outlined in Chapter 2 are as valid for Asia as they are for the Western world. The entire world has been on an unsustainable growth path, endangering the environment and the fate of future generations. Moreover, the economic

---

[9]"How Shenzhen Battles Congestion and Climate Change," Chia Jie Lin, GovInsider, July 2018, https://govinsider.asia/security/exclusive-shenzhen-battles-congestion-climate-change/.

growth that China, India, and others achieved in recent years was often shared just as unequally as in the West.

For China, the inequality challenge is equally present, but the greater problem may be the looming burden of its debt. Until the financial crisis in 2008, China's total debt-to-GDP ratio of 170 percent was in line with that of other emerging markets, as Martin Wolf of the *Financial Times* noted in a 2018 essay.[10] But in the decade since then, it has risen explosively. In July 2019, it stood at 303 percent, according to an IIF estimate, and after the first few months of the COVID-19 crisis it ballooned to 317 percent.[11]

This is a dangerous trend because much of Chinese debt is owned by nonfinancial state-owned enterprises and local governments who may use debt to boost economic output in the short run. However, with marginal returns on public and private investments sharply decreasing in recent years, top-line economic growth is decelerating as a result, and the debt overhang is becoming increasingly concerning. Trade tensions, a decline in population growth, or other factors may trigger a further slowdown in growth. If that happens, a Chinese crisis may reverberate globally.

Finally, while China led the world in installing new wind and solar facilities in the past few years, and President Xi at the UN General Assembly in September 2020 announced it wanted to achieve carbon neutrality before 2060,[12] there are still some major hurdles left to get there. First, in spite of the new Chinese ambitions, the building of new renewable energy facilities in the country slowed in 2019, a trend that continued into the new decade.[13] Second, China saw its oil demand rebound quicker than elsewhere after the COVID crisis, with 90 percent of its pre-COVID demand recovered by early summer of 2020. It was a good sign for the global economic recovery but less good news for emissions, as China is the world's second-largest consumer of oil, behind

---

[10]"China's Debt Threat: Time to Rein in the Lending Boom," Martin Wolf, *Financial Times*, July 2018 https://www.ft.com/content/0c7ecae2-8cfb-11e8-bb8f-a6a2f7bca546.

[12]"China's Debt-to-GDP Ratio Surges to 317 Percent," The Street, May 2020, https://www.thestreet.com/mishtalk/economics/chinas-debt-to-gdp-ratio-hits-317-percent.

[12]"Climate Change: Xi Jinping Makes Bold Pledge for China to Be Carbon Neutral by 2060," *South China Morning Post*, September 2020, https://www.scmp.com/news/china/diplomacy/article/3102761/climate-change-xi-jinping-makes-bold-pledge-china-be-carbon.

[13]"Current Direction for Renewable Energy in China," Anders Hove, The Oxford Institute for Energy Studies, June 2019, https://www.oxfordenergy.org/wpcms/wp-content/uploads/2020/06/Current-direction-for-renewable-energy-in-China.pdf.

the US. And third, Bloomberg reported,[14] Asia's share in total global coal demand will expand from about 77 percent now to around 81 percent by 2030. China, which produces and burns about half of global coal, and Indonesia were the world's largest coal producers, and each also produced significantly more in 2019 than the previous year, BP indicated in its 2020 Statistical Review of World Energy.[15]

Emerging Markets in China's Slipstream

China wasn't the only economy to make enormous leaps forward in the past few decades. In its slipstream, countries from Latin America to Africa and from the Middle East to Southeast Asia also rose. China needed commodities, and many of its fellow emerging markets could provide them.

Indeed, while China is a giant in both geographical and demographical terms, it is more modest in its possession of the world's most important resources, with the exception perhaps of rare-earth minerals. As it grew, constructing new cities, operating factories, and expanding its infrastructure, it needed the help of others to supply it with the necessary inputs.

This was a blessing for other emerging markets, especially those in China's immediate vicinity (including Russia, Japan, South Korea and the ASEAN region, and Australia) and those who had struggled to attain high growth rates before (including many developing countries in Latin America and Africa).

China's rise, in fact, fueled a great emerging-markets bonanza. A glance at the World Bank's and UN's trade databases for 2018[16] gives an insight into just how much China's rise contributed to that of other countries. China today is the world's second-largest importer of goods and services, to the tune of some $2 trillion. In reaching that size, it gave more than one economy a huge boost, buying loads of commodities every year.

---

[14]"Everyone around the World is Ditching Coal—Except Asia," Bloomberg, June 2020, https://www.bloomberg.com/news/articles/2020-06-09/the-pandemic-has-everyone-ditching-coal-quicker-except-asia.

[15]"Statistical Review of World Energy 2020," BP, https://www.bp.com/en/global/corporate/energy-economics/statistical-review-of-world-energy.html.

[16]"World Integrated Trade Solution," World Bank, 2018, https://wits.worldbank.org/CountryProfile/en/Country/CHN/Year/LTST/TradeFlow/Import/Partner/by-country/Product/Total#.

In 2018,[17] for example, it imported huge amounts of oil from Russia ($37 billion), Saudi Arabia ($30 billion), and Angola ($25 billion). For mining ores, besides Australia ($60 billion), it counted on Brazil ($19 billion) and Peru ($11 billion). Precious stones such as diamonds and gold were imported mostly through Switzerland, with South Africa a runner-up. China also bought copper from Chile ($10 billion) and Zambia ($4 billion), while various types of rubber came mostly from Thailand ($5 billion).

Those were just the raw materials. As China climbed up the value chain, it started to outsource some of its production, moving factories to the new low-cost economies of Vietnam, Indonesia, and Ethiopia, to name but a few. The technology it once needed to import through foreign joint ventures, China now created itself, allowing it to become an importer of the finished goods it had produced abroad and an exporter of them to consumers in other countries.

It is no surprise then, that just like China, many emerging markets experienced their own wonder years in the past two decades. The trend started slowly in the 1990s, when the world moved toward free trade, and it accelerated in the years following China's inauguration into the WTO in 2001. For over a decade, from 2002 to 2014, the *Financial Times* calculated,[18] emerging markets consistently outperformed their developed world peers, not just in growth but in *per capita* GDP growth (Figure 3.1). The result was, as economist Richard Baldwin dubbed it, "the great convergence":[19] the incomes and GDP of poorer, emerging markets, moved closer to that of richer, developed markets.

Unfortunately, that trend in recent years has come to an end for most emerging markets, bar China and India. Since 2015, per capita GDP growth in the 30 largest emerging markets fell back below that of the 22 largest developed ones. The fact that China's growth in those years fell to under 7 percent is no exception. Its appetite for commodities is no longer insatiable, which put the brakes on their prices and trading volumes.

That doesn't mean growth has petered out everywhere. Three regions in particular continue to perform well:

---

[17]"China Imports," Comtrade, UN, 2018, https://comtrade.un.org/labs/data-explorer/.

[18]"Does Investing in Emerging Markets Still Make Sense?" Jonathan Wheatley, *The Financial Times*, July 2019, https://www.ft.com/content/0bd159f2-937b-11e9-aea1-2b1d33ac3271.

[19]*The Great Convergence*, Richard Baldwin, Harvard University Press, https://www.hup.harvard.edu/catalog.php?isbn=9780674660489.

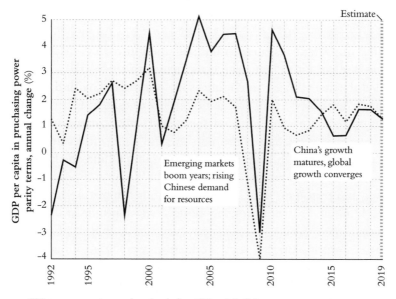

5

4

3

GDP per capita in pruchasing power parity terms, annual change (%)

2

1

0

-1

-2

-3

-4

Estimate

Emerging markets
boom years; rising
Chinese demand
for resources

China's growth
matures, global
growth converges

1992 1995 2000 2005 2010 2015 2019

—— 30 Largest emerging markets (excluding China & India)

···· 22 Largest developed economies, as defined by the IIF

Figure 3.1 After a China-Fuelled Boom in the 2000s, Emerging Markets Growth Lags That of Developed Economies Again

Source: Redrawn from IMF, Real GDP growth, 2020.

First there is the ASEAN economic community, home to some 650 million people, including from large and growing countries such as Indonesia (264 million people), the Philippines (107 million), Vietnam (95 million), Thailand (68 million), and Malaysia (53 million).[20,21] Though an extremely diverse group of nations, both culturally and economically, the whole ASEAN community is set to return to the GDP growth path it had built up in the last few years before the COVID crisis hit, averaging some 5 percent per year.[22] In the IMF's latest World Economic Outlook, dating from October 2020, the five largest ASEAN economies were in fact expected to experience a smaller than global

---

[20]"Member States," ASEAN, https://asean.org/asean/asean-member-states/.

[21]"Total Population of the ASEAN countries," Statista, https://www.statista.com/statistics/796222/total-population-of-the-asean-countries/.

[22]"Economic Outlook for Southeast Asia, China and India 2019," OECD, https://www.oecd.org/development/asia-pacific/01_SAEO2019_Overview_WEB.pdf.

average economic contraction in 2020 (–3.4 percent) and return to a 6.2 percent growth in 2021.[23]

One important reason for their sustained growth is that as a group, they are the closest to being the next factory of the world, a title China held before them. Wages in countries like Vietnam, Thailand, Indonesia, Myanmar, Laos, and Cambodia are often lower than in China, and their proximity to China and some of the world's most important sea lanes make for easy export to consumers around the world. Already, hundreds of multinationals from countries including China, the US, Europe, Korea, and Japan are producing there.

Another reason for their sustained economic success is that they're an agreeable neutral territory for the world's two major economic powers. Because of the ongoing trade tensions between the US and China, many companies are looking to shift production away from China to avoid tariffs. ASEAN, which has so far stayed out of the trade wars, has proven an attractive alternative. Vietnam has been a clear winner in this regard.[24]

The third and final reason for its continued positive outlook is the mix of regional integration and technological innovation. ASEAN is arguably the most successful regional economic community after the European Union. Regional trade is rising and integration increasing. And it also created several homegrown tech unicorns, a term to describe privately held companies with a valuation of $1 billion or more. Singapore-based ride hailing app Grab is the most famous, but Indonesia's Go-Jek, Tokopedia, and Traveloka, several Singaporean startups, Vietnam's VNG, and the Philippines' Revolution Precrafted also achieved that hallowed status (at least before the COVID crisis), according to consulting firm Bain & Company[25] (Figure 3.2).

Growth in India

Another country that was experiencing strong growth prospects before the COVID crisis hit is India, though it was harder hit than

---

[23]"World Economic Outlook: Latest World Economic Outlook Growth Projections," International Monetary Fund, October 2020, https://www.imf.org/en/Publications/WEO/Issues/2020/09/30/world-economic-outlook-october-2020.

[24]"Vietnam Emerges a Key Winner from the US-China Trade War," *Channel News Asia*, https://www.channelnewsasia.com/news/commentary/us-china-trade-war-winners-losers-countries-vietnam-hanoi-saigon-11690308.

[25]"Southeast Asia Churns Out Billion-Dollar Start-Ups," Bain, https://www.bain.com/insights/southeast-asia-churns-out-billion-dollar-start-ups-snap-chart/.

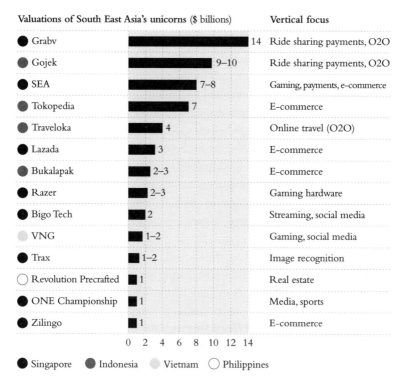

Figure 3.2 By 2019, Southeast Asia Had at Least 14 Tech "Unicorns"

Source: Redrawn from Bain & Company, November 2019.

most during the pandemic. For decades after its independence, the country struggled with the so-called Hindu rate of growth, a euphemistic way of saying "low growth." Despite enthusiasm about its independence and young workforce, India's economy never achieved the runaway success of the Asian Tigers or China. The protectionist policies it pursued, alongside the red tape of the so-called Licence Raj system, which effectively created monopolies, precluded it from making such progress.

India also remained largely unindustrialized, with hundreds of millions of people living on the countryside, earning only what they could get from small-scale farming. The resulting socioeconomic picture until well into the 1990s was one of a massive rural population living close to or under the poverty line and another large part of the population trying to come by in the country's mega-cities, which nevertheless offered less opportunities for advancement than those in Japan, the Asian Tigers, or China.

Starting the 1980s, however, some entrepreneurs started to gradually change the face of this rural, under-industrialized India. As the computer revolution took off, some entrepreneurial individuals, often hailing from the country's Indian Institutes of Technology (IIT), managed to build some of the world's most successful IT outsourcing firms, such as Infosys and Wipro. Leading industrialists also added to the burgeoning tech scene with the creation of offshoots such as Tata Consultancy Services (TCS) (founded already 1968) and Tech Mahindra.

A number of industrial companies also emerged, initially focusing on basic products in raw materials, chemicals, and textile but later expanding to modern technologies such as telecommunication and the Internet. The best-known and largest example is probably Reliance Industries, led by Mukesh Ambani. By diversifying and investing in large new projects centered on Fourth Industrial Revolution technologies, Reliance and other large Indian conglomerates are playing a substantial role in ushering in the digital era in India. Their scope is comparable to that of the large Chinese tech firms, as they offer everything from e-commerce to banking and from Internet to TV.

Before India got hit by COVID, the country was making structural efforts to do away with its checkered macroeconomic legacy. Under Prime Minister Modi, in office since 2014, the central government made substantial market reforms, including a unified tax on goods and services, allowing for foreign investment in a variety of industries, and running a more transparent auction of the telecom spectrum.[26] GDP growth in years before 2020 hovered between 6 and 7 percent per year, putting it on par or even higher than that of China.

COVID, however, halted that ascent abruptly. India's economy was expected to contract by over 10 percent, putting it on par with Spain and Italy as the worst hit economies, the IMF said in late 2020.[27] And that top-line economic decline hid an even more dramatic situation on the ground, as millions of the country's poorest city dwellers felt forced to return to rural home villages on foot when the country went in lockdown on March 24. With 10 million migrant workers returning home,[28]

---

[26]"India's Economic Reform Agenda (2014–2019), a Scorecard," Center for Strategic and International Studies, https://indiareforms.csis.org/2014reforms.

[27]"World Economic Outlook," International Monetary Fund, October 2020, Chapter 1, p. 9, https://www.imf.org/en/Publications/WEO/Issues/2020/09/30/world-economic-outlook-october-2020.

[28]"India's Harsh Covid-19 Lockdown Displaced at Least 10 Million Migrants," Niharika Sharma, Quartz India, September 2020, https://qz.com/india/1903018/indias-covid-19-lockdown-displaced-at-least-10-million-migrants/.

it became one of the largest intra-country migrations of the 21st century so far. Many of them walked for weeks to their home provinces, in the hopes of being better off there during the crisis. But the long journey brought many additional problems, not in the least for their physical health and safety.

Yet there are also a few reasons to remain optimistic about India in the longer term. The country will soon have the largest working-age population in the world (25 years old on average), and its government has done away with some of the biggest impediments to growth. The Licence Raj, which effectively rationed supplies and limited competition for many goods before, was abolished, and more steps toward a unified internal market are underway.

Still, many of its 1.3 billion people are underprepared to join a modern workforce. One major reason for this is the literacy rate in India, which is still only 77.7 percent in 2020,[29] caused in large part by a low schooling rate among girls. It does not need to be this way. In the US, Indian immigrants are already heading some of the largest tech firms in the world, leaders like Sundar Pichai at Google, Satya Nadella at Microsoft, and Shantanu Narayen at Adobe Systems. In recent years, tech unicorns such as Paytm and Flipkart were started in India.

But to really reach its potential, the country will have to make strides in education, health care, and infrastructure, so that all its people have a chance to reach their full potential and the country can do away with its ever-rising inequality. Because even as the top-line growth in the country accelerated in recent years and decades, income and wealth inequality in the country got out of hand as well. The macroeconomic reforms the country made helped unlock a more competitive economy in many industries, both domestically and internationally. But they did little to help the many rural farmers and the urban working class get ahead, whether in education, health care, or income.

The Bigger Picture

The 2020s onward may also see the continuation of the deepening Afrasian ties, which could complement the rise of China. Basic infrastructure, education, and health care, as well as sufficient access to finance have for

---

[29]"International Literacy Day 2020: Kerala, Most Literate State in India, Check Rank-Wise List," *The Hindustan Times*, September 2020, https://www.hindustantimes.com/education/international-literacy-day-2020-kerala-most-literate-state-in-india-check-rank-wise-list/story-IodNVGgy5hc7PjEXUBKnIO.html.

decades been lacking in many African economies. But thanks to China's transformation to a quasi-advanced economy and the country's willingness to invest in Africa, some of those constraints are now disappearing.

China may consider Africa to be the next major manufacturing hub once Southeast Asian opportunities have dried up. In effect, Africa could be for China what China was for Western countries. Already, countries such as Angola, Ethiopia, and Kenya are major recipients of Chinese investments.[30] According to the Brookings Institution, these investments are largely focused on transport and energy, but once the roads, railroads, and electricity are available, they could also provide the basis for manufacturing.

So, while emerging market growth overall may be slowing, some of Africa's markets may continue to develop quickly,[31] including those where China has a major stake. In East Africa, for example, Ethiopia, Kenya, Tanzania, and Uganda are expected to hit between 6 and 8 percent growth in the coming years, in part thanks to their ties with China. In West Africa, the outlook for Côte d'Ivoire, Ghana, and Niger are also positive. Nigeria and South Africa, on the other hand, the two most populous countries in Africa, have narrower paths to growth. The COVID crisis hit South Africa particularly hard, and Nigeria had been growing slower even before the pandemic hit.

In contrast to the picture we painted in previous chapters regarding Western growth, the overall track record of economic development in other parts of the world, particularly East and Southeast Asia, has been a hugely positive one. This was in large part thanks to China, which boosted the fortunes of many both at home and abroad. As we have seen in this chapter, China, by its own calculation, lifted 740 million of its own citizens out of poverty. And it helped many other emerging markets achieve higher growth rates, leading at its peak to a global convergence—though it has since ebbed somewhat.

The greatest consequence of this China effect is that what many people call "the Asian Century" has already begun, according to some measures. In a March 2019 essay,[32] *Financial Times* writers Valentina

[30]"Chinese Investments in Africa," Brookings Institution, https://www.brookings.edu/blog/africa-in-focus/2018/09/06/figures-of-the-week-chinese-investment-in-africa/.

[31]"Global Economic Prospects, Sub-Saharan Africa," The World Bank, January 2019, http://pubdocs.worldbank.org/en/307811542818500671/Global-Economic-Prospects-Jan-2019-Sub-Saharan-Africa-analysis.pdf.

[32]"The Asian Century Is Set to Begin," *Financial Times*, March 2019, https://www.ft.com/content/520cb6f6-2958-11e9-a5ab-ff8ef2b976c7.

Romei and John Reed pointed to a remarkable statistic: as a share of world GDP at purchasing power parity (PPP), 2020 was going to mark the first time in two centuries that Asian GDP will be higher than that of the rest of the world (Figure 3.3). And the COVID crisis confirmed that outlook. By October 2020, the IMF forecasted[33] that China would be the only major economy that would see full-year economic growth in 2020, with ASEAN the only other region able to limit its losses. Most of the Western advanced economies, by contrast, particularly those in Europe, were expected to see historic economic contractions.

The importance of this statistic, depicted in Figure 3.3, should not be underestimated: The last time Asia dominated the world economy was in the early 19th century, just as the First Industrial Revolution commenced. Back in 2000, Asia still only counted for one third of global output. Today, at the dawn of the Fourth Industrial Revolution, Asia is reconquering the dominant position it held for millennia. And, going by the advances in China, it may well outperform the rest of the world on

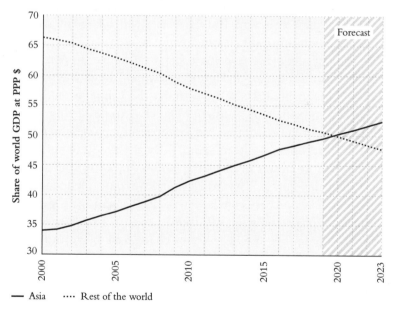

— Asia ···· Rest of the world

Figure 3.3 By Some Measures, the Asian Century Has Already Begun

Source: Redrawn from *The Financial Times*, Valentina Romei, International Monetary Fund.

---

[33]"World Economic Outlook: Latest World Economic Outlook Growth Projections," International Monetary Fund, October 2020, https://www.imf.org/en/Publications/WEO/Issues/2020/09/30/world-economic-outlook-october-2020.

everything from the Internet of Things to artificial intelligence, locking in its advantage for decades.

The rise of China—and of other emerging markets in its slipstream—does represent an incredible milestone. But it shouldn't deflect us from the even bigger picture: the global trends we outlined in Chapter 2 are as valid for Asia as they are for the Western world. The entire world has been on an unsustainable growth path, endangering the environment and the fate of future generations. Moreover, the growth that China, India, and others achieved in recent years was often just as lopsided as that in the West.

Consider first the environmental realities in Asia. Many cities in China, Southeast Asia, and other emerging markets are among those experiencing the worst effects of environmental degradation, pollution, and climate change. Over 90 percent of the world's population breathes air the World Health Organization deems unsafe, the organization said in 2019.[34] But the 20 most polluted cities are all in Asia: 15 in India, including the capital, New Delhi, 2 each in China and Pakistan, and the final one is Dhaka, the capital of Bangladesh. In recent years, awareness about the severity of the situation in China has grown a lot, and recent policy changes reflect these concerns. But no matter which large industrial city you walk in, pollution is still clearly a major issue.

The issue of inequality remains a major challenge for Asian economies as well, as can be seen in Figure 3.4, which shows the two graphs of the World Inequality Lab (WIL). In India, the Lab reported, "inequality has risen substantially from the 1980s onwards, following profound transformations in the economy that centered on the implementation of deregulation and opening-up reforms."[35] By the time the current government came into power in 2014, the country faced "historically high" income inequality levels. Similarly, China's income inequality almost continuously increased between the start of its Reform and Opening-Up and around 2010. The policies, WIL wrote, caused "unprecedented rises in national income" but also "significant changes to the country's distribution of income." Almost every segment of the population advanced, but the higher income groups were progressively benefiting more from the opening up. Since almost a decade, however, this evolution toward ever-more inequality does seem to have slowed or stopped, but the resulting picture is still one of high inequality.

---

[34]"Air Pollution," World Health Organization, https://www.who.int/airpollution/en/.

[35]"World Inequality Report 2018: Income Inequality in India," World Inequality Lab, https://wir2018.wid.world/.

Inequality in India and China
(top 10% and bottom 50% income shares, 1978–2014)

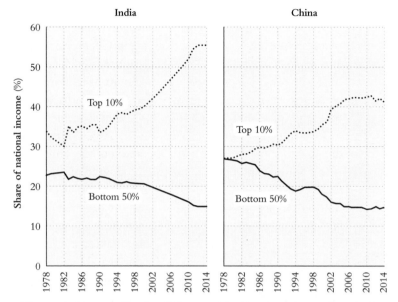

Figure 3.4 Inequality in China and India Has Risen Sharply in Recent Years

Source: Redrawn from World Inequality Report, Chancel, Piketty, Yang and Zucman.

Finally, the COVID-19 crisis caused an additional short-term disruption in the entire global economy, including Asia. If early indicators are proven correct, China, some ASEAN economies, and East Asia did bounce back faster from this crisis than many Western nations, completing as such a so-called V-shaped recovery. But, as we have seen, the challenges of inequality, lack of sustainability, and possible lack of resilience will still be shared by both Western and Asian societies after the COVID crisis recedes.

We can hope that Asia will use its regained economic and political strength to help address the key global challenges we are facing, including climate change, the lack of multilateralism, and social and economic inequalities. In principle, the Confucian spirit of searching for harmony could be Asia's contribution to a more virtuous world. But we are not yet there. Our global economic system has spiraled out of control, and before we can change course, we must confront another painful reality. We are living in split societies.

4

Divided Societies

On the morning of August 12, 1961, Berliners woke up to a harsh new reality. A wall had appeared in their city, dividing it right through the middle. It was a culmination of a long process of diverging geopolitical interests—yet a brutal shock to many. The Berlin Wall would last for nearly 30 years and scar several generations of Germans.

Fifteen years earlier, at the end of World War II, Germany had been overrun by the Allies. The Soviet Union, the United States, the United Kingdom, and France brought down the Nazi leadership and ended the most devastating war in history. But the end of one war also marked the beginning of another. Germany was split in two, and so was Berlin. East Berlin eventually became part of the Deutsche Demokratische Republik (DDR), a country under Soviet influence in the Eastern part of Germany. And West Berlin, which had been occupied by the Allies, became part of the Western-oriented Bundesrepublik Deutschland (BRD), which encompassed the western and southern parts of Germany.

Berlin was in an awkward position. As capital of the entire country until then, it was home to both *Wessies* (inhabitants of West Germany) and *Ossies* (citizens of East Germany), who lived respectively in the American, French, and British quarters and in the Russian quarter of the city. That situation wasn't to last. As the tensions between the two newly formed nations grew, and defection from the communist East to free West increasingly became a problem, the DDR in 1961 decided to build a border wall. The wall divided the city right through the middle and blocked the access to the West for all DDR citizens. It settled the geopolitical division in the region for decades.

German Division and Reunification

I vividly remember the moment the wall appeared, as do probably all Germans, and many other people around the world. I was 23 and had been very aware of the political reality in my country of birth and Europe at large. In my youth, I had spent a great number of months traveling throughout the free Western Europe and joined youth movements that celebrated the common European identity we all shared—whether we were German, French, English, or Italian. We wanted to translate that shared identity in a political and social reality, a project epitomized by the European Economic Community, which later turned into the European Union.

But there was another reality emerging too at that time, in which countries didn't come together but were going their separate ways. The building of the Berlin Wall fit into that evolution. It was part of the Cold War between the Soviet-led Eastern part of the world and the United States–led Western bloc. That conflict took place all over the world. A few months before the Wall was built, Cuban exiles aided by the US government attempted a *coup d'état* of the newly communist Cuba of Fidel Castro. The botched attempt became known as the Bay of Pigs. It led to the Cuban Missile Crisis two years later. In the months and years that followed, the Soviet Union and the United States each ramped up their stock of weapons of mass destruction and brought the world to the brink of a nuclear war. It was only narrowly avoided.

Back in Berlin, the Wall's starkest division between these two worlds was in front of the Brandenburg Gate. The Wall passed right by the iconic gate, literally blocking the road from the democratic West Berlin to the Eastern province of Brandenburg that surrounded the city. Inaccessible behind the Wall and barbed wire, the Gate became a true reference point. Political leaders from Germany and the rest of the world gave speeches with the Brandenburg Gate symbolically behind it. It was here that US President John F. Kennedy in 1963 said, "*Ich bin ein Berliner,*" signaling his support to all Berliners.[1] It was here that West Berlin mayor Richard von Weiszacker in 1985 said that "the German question

---

[1] "Rede von US-Präsident John F. Kennedy vor dem Rathaus Schöneberg am 26. Juni 1963", City of Berlin, https://www.berlin.de/berlin-im-ueberblick/geschichte/artikel.453085.php.

is open as long as the Brandenburg Gate is closed." And it was here that US President Ronald Reagan in 1987 asked Soviet leader Mikhail Gorbachev to "open this gate" and "tear down this wall[2]."

But for almost three decades, it was to no avail. Wessies, the inhabitants of West Berlin, could only see the Brandenburg Gate in the distance, and those who had Ossie friends or family in the East-German state of Brandenburg would not see them for decades. In the years following its construction, hundreds of people even died trying to cross the Wall. In this way, the Wall was a physical manifestation of the Iron Curtain that soon divided not just Berlin and Germany but Europe as a whole. Only West Berliners would continue to experience freedom and democracy. East Berliners and those living in the surrounding regions, like Brandenburg, would live under markedly different circumstances. This was literally a divided society.

It all changed on November 9, 1989. That day, thousands of people climbed the Wall from both sides, after rumor spread that the border might re-open sometime in the future. The Soviet Union had become a giant with clay feet, and from Poland to Hungary its borders had started to crack. In a society that had been divided for so long, it was the straw that broke the camel's back. As the military guard stood by, a buoying crowd climbed on to the Wall overlooking the Brandenburg Gate, reaching over to the other side for the first time in two generations. In mounting the Wall, these men and women mounted more than a physical barrier. The message the Ossies and Wessies sent was clear: From now on, we are a people united. The images of the people on the Wall spread around the world—and throughout the still communist-ruled East Germany.

That night in November set in motion a cascade of historical events that many readers will remember. In the following months, the so-called Iron Curtain crumbled, and so did the governments behind it, including those of the Central and Eastern Europeans nations of the Warsaw Pact. The volte-face in East Germany was particularly impressive. In December 1989, the Berlin Wall was completely torn down, and the Brandenburger Gate officially re-opened. Hundreds of thousands of people crossed from East to West and vice versa, often seeing friends and family for the first time in decades. It was an important moment in the history of the World Economic Form too. As I recalled in a previous book on the Forum history:[3]

---

[2] "Ronald Reagan, Remarks at Brandenburg Gate, 1987", University of Bochum, https://www. ruhr-uni-bochum.de/gna/Quellensammlung/11/11_reaganbrandenburggate_1987.htm.

[3] "A Partner in Shaping History, The First 40 Years," The World Economic Forum, http:// www3.weforum.org/docs/WEF_First40Years_Book_2010.pdf.

The 1990 Annual Meeting [in Davos] became an important platform for facilitating the process of German reunification. The first encounters between West Germany's Federal Chancellor Helmut Kohl and the newly elected East German Prime Minister Hans Modrow in Davos were decisive in determining the course of the reunification process of Germany. Kohl recognized the urgency to act. The [DDR] was in the process of imploding and needed immediate economic support to maintain financial stability. For his part, the deeply affected Modrow realized that he could no longer insist on German postreunification neutrality. On his return to Bonn, Chancellor Kohl moved quickly. Days later, on 7 February, his cabinet confirmed officially the proposal for the monetary union of the two Germanies. Eight months later the process was complete and, on 3 October 1990, Germany was reunified.[4]

In the years after the German reunification, people supported government policies to truly mend the ties between East and West and to reunify a divided country. In Brandenburg, the province surrounding Berlin, people voted en masse for the two major Big Tent parties, the Christian-Democrats of CDU and the Social-Democrats of SPD. Together, they got two thirds of the Brandenburg vote in the first free elections (the former Communists came in third). The same was true in other German states. Thanks to this broad popular support, Germany could become one political, social, and economic union. East Germany did need substantial financial aid to recover from the shock of economic integration, and people had unavoidably grown apart during 40 years of separation. But the enthusiasm for unity was overwhelming.

In these circumstances, no one could predict that within the next thirty years, the tide would once again turn, and division would return. Yet it did.

After two decades of support for the major parties of the center and the shared progress they advocated for, things took a dramatically different turn in the former East German states. In the span of only a couple of years, a breakdown of the political center ensued. After the most recent elections in September 2019, the once unthinkable happened. The two major parties received far less than half of the vote, coming at 42 percent. Even adding in the third traditional party, the Left (the former Communists), didn't change the calculation much. From peak to zenith to nadir, the Big Three lost almost half of their voters in Brandenburg.

[4]"A Partner in Shaping History, German Reunification and the New Europe," World Economic Forum, p. 108, http://www3.weforum.org/docs/WEF_A_Partner_in_Shaping_History.pdf.

The winners were two parties on opposing sides on the social and political spectrum. The climate-centered party *Die Grünen* (the Greens) got about 10 percent of the vote in Brandenburg. They embodied the growing concern in society over climate change, and their entry in the political arena was mostly welcomed by the other parties. More worryingly however, the radical right and anti-immigration party Alternative for Germany (AFD) got a historic 23.5 percent of the vote as well—the highest result for a radical right party since the last democratic elections of 1930s Germany.

In Germany as a whole, the evolution was similar, until a well-managed COVID crisis response allowed the Christian Democratic Union (CDU) of Chancellor Merkel, traditionally the centrist party in Germany, to surge again in the polls. But even that resurgence of the center could not hide the growing radicalization on the right and the splintering of the left. Despite her managing the COVID crisis to great critical and popular acclaim, a significant portion of the population grew skeptical of both government as a whole and public health measures in particular, including mask wearing, distancing, and the prospect of vaccination.

The 2019 state elections and the COVID crisis in that way capped a 30-year cycle. Brandenburg, whose Gate had once stood as symbol of unity and hope, now symbolized an entirely different reality: that of a more polarized and highly skeptical society. There is no wall dividing society right through the middle anymore, yet many people ran away from the political center, seeking refuge in more extreme, radical, or more divisive parties.

What happened?

The collapse of the political center and the surge of populism, identity politics, and other divisive ideologies is not one that is limited to Brandenburg or even Germany. Across the world, people are voting in ever-smaller numbers for major centrist parties and in ever-greater numbers for parties and candidates with more extreme or divisive views, which ends up polarizing and paralyzing politics and society. This is a break with a longstanding post-war trend in the West, where most leading parties tended to be inclusive both in their membership and views. And as we should know from experience, choosing for more divisive alternatives often leads to further rifts, rather than a more harmonious future. Once put in motion, it is hard to stop these centrifugal forces.

It is hard to single out one factor that explains this polarization entirely. (We'll look at some social and economic causes in the next part of this book.) But polarization is quite likely both a consequence of existing socioeconomic issues and a contributor to them.

So how widespread is the societal divide we are facing, and where does it come from? To answer those questions, let's look at some more examples from Europe and around the world.

The Erosion of the Political Center

Most people are familiar with the societal and political developments in the United States and the United Kingdom, two of the most mediatized societies in the West. In the United States a non-establishment figure was elected president for the first time in living memory in 2016. And in the UK the people's vote on whether to remain in or leave the European Union (Brexit) in 2016 also split society almost right through the middle. In both countries the societal divide has persisted and even grew since. But the trend toward polarization goes beyond the Anglo-Saxon world, and it is deeper and more profound than it may appear at first sight.

Consider the situation in Continental Europe, with its parliamentary democracies. Here, the political landscape was for a long time dominated by center-left and center-right parties, similar to those in Germany. But in recent years, the once leading *Volksparteien* have often disintegrated and been replaced by more extreme ones. Or they went through a transformation from within and reincarnated as more radical versions of themselves.

Consider first the center-left. Following the fall of the Iron Curtain and the disintegration of communism in Europe, many former socialist parties in Europe initially rebranded as more pragmatic and center-left parties. They received votes from a wide array of people and in doing so, became true Big Tent parties: major political forces with a broad and often non-ideological appeal. But that newfound equilibrium did not last. Starting in the late 2000s, the Social Democrats in many European countries started losing ground. Having been part of government in the build-up to or during the sovereign debt crisis, and the steep economic recession that followed it, voters lost their confidence in their center-left brand of politics.

Their subsequent fall in the polls has been nothing short of dramatic. In Germany, the SPD of Chancellor Gerhard Schroder received more than 40 percent of votes in 1998, a post-reunification high. By 2019, by contrast, it polled below 15 percent. In France, the social-democratic *Parti Socialiste* went from regularly winning a majority as well as the presidency until 2012 to near-disintegration in 2017. (Though a new center force did emerge, in President Macron's *La Republique en Marche*.) In Italy, the collapse of the center-left Democratic Party was even swifter. In 2013, Prime Minister's Renzi social-democratic *Partito Democratico* held almost half of parliamentary seats, and his center-left coalition held a comfortable majority in parliament. Five years later, the party crumbled, winning only a sixth of seats in parliament.

Where these voters went varies by country, but the parties that gained the most often came from outside the traditional center, advocating for radical reforms domestically and being dismissive of the European Union and the global economic system abroad. In France, for example, the left-wing populist party *La France Insoumise*, or "Insubmissive France," fell just short of a second-round run-off place in the 2017 presidential elections, outscoring the PS candidate by 3 to 1. One of its aims is to install a Sixth Republic to replace the postwar "Fifth Republic." In Greece, the left, anti-austerity Syriza party came to power after the country's debt crisis spun out of control in the early 2010s. It famously sparred with its creditors, including the IMF and the EU, objecting to their financing conditions. And in Spain, a new political party called *Podemos*, or We Can, successfully challenged the Spanish Social Democrats on their left flank, coming to the forefront shortly after the street protests of indignant youth. What bound all these parties together was a wish to withdraw from existing international trade agreements, demands to reform or leave the European Union, and a general dislike for elites.

The second and more drastic move away from the center in Europe happened on the center-right. For much of their recent history, the conservative Christian-Democratic parties were the true *Volksparteien* of Europe. They did not adhere to either of the ideologies born out of the Industrial Revolution or Enlightenment—socialism or liberalism—but instead put forth a humanistic vision of society, as well as a more centrist role in politics. No person embodies this pragmatic style of politics in recent history better than Chancellor Angela Merkel. But long before she came to power, her CDU-CSU alliance was Germany's major *Volkspartei*. Its dominance went back to Helmut Kohl being German Chancellor for 16 years in the 1980s and 90s and even Chancellor Konrad Adenauer, who led Germany during nearly 15 years following the Second World War, often with support of nearly or over half of the vote in elections (an impressive feat in the multi-party, representative democracy).

In recent years however, the CDU has been pressured from the right to shed its humanistic and centrist reflexes. The European refugee crisis provided a major trigger. In 2015 and 2016, over a million political and economic refugees fled from the Middle East and Africa to Europe, posing a major societal and political challenge for the recipient countries. Merkel and her CDU-CSU initially reacted with an open hand. She advocated to keep borders open, having in mind no doubt the drama of the Iron Curtain and Berlin Wall just decades earlier. "*Wir Schaffen Das*," or "We'll manage it," declared the Chancellor. We have done it before, during East-West migration following German reunification, and we can do it again. But popular support for that inclusive and welcoming approach quickly eroded, as the challenges of integration proved to be more than many local communities could handle. Many young, male, non–German-speaking immigrants had to go through a rather long process of reskilling, language learning, and administrative hurdles before they could join the workforce, putting a strain on many cities' social programs. Moreover, heavy media coverage of crimes committed by immigrants[5] early in the migrant crisis, including reported gang assaults of women[6] during New Year's celebrations in various cities, turned public opinion against the new immigrants. The Alternative for Germany (AfD) party emerged, demanding closed borders and harsher integration policies, which led to it rising in the polls. Outflanked on the right, the CDU-CSU was forced to take on a harder stance of its own, and in 2016, Chancellor Merkel retracted the "*Wir Schaffen Das*" slogan. "I sometimes think this phrase was a little overstated, that too much store was set by it—to the extent that I'd prefer not to repeat it," Merkel notably told the magazine *Wirtschaftswoche*. It seemed like it could be the beginning of the end for Europe's leading *Volkspartei* and the European People's Party it belonged to, as similar events took place elsewhere in the European Union. But the pragmatic and inclusive approach of Merkel did in fact make a major and unexpected comeback in 2020, as her leadership during the COVID crisis proved remarkably successful. Merkel, a scientist by training, followed a rigorous, data- and evidence-based approach to managing the public health crisis. As a result, the country felt the consequences of the pandemic much less severely than many other countries,

---

[5]"Reality Check: Are Migrants Driving Crime in Germany?" BBC News, September 2018, https://www.bbc.com/news/world-europe-45419466.

[6]"Germany Shocked by Cologne New Year Gang Assaults on Women," BBC, January 2016, https://www.bbc.com/news/world-europe-35231046.

including France, Spain, and Italy, and the public rallied once again behind its pragmatic and centrist leader.

Fellow Christian-Democratic parties in other European countries, however, did not bounce back as well during the COVID crisis, lacking an equally resilient government apparatus and public health system and the steady hand of an experienced leader like Merkel. Instead, leading center-right major parties everywhere on the continent were confronted with an impossible dilemma: take a hard turn to the right to maintain popular support or lose a majority of voters to an alternative hard-line party. Either outcome meant the end of the Christian-Democrats as leading centrist *Volksparteien*.

The result has been a hollowing out of the humanistic center. In Italy, a center-right coalition in theory remains the strongest political force to this day, as it has been for most of Italy's post-war history. But its internal setup changed dramatically. In the first post-fascist elections, the coalition was led by *Democrazia Cristiana*, a conservative, center-right party. But in the 2000s, Silvio Berlusconi's populist *Forza Italia* took over.

In recent years, Italy's leading coalition, kept together by Giuseppe Conte, an independent prime minister who enjoys strong popular support,[7] has taken an even stronger turn to the right. The right wing and nationalist *Lega* (League), formerly the junior partner in *Forza Italia's* coalition, took Italy's general elections by storm in 2018. At the same time, the anti-establishment, non-ideologically bound Five Star Movement became the other leading party in Italy, giving the country an untested government coalition of right wing and anti-establishment parties.

In many other European democracies, something similar happened. In Poland, where Lech Walesa's Solidarity movement had opened the door to democracy in the 1980s, the right-wing Law and Justice party emerged in recent years as the leading political party. The party technically still labels itself Christian-Democratic, but it is much more right wing and much more popular and populist than any previous one in Poland. In Hungary, the picture looks similar. "Fidesz-KNDP," a coalition of right wing and Christian Democratic parties, is by far the dominant political force. Fidesz too is technically a Christian-Democratic party and as such is affiliated to the European People's Party in the European Parliament. But the party's hard line against immigration and its

---

[7]"Why Italy's Technocratic Prime Minister Is So Popular," *The Economist*, June 2020, https://www.economist.com/europe/2020/06/25/why-italys-technocratic-prime-minister-is-so-popular.

anti-EU campaign in the previous elections caused considerable friction with the more centrist parties in the EPP.

Economist Branko Milanovic summarized this ever-more worrying trend in a graph (see Figure 4.1). Besides the center-right parties moving further to the right, radical right parties that were on the fringes of democracies as recently as 2000 are now rapidly becoming mainstream all over Europe, he showed.

Some parallels can also be drawn with what is happening elsewhere around the world, with nationalism, populism, and a more authoritarian style of leadership on the rise in many places. While it is hard to compare political trends across regions, especially when socioeconomic circumstances differ, in many places voters do seem to lean more toward nationalism instead of humanism, protectionism instead of openness, and a world vision of "us" versus "them," with perceived outsiders both within a society and the world at large.

In Brazil, for example, Latin America's most populous country, the conservative member of parliament Jair Bolsonaro was elected president

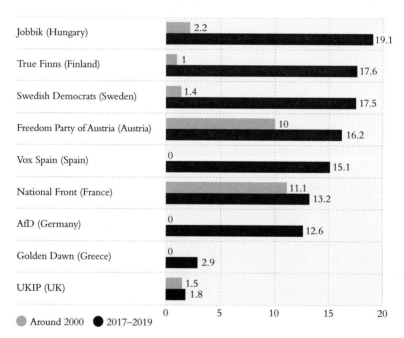

Figure 4.1 Percentage of Vote for Right-Wing Populist Parties in Parliamentary Elections around 2000 and the Most Recent Elections (2017–2019)

Source: Redrawn from Branko Milanovic.

on the premise of being a political outsider, who would bring "rule and order" back to Brazilian society and politics. Though he had served several terms in congress, his nationalist and traditionalist stances were not majoritarian until the 2018 election. Since the military dictatorship fell in the country in 1988, Brazil had had instead center-left or left-leaning presidents. Bolsonaro's election changed that, as voters gave a strong mandate for his brand of radically conservative politics at the ballot box.

Others have pointed to the nationalist and authoritarian turn taken by political leaders in other G20 countries such as China, India, Russia, and Turkey. In each, the societal and economic background is different, but the trend toward stronger, more domestically and ethnically focused political leadership is similar. It begs a second question: What caused the societal divide that led to this more divisive style of politics?

Societal Unrest

The seeds for these societal divides have been present since at least the 1990s and can be found to a large degree in the economic model that has prevailed for the last decades. The signs were there for anyone to see. But before they became properly mainstream, a few more decades passed.

In 1996, for example, one of us (Klaus Schwab) already noted in a *New York Times* op-ed that "economic globalization has entered a critical phase. A mounting backlash against its effects, especially in the industrial democracies, is threatening a very disruptive impact on economic activity and social stability in many countries. The mood in these democracies is one of helplessness and anxiety, which helps explain the rise of a new brand of populist politicians."[8] That observation came as centrist parties were only just being challenged on their flanks and most people were still well off economically, leaving the protesting voices in the margins.

But with the centrist governments not addressing the underlying issues, the division was destined to grow further. In the years following, I spoke to many of the protestors and activists present at World Economic Forum events. I realized they were the canaries in the coal mine, signs of

---

[8]"Start Taking the Backlash Against Globalization Seriously," Klaus Schwab and Claude Smadja, *The International New York Times*, February 1996, https://www.nytimes.com/1996/02/01/opinion/IHT-start-taking-the-backlash-against-globalization-seriously.html.

a coming broad-based societal discontent, and that systemic reforms to capitalism, globalization, and our economic development models were needed. As indicated earlier, however, the calls for stakeholder capitalism and other more inclusive policies I and others raised largely fell on deaf ears. And, looking back, we could and should have done more to make our case. But until the global financial crisis that started in 2008, the cracks that appeared in many industrialized societies were often still overcome by the prosperity of the majority.

When the financial crisis of 2008 hit, however, a deep and long economic recession ensued, and the popular uproar against the system, elites, and immigrants became an unstoppable avalanche. Many of the societies that were hurt by the financial crisis saw *Indignados* and Occupy Wall Street–inspired protests. And they also saw anger boil up from other parts of society. In Italy, for example, "lorry drivers, farmers, small business owners, students and unemployed people" came on the street in December 2013 to rally against Italy's leading polit ical class, the European Union, taxation, and globalization.[9] The so-called Pitchfork protestors had started off as a nationalist movement of farmers in Sicilia but quickly gained traction in the north of Italy and there also "attracted rightist groups and hard-core 'ultra' soccer fans," Italian news agency ANSA reported.[10]

Starting in 2017, yet another factor came to the forefront: the environmental crisis. But here, not everyone stood on the same side of the debate. Take the example of France. There, on the one hand, young protestors of the Youth for Climate movement advocated for much stronger action on climate by governments and lawmakers. The most prominent among them, the Swedish Greta Thunberg, was even invited to make her case in the French Parliament. But on the other hand, *Gilets Jaunes*, or Yellow Vests, hit the streets of Paris to oppose an environmentally driven fuel tax hike of the Macron government. The Yellow Vests were initially not ideologically driven either. They advocated neither traditional leftist nor rightist policies and disavowed

---

[9]"Italy Hit by Wave of Pitchfork Protests as Austerity Unites Disparate Groups," Lizzie Davies, *The Guardian*, December 2013, https://www.theguardian.com/world/2013/dec/13/italy-pitchfork-protests-austerity-unites-groups.

[10]"Clashes with fans as Pitchfork protests enter third day," ANSA, December 2013, http://www.ansa.it/web/notizie/rubriche/english/2013/12/11/Clashes-fans-Pitchfork-protests-enter-third-day_9763655.html.

political parties. As the movement gained traction abroad though, it was often co-opted by the alt-right.[11]

In 2020, lastly, a final group of dissenting voices emerged: those that grew angry and mad at the global government responses to the COVID-19 pandemic, which caused the greatest combined devastation to lives and livelihoods since the Spanish flu in 1918–1919. Around the world, people started spreading conspiracy theories about the alleged true nature of the pandemic. Some believed it was intentionally created and spread by China. Others saw in it an effort by their own governments to suppress the population and opposed public health measures on those grounds. Some even went so far as to suggest the World Economic Forum, the organization we work for, had a hand in the pandemic. In Germany, media reported that neo-Nazi elements were involved in the protests for freedom from government measures against the pandemic.

Looking at the many protestors, voters, and parties that emerged in recent years with only an ideological lens, however, does not explain entirely what is going on. It isn't so much that the extreme right or extreme left is replacing the center right or center left in society and politics. It is that voters often simply no longer support and believe in any establishment political parties or even the current democratic system itself. Many either don't show up to vote or opt for non-democratic parties. Even more problematically, attacks on democratic institutions are widespread around the world. That should be a crucial concern for all advocates of democracy, regardless of their economic ideology. In addition to the economic foundations that were laid in the post-war era, the notion of democratic government formed the foundation of the prosperous Western societies we have come to live in. That foundation is now shakier than ever before.

In Italy, for example, the junior coalition partner in government at the time, the Five Star Movement, supported the Yellow Vest movement. It may seem odd for a governing party, knowing the movement opposed precisely government. But it wasn't even such an unnatural move. The party had originated out of a popular, anti-elite movement itself and was in government for the first time in its young history. The senior coalition

---

[11]In Canada, for example, the movement gained a lot of traction online, as it assembled people who opposed immigration, multiculturalism, and the elites in power. See: « Le mouvement "gilet jaune" s'enracine à droite au Canada », *Le Courrier International*, January 2019, https://www.courrierinternational.com/article/le-mouvement-gilet-jaune-senracine-droite-au-canada.

partner, the right-wing *Lega*, subsequently also spoke out in support of the protests. Or take the case of Germany. There, the Yellow Vest movement got endorsed by both left and right, making it harder to put a specific political color to the protests. *Pegida*, an alt-right movement, mostly saw in the Yellow Vests an opportunity to reinforce its anti-immigration message. *Aufstehen*, on the other hand, used it to call for international solidarity and end to wars. Cases like these show the complexity of the new societal divides and the limited application of old ideologies in these new dividing lines.

As indicated earlier, it will be hard to find common ground in a divided society. Precisely on the topics that matter most to them, the loudest voices often take opposing stances. And even when they coalesce around specific topics, enacting the solutions they propose may in fact weaken democratic institutions and the political system as we know it.

The Lesson to Draw from a Divided Society

There is an important lesson we must draw from the more radical voices that emerge from divided societies, whether one agrees more or even wholeheartedly with one side or another or neither. That is that the leading political and economic class has failed to bring them into the fold, both economically and socially. The initial response, then, should be one of humility and introspection, rather than outright condemnation or indignation.

Seventy-five years have passed since World War II came to an end, and the pledge to have "Never Again War" was made. Fifty years also have passed since the first World Economic Forum Annual Meeting in Davos. For much of its history, the so-called Davos Manifesto participants approved in 1973 was the main inspiration for meeting. In the Manifesto, business leaders promised to look after all their stakeholders, not just shareholders. And 20 years have passed since the fall of the Berlin Wall. We then believed we would soon achieve prosperity for all in all nations.

But as we saw in previous chapters, income inequality in many countries has reached levels not seen in recent history,[12] our growth

---

[12]For a full discussion of the state of global inequality, both within various countries and around the world, I refer to the excellent book *Global Inequality: A New Approach for the Age of Globalization*, by Branko Milanovic. He discusses the state and evolution of income, wealth, and opportunity inequality in a global and historical context and includes many qualifications I have left out of my analysis for the sake of brevity and clarity.

model is broken, and the environment is degrading further every day, leading to devastation as well as conflicts. We must acknowledge that we have not lived up to the expectations of the current and future generations.

It should come as no surprise then that many Western societies have become deeply polarized, people have become wary of their institutions and leaders, and increasingly, these various factions only interact within their own echo chamber. For decades, their leaders promised things would get better for everyone, and many privileged observers stood by. If only we let the free market run its course, they said, an invisible hand would allocate all resources optimally. If only companies were unshackled of regulation, they would create unmatched prosperity. And if only financial and technological innovators could blossom, we'd reach endless GDP growth, which would have benefits for all.

Many leading economists believed in these dogmas, and they increasingly influenced government and central banks. Some business leaders did sign up for stakeholder capitalism, looking after all those who matter to their businesses, but most adhered to shareholder capitalism, maximizing profits over other priorities. And especially in the wake of the fall of the Berlin Wall, many political leaders became more and more indistinguishable on the economic front, believing that there was only one right set of economic policies, one which favored top-line GDP growth over inclusive development. The rest of this book explores the causes of this fundamental error so we can find a way forward.

As one of the people who had a first-row seat on the creation of the current global economic system, hindsight provides a mixed verdict. Our best intentions don't always lead to the desired outcomes. But past failures should not deter us from creating a better economic system for the next 50 years and beyond. This won't be an easy feat. Many societies no longer have a majoritarian political center, as radical figures have taken over the political system, a consequence of the societal divide we've seen in many places. And this societal divide, in turn, is consequence of the crises in our economic and environmental systems, as well as an obstacle to overcoming them.

That bring us back to the Brandenburg Gate. Thirty years ago, Germans of East and West, younger and older generations, left and right, gathered there to celebrate their unity. But in recent years, the Gate saw protests in favor of climate action and against it, in favor of open societies and against them, in favor of community and against it, and in favor of COVID-related public health policies and against them. The Gate behind them once united Germans, Europeans, and global citizens from all political beliefs, from every generation, and every background. No longer. If we want to rebuild that kind of unified society, we'll first have to agree on the causes of our societal and economic ills and then take joint action to address them. It is what we'll do in the next chapters of this book.

PART II
DRIVERS OF PROGRESS
AND PROBLEMS

5

Globalization

In the summer of 2012, three university students, Annisa, Adi, and Arekha, were in Bandung, West Java. The students shared an entrepreneurial drive and found that their individual talents were natural complements. Annisa was studying economics, Adi architecture, and Arekha biotechnology. Bandung is a sprawling West-Javan city of about 2.5 million people. Despite being home to many creative minds, its action radius was mostly limited to Indonesia itself. Had Annisa, Adi, and Arekha followed in their parents' footsteps, they would have ended up working as public servants, teachers, or freelance consultants. But their curiosity, ambition, and academic connections to the world beyond Bandung gradually changed their outlook. Soon after meeting, the young trio became student-entrepreneurs: they started as mushroom farmers, aiming to help their fellow countrymen gain food security and selling an edible growing mushroom kit. By 2014, their dream grew even larger: having worked for all these years with mushrooms, they realized the fungi's potential as a sustainable material as well. They wanted to use it to make all-kinds of consumer products and potentially sell it all over the world.

To achieve their dream, the young graduates from Bandung found support abroad. Through an academic contact, the Swiss Institute of Technology (also known as ETH) decided to fund their scientific research and testing. After a few years, 500 Startups, a San Francisco–based venture capital firm became Annisa, Adi, and Arekha's first foreign investor. And today, their company, MYCL, is a successful SME. Its facilities are in a remote village an hour and a half outside Bandung, but they are bustling with action. When my colleague visited them in the summer of 2019, a handful of young college graduates sat in a multi-purpose room, working on R&D on their laptops. They were creating new types of mushroom-based products, including a low-impact leather and construction material, the company's current focus. In the manufac-turing facilities next door, workers—all young women—were turning the industrially produced mushrooms into the raw "leather" it became. Further down the street, a dozen or so mushroom farmers worked on supplying the company with the raw materials it needed to make its products. MYCL's clients varied from partner companies in the Bandung region to buyers from as far as Australia, the UK, and 14 other countries, who bought their mushroom-and-wood watch via Kickstarter.

The story of the Bandung entrepreneurs is not exceptional in Indonesia. Around the same time as MYCL took off, Winston and William Utomo were pursuing their own entrepreneurial dream. Born and raised in Surabaya, another large Indonesian city some 700 kilometers (430 miles) east of Bandung, the twentysomething brothers got inspired by new American media companies such as Disney and BuzzFeed, tech-nology companies such as Google and Facebook, and venture capital firms such as Andreessen Horowitz and Sequoia Capital. The Utomo brothers were in awe of Silicon Valley and wondered whether they could replicate a company in Indonesia that followed the start-up model they admired. They were determined to find out. After completing their college degrees in the United States, at the University of Southern California and Columbia University in New York, Winston got a job as an account strategist for Google in Singapore, and William, the younger brother, worked at an investment banking firm. Working for companies they admired was inspiring, and soon the two brothers quickly decided it was time to bootstrap a company of their own.

With Winston's salary from Singapore, they hired a couple of young talents in Surabaya and set up their company, IDN Media, at Winston's 2-by-3-meter apartment in Singapore. Its goal was "to democratize information and to become the voice of Millennials and Gen Z in Indo-nesia."[1] They wanted to solve the information gap that had been hap-pening in Indonesia for decades. It proved more successful than even the Utomo brothers could imagine. Investors from Singapore, New York,

---

[1]"Interview with Winston and William Utomo by Peter Vanham, Jakarta, Indonesia, October 2019".

Hong Kong, Japan, Korea, and Thailand soon joined in, thanks to the brothers' connections from Singapore and California, as well as several local Indonesian family offices. Six years after its founding, the company's content platform had grown to one of the leading content platforms in Indonesia, with over 60 million unique monthly users.[2] It had over 500 employees and hundreds of thousands of community members. And when we visited, the company had just opened its new marquee space in Jakarta: a skyscraper that held its name, IDN Media HQ.

Consider one more example of Indonesian millennials breaking through in the global economy. As the Utomo brothers' business expanded, Puty Puar was reflecting on her own future. A college friend of Annisa (the mushroom entrepreneur from Bandung), Puty had studied geological engineering and was now working on the island of Borneo as a geologist for Total, the French energy multinational. It wasn't an easy life. Her husband worked in Jakarta, and the two only saw each other every other weekend. Then, as Puty got pregnant, she made a major decision. She would resign, move back to Jakarta with her husband, and become a stay-at-home mom. Instead of being a geologist, she would try to work as an illustrator and graphic designer. She might not make the same as when she worked for Total, but her new plan would allow her to pursue her art hobby and be home with her child.

For Puty, this choice worked better than she expected. Her blogs and illustrations on life as a young mom quickly inspired moms her age throughout Indonesia, and even beyond, thanks to the viral power of Instagram. One of her projects even earned her a trip to New York. The international Emmy Awards organized a competition for one-minute videos, and Puty became a finalist. It launched her international career as a successful freelancer and artist. Working from home, she secured an assignment from Facebook's art director in San Francisco. The company wanted locally adapted "stickers" for the social media's vast Indonesian user base. In a separate project, a woman from the United Arab Emirates commissioned her to design personal greeting cards. Puty never met her client in real life, but the online interactions were flawless, and the client neatly paid for the project through PayPal. After that, a company from Singapore reached out to order illustrations for their clothing brand. Puty had given up her job at Total, but she had gained a large social following that helped national and international clients find her.

[2]IDN Times, IDN Media, consulted October 2020, https://www.idn.media/products/idntimes.

These stories from Indonesia all have one thing in common. They show how globalization works at its very best. Global networks of trade, technology, investments, people, and knowledge can help people create successful businesses and job opportunities and help regions and countries develop, while also being beneficial for the country at the other side of the bargain. Annisa and her co-founders used a global university and start-up network to gain knowledge and fund their research and company in a rural part of Indonesia. Winston and William used their ties to global tech and venture capital firms to build a similar company in a new and quickly emerging market, hiring dozens of young journalists, engineers, and marketers. And Puty made use of globe-spanning social networks to build a career as freelance illustrator and influencer. The investors and clients at the other side of the world too benefited from working with them. Often faced with only limited options to invest at home, they find in these Indonesian entrepreneurs the growth they are looking for or a supplier able to get them unique products at a good price. Their money helps these young entrepreneurs chase their dreams and earns them—if all goes well—a handsome return on their investment.

If everyone stands to gain, why has globalization gotten a bad reputation in some parts of the world? To answer that question, let's look a little deeper at the two sides of globalization.

Indonesia and Globalization

Consider first the case of Indonesia. What is true for the MYCL founders, the Utomo brothers, and Puty is also true for Indonesia as a whole. With an average age of about 29 and a GDP per capita of only $4,000, the country of 266 million people has a lot of youngsters who want to get ahead. To make that possible, Indonesia has embraced globalization over the past few decades,[3] before COVID put that openness on at least a temporary hold in 2020. Where did its enthusiasm come from?

Starting in the 1980s and 1990s, the Southeast Asian nation gradually opened up to foreign trade and investment, after a long period of protectionism. It lowered its export tariffs, attracted foreign investment, and started to grow its manufacturing and services sectors. The openness

---

[3]The following text has been adapted and updated from the World Economic Forum Agenda article by Peter Vanham, "Why Indonesians Fight like Avengers for Globalization," https://www.weforum.org/agenda/2018/12/why-indonesians-fight-like-avengers-for-globalization/.

paid off. Since the early 2000s to today, Indonesia's GDP growth rates were consistently between 4 and 6 percent per year. And as a percentage of GDP, trade doubled in importance: from 30 percent in the 1980s to 60 percent in the 2000s.

That openness to trade and foreign investment turned Indonesia into a newly industrialized nation and a member of the G20. Its entrepreneurs became more technologically savvy and its people more internationally minded. Today, the country is home to both domestic and foreign tech unicorns (start-ups with a valuation of over $1 billion): Ride-hailing firm Gojek was founded in Indonesia, and its Singapore-based rival Grab, is equally popular there. Indonesian travel booking sites Traveloka and online retail company Tokopedia are giving Booking and Amazon a run for their money, fueled by domestic as well as foreign investors. Indonesians, meanwhile, are among the most globalization-minded people anywhere. In a 2018 poll by YouGov and Bertelsmann (the most recent one available), a large majority (74% of Indonesians) said they considered globalization a force for good in the world. In the same poll, their peers in the United Kingdom (47%), the United States (42%), and France (41%) showed themselves to be much less enthusiastic.[4]

That is not to say Indonesia provides the proof globalization is always good. There are ample examples of when international trade didn't work out for the archipelago. The spices grown on its Maluku islands, notably, were the first goods to be widely traded around the world. That was true in ancient times and remained true until the dawn of the modern era. The Indonesian nutmeg, mace, and clove were so wanted around Europe, in fact, that they were the inspiration for merchants-discoverers such as Christopher Columbus and Vasco da Gama to find Eastern or Southern routes to "the Indies." It started the era of "mercantilist" globalization: one which favored individual European trading nations, while most other parties suffered (see more below). Indeed, when the Portuguese and Dutch were successful in reaching Indonesia, the local people paid the price. Instead of trading fairly, the newcomers subdued and colonized the Indonesians. Only after the Second World War did Indonesia become an independent nation, free from this one-sided trade and foreign occupation. And even then, it endured another four decades of authoritarian and isolationist rule before entering its liberal and democratic era. Finally, Indonesia's first attempt to benefit from global markets backfired in 1997, when the Asian financial crisis pushed its economy in a severe recession: starting in

---

[4]Ibidem.

Thailand, speculators massively bet against the ability of Southeast Asian nations to maintain their currency pegs, leading to severe devaluation, a soaring public debt, and an economic recession from Indonesia to Malaysia to the Philippines. It was financial globalization gone bad.

Still, the story of Indonesia in recent years can be called a success story of globalization. According to the World Bank, Indonesia's prudent economic management helped push poverty to a record low of under one in ten by the end of 2018, and trade was one of the sectors contributing most to Indonesia's growth.[5] Many people in the streets of Jakarta and Bandung won't necessarily name their country's openness to trade as the reason for their optimism—they simply are happy life is going better for them. But the two go hand in hand. Foreign investment and purchasers add to the stock of capital available to both the private and the public sector, and that in turn helps the country develop. If in Jakarta a new subway or new bridges get built, that visibly improves the quality of life for many of the capital's inhabitants. If Gojek and Grab, the ride-hailing companies, get more investors, that helps the companies expand their footprint and hire more drivers, giving more common Indonesians an income. And if MYCL finds foreign buyers for its products, it can hire more farmers and workers to manufacture its goods for export. It is a sentiment you hear everywhere in Indonesia—from the Grab driver to the civil engineer: life is getting better, so our economic policies must be getting something right.

A similar trend has played out in other parts of the world, and most dramatically so in Asia. As set forth in Chapter 3, the opening up of China to the world was the most important macroeconomic story of recent decades, rivaled only by the collapse of the Soviet Union and the emergence of its former member states as independent economies. Many other Asian economies were able to follow in China's slipstream, like the Four Asian Tigers (Hong Kong SAR, Singapore, South Korea, and Taiwan) did. In all, the transformation of Asia has been possibly the greatest triumph of globalization so far. But the positive picture from Indonesia and the rest of Asia stands in contrast to the perceived role of trade and globalization in some other parts of the world. In industrial areas in the United States, the United Kingdom, and continental Europe, people feel increasingly negative about globalization, openness, and free trade. It is remarkable that it has come to this. The West was the driving force behind the first

[5]"Indonesia Maintains Steady Economic Growth in 2019," World Bank's June 2019 Economic Quarterly, https://www.worldbank.org/en/news/press-release/2019/07/01/indonesia-maintains-steady-economic-growth-in-2019.

true waves of globalization—and its main beneficiary. To appreciate this, let's briefly look at its history and its effect on people's lives.

Early Beginnings and Spice Routes[6]

People have been trading goods for almost as long as they've been around. But as of the 1st century BC, a remarkable phenomenon occurred. For the first time in history, luxury products from China started to appear on the other edge of the Eurasian continent—in Rome. They got there after being hauled for thousands of miles along what came to be known later as the *Seidenstrassen*, or Silk Roads. Traders along those routes only traveled a limited distance. But the wares they bought and sold traveled half the world. That is not to say globalization had started in earnest. Silk was mostly a luxury good, and so were the spices that were added to the intercontinental trade between Asia and Europe. As a percentage of the total economy, the value of these exports was tiny, and many middlemen were involved to get the goods to their destination. But global trade links were established, and for those involved, it could be a gold mine.

The Silk Road could prosper in part because two great empires dominated much of the route: Rome and China. If trade was interrupted, it was most often because of blockades by their local enemies. If the Silk Road eventually closed up, as it did after several centuries, the fall of the empires had everything to do with it. When it reopened in Marco Polo's late medieval time, it was because of the rise of a new hegemonic empire, that of the Mongols. It is a pattern we'll see throughout history: trade thrives when nations protect it and falls when they don't.

The next chapter in trade happened thanks to Islamic merchants. As the new religion spread in all directions from its Arabian heartland in the 7th century, so did trade. The founder of Islam, the prophet Mohammed, was famously a merchant himself, as was his wife, Khadija. Trade was thus in the DNA of the new religion and its followers, and that showed. By the early 9th century, Muslim traders already dominated Mediterranean and Indian Ocean trade; afterward, they could be found as far east as Indonesia, which over time became a Muslim-majority region, and as far west as Moorish Spain.

---

[6]This section is adapted from "How Globalization 4.0 Fits into the History of Globalization," Peter Vanham, World Economic Forum Agenda, January 2019, https://www.weforum.org/agenda/2019/01/how-globalization-4-0-fits-into-the-history-of-globalization.

As we saw earlier, the main focus of Islamic trade in the Middle Ages were spices. Unlike silk, spices were traded mainly by sea, with a smaller overland portion from Arabia to the Mediterranean. Chief among these spices were the cloves, nutmeg, and mace from the fabled Spice Islands—the Maluku Islands in Indonesia. They were extremely expensive and in high demand, both locally and in Europe, where they were mainly used to preserve and spice food. Like silk, spices were a luxury product, and trade remained relatively low volume. By the Middle Ages, globalization still hadn't taken off, but the original belt (the overland Silk Road) and road (the overseas spice route) of trade between East and West had been established. (The notion of this "Belt and Road" would be revived hundreds of years later by Chinese President Xi Jinping, as he unveiled a modern "Belt and Road Initiative" to better connect China with Europe, Africa, and Central Asia through railroads, sea ports, pipelines, highways, and digital connections.[7])

Age of Discovery (15th to 18th Century)

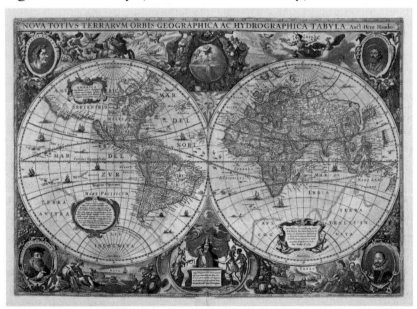

Figure 5.1 Nova Totius Terrarum orbis Geographica ac Hydrographica Tabula, Jan Janssonius Novus atlas i 1647–50

Source: Nasjonalbiblioteket/National Library of Norway.

---

[7]"The Belt and Road Initiative," Permanent Mission of the People's Republic of China to the United Nations Office at Geneva and other International Organizations in Switzerland, http://www.china-un.ch/eng/zywjyjh/t1675564.htm.

Truly global trade kicked off in the Age of Discovery. It was in this era, from the end of the 15th century onwards, that European explorers connected East and West—and accidentally discovered the Americas. Aided by the inventions of the so-called Scientific Revolution in the fields of astronomy, mechanics, physics, and ship making, the Portuguese and Spanish, and later the Dutch and the English, first "discovered," then subjugated, and finally integrated new lands in their economies.

The Age of Discovery rocked the world. The most (in)famous event of this period[8] was Christopher Columbus's voyage to America, which all but ended pre-Colombian civilizations, but the most consequential exploration was the circumnavigation by Magellan. It opened the door to the Indonesian Spice Islands, cutting out Arab and Italian middlemen. And while trade once again remained small compared to total GDP, it certainly did alter people's lives. In the Americas, millions of people died of diseases, were killed, or were subjugated after the arrival of the conquistadors. Potatoes, tomatoes, coffee, and chocolate were introduced in Europe, and the price of spices fell steeply, changing people's diets and longevity forever. The notion that the world most definitely wasn't flat and the realization that there were other peoples and cultures around the world also brought a shock to the social, religious, and political life of the times. In Europe, religious wars broke out, partially because of the upheaval that came with the Age of Discovery. By 1648, a few dominant nation-states arose from the web of hundreds of small city-states that used to characterize Europe.

As Europe opened its eyes to the vastness of the world, the motors of economic development were jump-started by international trade. Using joint stock companies, traders and financial investors pooled their risks to ensure the most advantageous outcomes of their overseas trade. The most famous of these were the English and Dutch East India Companies. European governments often granted monopoly privileges, giving particular companies exclusive trading access to colonies. This allowed joint stock companies to operate as states to become by some measures the largest companies the world has ever seen. This helped fuel the creation of stock markets, such as in Antwerp and

---

[8]We avoid the term "discovery" because native peoples had settled in the Americas long before any Europeans were aware of the existence of continents between them and Asia. It is also now widely understood and accepted that Columbus was preceded by Viking Leif Erikson, who is credited with being the first to make the journey from Europe to America.

Amsterdam, and financial products of credit and currency exchange. It would not be an exaggeration to say modern capitalism was founded in this era.

Despite this, economists today don't regard this era as one of true globalization. Trade had certainly started to become global, and the search for new trade horizons had even been the main reason for starting the Age of Discovery. But the resulting global economy was still very much siloed and lopsided. The European empires set up global supply chains, but most of these were limited to their own colonies and areas of control. Moreover, the colonial model was chiefly one of exploitation. Not only were local civilizations and societies subverted and dismantled, but the slave trade was integral to the new colonial economy. The empires had thus created both a mercantilist and a colonial economy but not a truly globalized one: the exchanges that happened on a global scale were not mutually beneficial or even agreed upon by all parties involved. For the most part, they also didn't happen freely between independent nations but rather between imperial powers and their own colonies only.

First Wave of Globalization (19th Century–1914)

This started to change with the first wave of globalization, which occurred over the century, roughly ending in 1914. By the end of the 18th century, Great Britain had started to dominate the world both geographically, through the establishment of the British Empire, and technologically, with innovations such as the steam engine, the industrial weaving machine, and more. It was the era of the First Industrial Revolution. Britain in particular positioned itself as a fantastic twin engine of global trade. On the one hand, steamships and trains could transport goods over thousands of miles, both within countries and across countries. On the other hand, its industrialization allowed Britain to make products that were in demand all over the world, such as iron, textiles, and manufactured goods. As the BBC described, "With its advanced industrial technologies, Britain was able to attack a huge and rapidly expanding international market."[9]

---

[9]http://www.bbc.co.uk/history/british/victorians/victorian_technology_01.shtml.

Figure 5.2 The machine works of Richard Hartmann in Chemnitz. Hartmann was one of the most successful entrepreneurs and largest employers in the Kingdom of Saxony

Source: Nortbert Kaiser, scan of 1868 original.

The resulting globalization was obvious in the numbers. For about a century, trade grew on average 3 percent per year.[10] That growth rate propelled exports from a share of 6 percent of global GDP in the early 19th century to 14 percent on the eve of World War I.[11] As John Maynard Keynes, the economist, famously observed, in *The Economic Consequences of the Peace*: [12]"What an extraordinary episode in the economic progress of man that age was which came to an end in August 1914! [...] The inhabitant of London could order by telephone, sipping his morning tea in bed, the various products of the whole Earth, in such quantity as he might see fit, and reasonably expect their early delivery upon his doorstep." Keynes also noted a similar situation was also true in the world of investing. Those with the means in New York, Paris, London, or Berlin could also invest in internationally active joint stock companies. One of those, the French Compagnie de Suez, constructed the Suez Canal connecting the Mediterranean with the Indian Ocean and opened yet

---

[10]https://ourworldindata.org/international-trade.

[11]https://edatos.consorciomadrono.es/file.xhtml?persistentId=doi:10.21950/BBZVBN/U54JIA&version=1.0.

[12]"John Maynard Keynes, The Economic Consequences of the Peace, 1919, quote can be found at https://www.theglobalist.com/global-man-circa-1913/".

another artery of world trade. Others built railways in India or managed mines in African colonies. Foreign direct investing, too, was globalizing.

While Britain was the country that benefited most from this globalization, as it had the most capital and the best technology, others did too, by exporting other goods. The invention of the refrigerated cargo ship or "reefer ship" in the 1870s, for example, allowed for countries like Argentina and Uruguay, to enter their golden age. They started to mass export meat, from cattle grown on their vast lands. Other countries, too, started to specialize their production in those fields in which they were most competitive.

But the first wave of globalization and industrialization also coincided with some darker events. By the end of the 19th century, "most [globalizing and industrialized] European nations grabbed for a piece of Africa, and by 1900 the only independent country left on the continent was Ethiopia."[13] Large countries such as India, China, Mexico, or Japan, which were for much of the preceding centuries economic powers to reckon with, were either not able or not allowed to adapt to the industrial and global trends. The British policy in India, for example, "was aimed not only at keeping Indian markets open for British cotton textiles, but also at preventing India's emergence as an export competitor."[14] Independent nations such as Japan, on the other hand, lacked the access to capital or technology required to compete with the European trading forces.

Even within industrialized nations, not all citizens benefited from globalization. Workers, some of whom were previously craftsmen with unique skills, became just another commodity, working in Fordist assembly lines at the rhythm of the new industrial machinery, or their output was undercut by foreign imports. Keynes may have written that an "inhabitant of London" could take part in globalized trade, but surely he knew it was only the privileged classes who could do so: The top 5 percent wealthiest citizens of the United Kingdom owned 90 percent of the country's wealth around the turn of the 20th century.[15] Most men and women and even children were resources for the industrial era, mostly as low-wage workers. (For more on the social effects of globalization, see Chapter 6.)

---

[13] "The Industrial Revolution," Khan Academy, https://www.khanacademy.org/humanities/big-history-project/acceleration/bhp-acceleration/a/the-industrial-revolution.

[14] "India in the Rise of Britain and Europe: A Contribution to the Convergence and Great Divergence Debates," Bhattacharya, Prabir Heriot-Watt University, May 2019, https://mpra.ub.uni-muenchen.de/97457/1/MPRA_paper_97457.pdf.

[15] "Top Wealth Shares in the UK, 1895–2013, Figure 4.6.1," World Inequality Lab, https://wir2018.wid.world/part-4.html.

It was a situation that was bound to end in a major crisis. In 1914, the outbreak of the Great War brought an end to just about everything the burgeoning high society of the West had gotten so used to, including globalization. The ravage was complete. Millions of soldiers died in battle, millions of civilians died as collateral damage, war replaced trade, destruction replaced construction, and countries closed their borders yet again. The writings of Karl Marx and others on the exploitative nature of this first globalized capitalist era also led to revolts in many countries and the overthrow of existing regimes. It led in a space of a few decades to a world marked by two systems: one where private ownership and management dominated the means of production (capitalism) and one where production facilities were owned and objectives set by the state (communism). In the years between the World Wars, the financial markets, which were still connected in a global web, caused a further breakdown of the global economy and its links. The Great Depression in the US led to the end of the boom in South America and a run on the banks in many other parts of the world. Another World War followed in 1939–1945. By the end of the Second World War, trade as a percentage of world GDP had fallen to 5 percent—the lowest level in more than a hundred years.

Second and Third Wave of Globalization

The story of globalization, however, was not over. The end of the Second World War marked a new beginning for the global economy. A new hegemon, the United States of America, entered the stage. It had seen a major influx of mostly European immigrants in the 19th and early 20th century. It had a baby boom in the middle of the 20th century. And it was aided by its dominance in industries of the Second Industrial Revolution, such as cars, aviation, and modern manufacturing industries. As a consequence, global trade started to rise once again. At first, this happened in two separate tracks, as the Iron Curtain divided the world in two spheres of influence: the liberal and democratic one led by the US and the communist led by the Soviet Union. In the early decades after World War II, institutions like the European Union and other free trade vehicles championed by the US were responsible for much of the increase in international trade. In the Soviet Union, there was a similar increase in trade, albeit through centralized planning rather than the free market. The effect was profound. Worldwide, trade once again rose to 1914 levels. By 1989, export once again counted for 14 percent of global GDP. This was paired with a steep rise in middle-class incomes in the West.

After the fall of the Berlin Wall and the collapse of the Soviet Union, globalization became an all-conquering force. The newly created World Trade Organization (WTO) encouraged nations all over the world to enter free trade agreements, and most of them did,[16] including many newly independent ones. As we saw in Chapter 2, even China, which for the better part of the 20th century had been a closed, agrarian economy, in 2001 became a member of the WTO and started to manufacture for the world. In this new economic world, the US still set the tone and led the way, but many others benefited in its slipstream. At the same time, new technologies from the Third Industrial Revolution, such as the Internet, connected people all over the world in an even more direct way. The orders Keynes could place by phone in 1914 could now be placed over the Internet and delivered through a global network of large ships, trains, and planes. Importantly, members of the middle class had access to the goods produced in the global supply chain. Global trade was no longer a luxury. Instead of having them delivered in a few weeks, they would arrive at one's doorstep in a few days. What was more, the Internet also allowed for a further global integration of value chains. You could do R&D in one country, sourcing in others, production in yet another, and distribution all over the world.

The result has been a globalization on steroids. In the 2000s, global exports reached a milestone, as they rose to about a quarter of global GDP.[17] Trade, the sum of imports and exports, consequentially grew to about half of world GDP. In some countries, such as Singapore, Switzerland, Belgium, and the Netherlands, trade is worth more than 100 percent of GDP (that is possible because GDP measures domestic product, adding only the difference between exports and imports). And much of the global population has benefited from this: more people than ever before belong to the global middle class, and hundreds of millions achieved that status by participating in the global economy.

Globalization 4.0

That brings us to today, when a new wave of globalization is once again upon us, in a world now dominated by a new pair of world powers, the US and China. This time, the new frontiers of globalization are the cyber world (including cybercrime), climate change, and the increased threat posed by viruses.

[16]https://www.wto.org/english/res_e/booksp_e/anrep_e/world_trade_report11_e.pdf.

[17]https://edatos.consorciomadrono.es/file.xhtml?persistentId=doi:10.21950/BBZVBN/U54JIA&version=1.0.

The digital economy, in its infancy during the third wave of globalization, has become a force to reckon with through e-commerce, digital services, and 3D printing. Digital globalization, in fact, has become a global economic power hiding in plain sight. While most countries still focus on physical trade when negotiating trade agreements or pursuing industrial policies, digital trade has become by some measures as large or even multiple times larger than physical trade—though there is no way of knowing. No uniform method currently exists to measure digital trade, and many statistical agencies do not even try to measure it. (The best effort, most likely, comes from the OECD, in its report "Trade in the Digital Era" from 2019.[18]) But as the example of Puty Puar shows, it is now not uncommon for an individual or company to sell their goods and services entirely online. This method of trade is becoming more common every day.

At the same time, a negative globalization is expanding too, through the global effect of climate change and the spread of viruses. They go hand in hand with our global economic development model. Pollution in one part of the world leads to extreme weather events in another. The cutting of forests in the few "lungs" the planet earth has left, such as the Amazon Rainforest, has further effect on not just the world's biodiversity but its capacity to cope with hazardous greenhouse gas emissions (see also Chapter 1 and Chapter 8).[19] The emergence of the novel coronavirus in 2019 should be considered in the context of our lack of sustainability. Human encroachment on natural habitats is the likely cause of the spread of many new viruses to humans from animals, from Ebola to the coronavirus that causes COVID-19. The pandemic's rapid spread around the world was made possible by international travel, which physically connects nearly every nation. Both of these trends are unsustainable.

As this new wave of digital, climate, and viral globalization is hitting us, many of the world's people are turning their backs on it. As a percentage of GDP, global exports had already started to reverse in the years following the global financial crisis. As a political ideology, globalism, or the idea that one should take a global perspective, is on the wane, especially in the Western societies that so passionately adhered to it in

---

[18]"Trade in the Digital Era," OECD, March 2019, https://www.oecd.org/going-digital/trade-in-the-digital-era.pdf.

[19]As the UK Centre for Ecology and Hydrology explained: " Tropical rainforests are often called the 'lungs of the planet' because they generally draw in carbon dioxide and breathe out oxygen," https://www.ceh.ac.uk/news-and-media/news/tropical-rainforests-lungs-planet-reveal-true-sensitivity-global-warming.

the late 20th century. The United States, the power that propelled the world to its highest level of globalization, is backing away from its role as international police and trade champion.

All these trends were already underway before 2020. Then, the novel coronavirus that causes COVID-19 put the entire global economic system literally on hold. The virus all but halted international travel, disrupted global supply chains, and made many people, companies, and governments reconsider their attitude toward globalization. Indeed, they didn't just pause and reflect on their own lives and careers but on the merits and shortcomings of our global economic system at large, and the potential of other ways of producing and consuming necessary goods and services. Should Europeans and Americans still procure goods from China or other overseas destinations, given their environmental footprint and the fragility of supply chains? Or can they near-shore or even re-shore production, thanks to advances in automation and 3D printing? Should countries with different labor, competition, and industrial policies be trading at all, given the tilted playing field that results from such policies? And, for that matter, has globalization stopped being a force for good? Or was it never one, after all?

Globalization Today

The history of globalization shows us in fact that trade can be an incredibly powerful force, which can connect people and generate enormous prosperity. But it also tells us that none of its positive effects are guaranteed. The opulence brought about by the East India Companies went hand in hand with the exploitation of the inhabitants of the colonies it traded with. The global trade links established in the First Industrial Revolution did little to aid the economic development of countries such as Mexico and India, and much more to benefit the industrialists of Britain and America. Even when more countries shared in the gains in later stages of globalization, the benefits were often distributed extremely unevenly. Finally, the increased connectivity and interdependence of a globalized world brings with them new risks and a loss of sovereignty, even if the economic gains are widespread. That is a lesson from the recent fears over cybersecurity and the rapid spread of the coronavirus.

The lesson is that globalization is, theoretically, a force for good, but in practice, it can be a positive force only if guardrails ensure that it benefits everyone and ensures resilience and sovereignty. In the history of globalization, there are only a few decades when the rising tide of trade lifted all boats and did not cause dangerous waves at the same time. For the West and a handful of Asian countries such as Japan, that period started immediately after the Second World War and lasted until the 1980s. For the East, and more broadly the so-called emerging markets, that period started somewhere in the 1990s, and even then, it was severely threatened during the 1997 Asian financial crisis. In countries such as Indonesia, Ethiopia, and Vietnam it is still ongoing, though the COVID crisis caused more than a hiccup. Taken together, globalization during this period did structurally raise wages for a large majority of workers and allowed records amounts of people to become part of the middle class, while allowing a more selected crop to rise even further.

By and large, economic globalization works best for everyone when at least three conditions are met. First, globalization can take off only if a social compact is in place. In post-war Europe and Japan, for example, the devastating experience of the war made people understand they were all in it together and that to progress economically as a nation, it was important everyone do their part and for everyone to get a share in the benefits. A broad tax base, with high compliance by companies and top marginal rates for wealthy individuals, supported public investments in education, health care, and housing. It also provided the conditions under which companies and people could work together and remain competitive. The long-term nature of the social compact meant that individuals were willing to leave short-term or selfish considerations aside, knowing that they would gain in the long run, just as the other stakeholders contributing to the pact. More recently, the close-knit societies of Scandinavia (including Denmark, Sweden, Finland, and Norway), provide an example of how countries can continue to benefit from and favor global trade, when the interests of all citizens are looked after (see Chapter 6 for the example of Denmark).

Second, globalization thrives when political leaders find a balance between providing direction to the economy and caring for their people on the one hand and opening up to the world in terms of trade and investment on the other.[20] Indeed, economists such as Dani Rodrik have argued convincingly that the optimal globalization policies do not necessarily consist of full-scale liberalization of trade, investments, and

---

[20]"The Globalization Paradox: Democracy and the Future of the World Economy, Dani Rodrik, W.W. Norton, 2011, https://drodrik.scholar.harvard.edu/publications/globalization-paradox-democracy-and-future-world-economy"

currency exchanges but in a more managed process, where a sovereign government retains a degree of control over its economy. In this regard, more gradual policies pursued by China and Indonesia today and by Europe, Japan, and America during the *Trente Glorieuses* after the war are more prone to shared progress than more dogmatic ones that favor liberalization and free trade over all other considerations.

And third, societies benefit from globalization when the reigning technology of the era is congruent with the comparative advantages an economy and society have. On the macro level, it explains why Argentina could become—for a short period of time—one of the world's wealthiest economies after the invention of the reefer ship. It could freeze and export its beef all over the world. On the micro level, it also explains why someone like Puty Puar in Indonesia can thrive as freelance illustrator today. The technology exists for her to exploit foreign markets from the comfort of her home.

In the absence of any of these three factors, however, globalization leads more often to unequal progress and sometimes even decadence or disruption. That has been the case in many emerging markets across Latin America, Africa, and Asia in previous waves of globalization. More recently, the United States, the United Kingdom, and other industrialized nations have been faced with the adverse effects of globalization as well. And, even when a social compact is in place, globalization and national sovereignty are well balanced, and technology advances play in a country's favor, things can still go wrong. A more connected global system is inherently less stable, as ripples in one country can more easily spread elsewhere. That is one of the lessons we should draw from the financial, health, and environmental crises of recent years. It is thus crucially important to make sure that globalization is a managed process, in which all precautions are taken to make the resulting economic system stable, resilient, and equitable. Sadly, however, this hasn't been the case. Let us look again at the factors previously identified and our performance on them in recent years.

In many of the large industrialized nations—the G7 consisting of Canada, France, Germany, Italy, Japan, the United Kingdom, and the United States—the social compact between people, government, and business has broken down in recent decades. Companies who once were proud to play a crucial role in communities they helped develop and build increasingly turned their backs on them, favoring instead to pursue higher profits and lower wages elsewhere in the world. The car industry, for example, which had been centered in Detroit, Michigan, moved much of its production to less expensive labor markets that could also easily serve US customers, such as Mexico, or ones that were closer to new international customers, such as China. The same has happened in the industrial heartland of Europe—Germany, Belgium, France, and Italy—where manufacturers moved production and jobs to new members of the European Union with significantly lower wages, such as Slovakia, the Czech Republic, or Romania, wreaking economic havoc on their former, higher-paid workers and the towns they lived in. Former automobile manufacturing towns such as Genk, Belgium, for example, to this day have not recovered from the loss of their car plants, suffering still from higher unemployment rates, lower wages, and a weaker economic growth path. For many of the companies deriving a lot of their profits from intellectual property, transfer pricing and differing tax rules across legislatures allowed them to move profits separately from production, depriving governments of oft much-needed tax incomes.

Free trade of course implies companies must be able to seek opportunities where they arise, and in fact they must do so at a healthy rate for globalization to work. But there is a point at which these actions stop being healthy for the communities these companies hail from or operate in. If the social compact is broken by one of the parties involved, it has a domino effect on the others. That is what has happened in many industrialized nations, where many ordinary workers stopped benefiting from globalization in its last wave—that of the 1990s and 2000s. As jobs disappeared, local tax bases eroded, leaving many local, regional, and sometimes even federal governments unable to meet their part of the social compact including paying for retirement or providing quality health care, housing, and education. The City of Detroit famously had to declare bankruptcy in 2013, no longer able to pay back its bonds, including those that guaranteed pensions to retired city government workers. While not a direct consequence of globalization, it certainly didn't help its manufacturing base had collapsed in the decades before. And countries such as Japan, Italy, and France increasingly had difficulties making the investments needed to secure not just functioning services to its people and companies today but also those that are needed to remain competitive in the future. In the face of this, it is no wonder people increasingly revolted against both the political and the economic system in these countries—and increasingly also against the multinationals who dominate the global economy and sometimes all too easily avoid paying taxes.

A second shortfall of globalization today is the policy environment governments created in the past three decades. Convinced of the organic benefits of a globalized world, many governments opted to embrace free trade and floating currency exchanges and eliminate barriers to foreign investment at an accelerated pace since the early 1990s. This seemed like a no-brainer following the victory of the American-led capitalist model over the Soviet-led communist one—what Francis Fukuyama famously called "the end of history." But it ignored the reality that the market does not always knows best—or[21] at least it doesn't automatically look after the interests of everyone involved. Economists such as Joseph Stiglitz, Mariana Mazzucato, Dani Rodrik, and many others observed in recent work that growing financialization and financial globalization in fact increases the instability in the economic system and increases both the likelihood and depth of financial crises. One country that can attest to the risks of unbridled financial globalization is Hungary. Zsolt Darvas, a native of Hungary and economist at think tank Bruegel (whose graphs on inequality we previously saw in Chapter 2), explained to us why he believed this was the root of many social, political, and economic problems the country faces today. As he wrote during the height of the global financial crisis in 2008:[22]

> Since Hungarian inflation was far higher than that in the eurozone, interest rates charged on loans in the Hungarian forint were also much higher. So, to get lower rates, many consumers and businesses switched to foreign currency loans—90% of new mortgage loans are now made in foreign currencies. In the Czech Republic and Slovakia, where interest rates were close to the eurozone rate, foreign currency loans only account for less than 2% of households' total.
>
> The global financial crisis arrived at high speed in late September [of 2008]. Many economists, including this writer, thought that the effects of the crisis on central and eastern European EU countries would not be dramatic. Our banks were not exposed to US sub-prime losses and were well capitalised. But it soon became clear that no country can isolate itself from the effects of this global financial crisis. With rising risk aversion and fear of contagion, investors started to sell and pull out of investments in emerging economies.
>
> Hungary was the hardest hit of the central European EU members because so much of its massive government debt was foreign-owned. These foreigners wanted to sell their Hungarian forint-denominated bonds but no new buyers appeared on the market. Long maturity interest rates jumped from the already high 8% to around 12% and the government bond market dried up. Auctions to issue new government bonds were unsuccessful. Hungarian blue-chips on the equity market

---

[21]"The End of History and the Last Man, Francis Fukuyama, Penguin Books, 1993".

[22]"The Rise and Fall of Hungary," Zsolt Darvas, *The Guardian*, October 2008, https://www .theguardian.com/business/blog/2008/oct/29/hungary-imf.

were also heavily sold. Pressure on the forint intensified and last week the central bank hiked interest rates by three percentage points. The rate rise helped strengthen the forint but the situation remained fragile and the government bond market was still frozen.

The events Darvas described are now more than a decade behind us. But they continue to reverberate until today. In the years following the catastrophic embrace of this type of financial globalization by Hungary, its bankers, and its citizens, the country experienced a major economic and debt crisis in 2008 and a smaller one five years later. Despite a return to growth afterward, disgruntled Hungarians increasingly showed their antipathy for the more liberal and Europe-minded politicians they believed got them into the situation. In recent years, they voted against European economic integration, against immigration, and against liberal trade and financial policies. Hungary notably closed its borders for immigrants, and it declined to participate in a European-wide solution for the migrant crisis in 2016. In an increasingly hostile environment, the Central European University, founded by George Soros, was forced to leave the country. The case of Hungary is peculiar and unique, but it does show how even well-intended policies in favor of globalization can lead to very undesirable outcomes. Globalization is a powerful force, and it can make a nation and its people better off, but it should be embraced pragmatically, not as a matter of blind ideology.

Finally, globalization's adverse effects can get amplified by technology. If people are not well skilled or educated to make the best use of the latest technologies, others in other countries will take their place in a globalized economy. In some cases, there are macro forces at play that are hard for a community to arm itself against. When the Internet was introduced, Richard Baldwin observed, communication costs fell drastically, and it made sense for profit-seeking companies to unbundle white-collar from blue-collar jobs. You could produce as well in one country (the one with the lowest combined production cost), ship the finished product, and sell it in another. It led to the rapidly advancing globalization of the 1990s and 2000s, which benefited many countries but harmed industrial communities in the West—something they could do little about. But that doesn't mean countries are powerless in the face of technologically driven globalization. Small, open economies such as Singapore, Denmark, the Netherlands, Belgium, who often trade goods worth well over 100 percent of their GDP, understand they live or die by their ability to adapt to the latest technologies driving globalization. If they invest in these technologies, or the skills to harness them, they can come out on the winning side. The Port of Rotterdam in this case is a good example. Understanding digital technologies such as blockchain will only intensify in their applications, the Port authority invested heavily in this technology.[23] It makes Rotterdam now possibly the most technologically advanced port in Europe, giving it and its workers a digital edge over its competitors in cities like Hamburg and Antwerp.

In the future, it won't just be physical trade that gets affected by technology. As indicated above, digital trade has begun an ascent that has not fully been appreciated anywhere and that is unlikely to halt anytime soon. Today, foresighted countries and communities still have a window of opportunity to plan to benefit from the rise in digital globalization. But they must be quick to act. Some aspects, such as the physical infrastructure of 5G, can be implemented relatively fast provided the funds are available. But some others, such as training the current and future workforce to become the Puty Puars of tomorrow, take a lot more advance planning.

■ ■ ■

Considering these realities, I believe globalization should be embraced, not foolishly or blindly, but rather in a pragmatic way that keeps the interest of the greatest number of stakeholders—people and companies—in mind first.

It is clear that such an approach can work. Annisa and her fellow founders of MYCL are an example of that, and so are Puty and the Utomo brothers who founded IDN Media. Aided by a substantial investment by their government in education, they were able to reap the benefits of global markets at home and help others in their country get ahead as well. It makes them convinced of the benefits of globalization, just as a majority of their countrymen and women. Or, as William, the younger Utomo brother told us, overlooking Jakarta from their company's offices:[24] "Trade and technology is how a country grows. If you specialize, you can grow." If all stakeholders of a country have a similar mindset and are aware of their responsibilities and the pitfalls of globalization, we could ensure the benefits of globalization once again outweigh its risks. But to do so, as William indicates, it is important also to get the second part of that equation right: technology.

---

[23]"How Rotterdam Is Using Blockchain to Reinvent Global Trade," Port of Rotterdam, September 2019, https://www.portofrotterdam.com/en/news-and-press-releases/how-rotterdam-is-using-blockchain-to-reinvent-global-trade.

[24]Interview with William and Winston Utomo by Peter Vanham, Jakarta, Indonesia, October 16, 2020.

6

Technology

A Changing Labor Market

The press release touted a most remarkable headline: **"Denmark in the world's top 10 for robots."**[1]

The organization behind the release was not a Danish tech firm, media outlet, or politician. It was Dansk Metal, the union representing blue-collar workers in the Danish metal manufacturing and processing industry. It was clear that the union was proud of this achievement: "An increasing number of employees in the industry work side by side with robots," the press release read. "Dansk Metal has a target of rounding 10,000 industrial robots in Denmark by 2020."

I was intrigued by this stance. From visiting other parts of the world, and reading about other times in history, I knew of many more instances where workers opposed new technologies, especially when they threatened to replace their jobs. The most famous case may have been that of the Luddites in England, a group of textile workers in 19th century England who destroyed the new machinery that was disrupting their industry. But throughout the world, including in our time, many others also protested new technologies and the new ways of working they promoted, whether through street protests against

---

[1] « Danmark i verdens robot top-10 », Dansk Metal, January 2018, https://www.danskmetal. dk/Nyheder/pressemeddelelser/Sider/Danmark-i-verdens-robot-top-10.aspx.

ride-hailing firms such as Uber or intellectual protests by politicians[2] or academics[3] in media.

I too share the concern over the future of work in this era of automation. Back in 2015, I realized we were at the dawn of a new era—one of artificial intelligence, advanced robotics, and integrated cyber-physical systems—and that together they constituted a Fourth Industrial Revolution. The new technologies we were witnessing, including also 3D printing, quantum computing, precision medicine, and others, I came to believe, were on par with that of the First Industrial Revolution—the steam engine—those of the Second Industrial Revolution—the combustion engine and electricity—and that of the Third Industrial Revolution—information technology and computing. They were leading to a disruption of the workforce, changing the nature of not just what we do but who we are, something I previously described in my book *The Fourth Industrial Revolution*.[4]

In their landmark 2013 study "The Future of Employment," Carl Frey and Michael Osborne of Oxford first warned of the kind of disruption this could bring about.[5] They notoriously estimated up to half of jobs would be altered in the coming years because of these new technologies, with many of them disappearing altogether. In 2019, Frey followed up on his original study with the equally eye-opening book *The Technology Trap*,[6] showing how today's labor-replacing technologies fit into the longer history of industrial revolutions. It is no wonder then that many people in today's global economy are fearful of what the future may bring and that they prefer instead to hold on to the more familiar world of the past. It explains why political leaders around the

---

[2] "Why American Workers Need to Be Protected From Automation," Bill de Blasio, *Wired*, September 2019, https://www.wired.com/story/why-american-workers-need-to-be-protected-from-automation/.

[3] "Robots Are the Ultimate Job Stealers. Blame Them, Not Immigrants," Arlie Hochschild, *The Guardian*, February 2018, https://www.theguardian.com/commentisfree/2018/feb/14/resentment-robots-job-stealers-arlie-hochschild.

[4] *The Fourth Industrial Revolution*, Klaus Schwab, Penguin Random House, January 2017, https://www.penguinrandomhouse.com/books/551710/the-fourth-industrial-revolution-by-klaus-schwab/.

[5] "The Future of Employment: How Susceptible Are Jobs to Computerization?" Carl Frey and Michael Osborne, Oxford University, September 2013, https://www.oxfordmartin.ox.ac.uk/downloads/academic/The_Future_of_Employment.pdf.

[6] *The Technology Trap: Capital, Labor, and Power in the Age of Automation*, Carl Frey, Princeton University Press, June 2019, https://press.princeton.edu/books/hardcover/9780691172798/the-technology-trap.

world, egged on by voters, are trying to save or revive manufacturing jobs and why they are increasingly retreating into more autarkic ways of running their economy. Technology is an awesome force, in every sense of the word.

But the news from Denmark seemed to suggest that such fears can be overcome and that the newest and best technologies can help workers too, without necessarily replacing them. How was this possible? To find out, I asked a colleague to go to Copenhagen and find out what explained this attitude.

Dansk Metal President Claus Jensen gave us a first convincing argument.[7] "Have you ever known of a country or company," he asked, "that implemented *old* technology to get rich?" He was convinced that wasn't possible. And he didn't share the doom and gloom vision of some on the future of work: "Maybe Singularity University will think that everyone will be replaced by technology," he said.[8] "Maybe they think everyone will be standing at the sea, looking at robots making everything. But not everyone would say that." He certainly didn't believe it. It went against his own experience and that of his predecessors at the union in the past 150 years. "Every time we introduced new technology in Denmark in the past," he said, "we've had more employment." So to Jensen, it was clear. "We should not be afraid of *new* technology," he said. "We should be afraid of *old* technology."[9]

This optimistic perspective wasn't only consistent among the leadership of the union for over a century (the union was founded in 1888, and its first president held the same view as Jensen today), it was also widely shared by the base of the organization—the union members themselves. Robin Løffmann, a 32-year-old ship equipment technician for MAN Energy Solutions in Copenhagen, was one example of that. The son of a car mechanic, Løffmann had the love for cars and engines in his blood.

---

[7] "If Robots and AI Steal Our Jobs, a Universal Basic Income Could Help", Peter H. Diamandis, Singularity Hub, December 2016, https://singularityhub.com/2016/12/13/if-robots-steal-our-jobs-a-universal-basic-income-could-help/.

[8] Interview with Claus Jensen by Peter Vanham, May 2019

[9] Even if jobs disappeared in one part of the industry, which happened when ships were no longer mainly built by humans but by robots, having a long-term vision of change helped him keep a positive and constructive outlook. Workers still need to oversee construction, they still need to repair engines, and they still needed to make sure all parts fit together. If Danish workers were the best in the world, Denmark could remain the global center of ship building and repair. It was in the DNA of his union to have such a positive perspective. "My union was founded in 1888, and our first chairman said the same things that I do today," he said. "We change technology, but we don't change our opinion."

When it was time to choose a profession at age 18, he chose to become an industry technician. Aided by a four-year technical education and a concurrent apprenticeship at a small manufacturer, he easily found a job upon graduating making fuel injection pumps for MAN.

Four years later, in 2012, things could have gone the wrong way for him. His boss told him the company would buy new machinery, which would bring down construction time for the parts from 20 minutes to five or six minutes and drastically reduce the need for human intervention in quality control. Yet Løffmann didn't oppose the new machinery. He loved it. "In other places, they don't want machines to do the heavy lifting," he told us in an interview for this book.[10] "But not so in Denmark," Løffmann said. Here, "the company will say: can we reskill you to be an operator on a different kind of machines?" In his specific case, Løffmann was sent to Bielefeld, Germany, where the new machinery was made, and asked to "sign off" on the new equipment on behalf of his company. A month later, a specialist of the German company came to Copenhagen and retrained him and three other workers to work with the new machinery.

Løffmann's story is typical for the broader industry. Dansk Metal Chief Economist Thomas Søby told us: "People aren't afraid to lose their jobs, because they have retraining possibilities. We have a very functioning system. When you lose your job, we at the union will send an e-mail or call you within one or two days. We'll have a meeting to talk about your situation, see if you need upskilling, if there are any companies in the area looking for their profile. And we are very successful in placing our members in another job, immediately or after re-skilling. We have established schools all over the country. The curriculum is decided by employers and employees. And they are open to retraining and re-education of the workforce."[11]

The constructive and trusting relationship between workers and companies is paying off for Denmark. While the country long ago stopped being the shipyard of the world—that place was taken by mega firms in South Korea, Japan, China, and Turkey—it still produces the engines that keep new and old ships running around the world (the oldest ship engine Løffmann's company maintains dates from 1861; the newest ones are still being made). And the cost advantage it loses in high wages it makes up in the productivity and can-do attitude of its workers.

---

[10]Interview with Robin Løffmann by Peter Vanham, Copenhagen, November 2019.

[11]Interview with Thomas Søby by Peter Vanham, Copenhagen, November 2019.

Just before the COVID pandemic hit in early 2020, Denmark had an unemployment rate of 3.7 percent,[12] and in the metal union it stood even lower at 2 percent (the fact that the union pays unemployment benefits, and thus has incentives to have as little people unemployed as possible, certainly plays a role). Perhaps more importantly, Denmark's wages are high and relatively equal. A member of the metal union, Søby said, makes about $60,000–70,000 per year, for a maximum 40-hour workweek, while union participation still stands at about 80 percent. Overall, Denmark is also one of the most equal countries in the world in terms of income, though its inequality has been trending upward in recent years.[13]

This story from Denmark is more remarkable because it contrasts with the narrative in other industrialized nations. The Danes look at it with astonishment. Not too long ago, American, German, French, Spanish, and Italian social security and education systems were on par with those in Scandinavia. But today, Søby told us, he looks with astonishment to what has happened in these countries. While Denmark maintained and updated its social security and education system, others have done much less. The Danish system, he says, works well for both companies and workers. The "pact" between them is that companies can fire workers with relative ease—but that they do pay high wages, contribute to taxes, and participate in reskilling efforts. With salaries taxed at up to 52 percent, there is certainly a price to pay for this "flexicurity" model. But, he said, "In Scandinavian countries, we offer reskilling for fired workers, and are able to place most workers again in a new job. You don't have that [to the same degree] in Germany, Spain, Italy or France."

The country he is most shocked by is the United States. America dominated the two previous Industrial Revolutions. With its Great Society it was also a place where blue-collar workers could achieve the American Dream. But today, it is no longer a Mecca for workers—at least not from Søby's perspective. Of course, the decline in manufacturing and the rise of the service sector is a global mega-trend, stretching decades and affecting the entire industrialized world. But the pace at

[12]Unemployment, Statistics Denmark, consulted in October 2020, https://www.dst.dk/en/Statistik/emner/arbejde-indkomst-og-formue/arbejdsloeshed.

[13]"Inequality in Denmark through the Looking Glass," Orsetta Causa, Mikkel Hermansen, Nicolas Ruiz, Caroline Klein, Zuzana Smidova, OECD Economics, November 2016, https://read.oecd-ilibrary.org/economics/inequality-in-denmark-through-the-looking-glass_5jln041vm6tg-en#page3.

which people lost jobs in the US manufacturing sector is extraordinary. Between 1990 and 2016, the *Financial Times* calculated, some 5.6 million jobs were lost in manufacturing.[14] The workforce of entire industrial cities was decimated. Some company towns, cities which all but depended on one industrial employer, were particularly hard-hit. And while many of these jobs didn't disappear altogether but were rather offshored to China or nearshored to Mexico, about half of the jobs did get lost because of advancing automation. At best, low-paid service jobs replaced these well-paid blue-collar jobs. At worst, no new jobs became available at all, at least not for workers without a college degree. Inflation-adjusted wages since 1980 have barely risen in certain sectors. And, despite having very low official unemployment numbers until the pandemic hit, the US labor force participation dropped from an all-time high of over 67 percent in 2000, to around 62 percent in 2020,[15] meaning many people stopped looking for work altogether. In Denmark, by contrast, the labor force participation continued to hover around 70 percent even after the pandemic hit in early 2020.[16]

Why did this happen? "One of the major problems in the American economy," Søby said, "is a lack of education of the workforce."[17] Unlike in Denmark, there is no widespread system for upskilling workers. It is an issue that becomes obvious in the figures of the Organization for Economic Cooperation and Development (OECD).[18] Denmark is the OECD country that spends the most per head on so-called "Active Labour Market Policies," to help unemployed back into the labor market. Comparatively speaking, the US spends a factor of 15 times less. The Danish system is also more inclusive (accessible to a greater percentage of people, regardless of their age, gender, education level, or employment status) and more flexible. And most significantly, the Danish system is the

---

[14]"How Many US Manufacturing Jobs Were Lost to Globalisation?" Matthew C. Klein, *Financial Times*, December 2016, https://ftalphaville.ft.com/2016/12/06/2180771/how-many-us-manufacturing-jobs-were-lost-to-globalisation/.

[15]Trading Economics, United States Labor Force Participation Rate, with numbers supplied by the US Bureau of Labor Statistics, https://tradingeconomics.com/united-states/labor-force-participation-rate.

[16]Trading Economics, Denmark Labor Force Participation Rate, https://tradingeconomics.com/denmark/labor-force-participation-rate.

[17]Interview with Thomas Søby by Peter Vanham, Copenhagen, November 2019.

[18]OECD, Directorate for Employment, Labour and Social Affairs, Employment Policies and Data, Skills and Work dashboard, http://www.oecd.org/els/emp/skills-and-work/xkljljo-sedifjsldfk.htm.

best adapted to labor market needs of all OECD countries, while the US lags behind 19 of the 32 studied countries.

It leads to a chronic mismatch in the American labor market. Even when reskilling is available in the US, economic journalist Heather Long of the *Washington Post* told us, workers either are often not incentivized to enroll, fearing it won't lead to a job anyway, or they register for some of the most basic IT courses, such as working with Microsoft Word or Outlook. "That's eye-opening to me," Long said,[19] recounting an anecdote.

> I tracked workers who were laid off from auto factory in Ohio. They all qualified for the "Cadillac" retraining, getting paid for two years to go to school and retrain. They could get a trucking or nursing license, go to community college, become an advanced machinist, or operate a 3D printer, one of the most advanced blue-collar jobs. People who qualified in their twenties or thirties felt great about it. But those in their forties, who hadn't been in a classroom for 20 years, they didn't. There was a major skills gap. Some of them didn't even know what a flash drive was. When I go to Davos, and I hear CEO says: we just need to upskill! That sounds great, but it is not at all possible. I don't think it's malign. But at the Ohio factory 2,000 workers were eligible. Fewer than 30% applied. And only 15% completed a programme.[20]

The problem here, to be clear, is not with the attitude of older workers. It is that when a culture of constant retraining does not exist and workers have not been upskilled once in their career, even a well-funded shock therapy won't suffice. That is also how Thomas Søby sees it, looking at the situation from Denmark: "I understand why workers have something against new technology and robots, because if they were to lose their jobs, they are pretty much doomed. Their skills are very company specific. If you don't have system for re-education or upskilling, you have a very fierce anger. It is very difficult to solve, and they are trying to do it in the wrong way. What you need is better education, and higher unionization.[21]" In advocating for this type of solution, Søby is not alone. Across the ocean, in Washington, DC, it is also what economists like Joseph Stiglitz propose, or think tanks such as the Economic Policy

---

[19]Interview with Heather Long by Peter Vanham, Washington, DC, April 2019.

[20] Ibidem.

[21]Interview with Thomas Søby by Peter Vanham, Copenhagen, November 2019.

Institute (EPI, founded by a group of economists including former US Labor Secretary Robert Reich). Josh Bivens, director of research at EPI, made this point in a 2017 study: While in Denmark union participation remains very high, guaranteeing that demands of workers on issues such as pay and training are taken into account, in the US it dropped from about one-third of workers in the 1950s, to about 25 percent in 1980, and barely 10 percent today. That drop in union participation coincided with a rise in economic inequality, and, as EPI argues, with a drop in training programs that keep workers skilled in this age of the Fourth Industrial Revolution and the US workforce productive and competitive.[22]

In the United States and the United Kingdom, two countries where workers have been hit hardest by the changes in the economic system, advocating for unions and education has become politically polarizing. In the 1980s, conservative Prime Minister Margaret Thatcher in the UK and Republican President Ronald Reagan in the US embraced a neoliberal agenda that proved anathema to public investment in fields like education and the power of unions. Under this ideology, collective bargaining by unions was a barrier to establishing free markets, and the state with its taxes and services was a drag on high economic growth. In the US, President Reagan famously fired all air traffic controllers who participated in a union-organized strike, thereby breaking the back of unions in the US. And in the UK, Prime Minister Margaret Thatcher broke a major miners' strike, ending the dominance of unions in her country. Both leaders also significantly lowered top tax rates. This was supposed to free up money for investment by companies and high net worth individuals and realize a trickle-down economy. But it also deprived the state of income to fund public services including education programs. For a long time, it seemed like those kinds of policies indeed helped the economies of the UK and the US. The next years marked a period of high growth in both countries, and by the 1990s, the neoliberal ideology was even adopted by the Democrats and New Labour. But by the Great Recession of 2008–09, it became clear neoliberal policies had had their best years. As we saw in Part I, economic growth remained sluggish in recent years, and wages for many

---

[22]"How Today's Union Help Working People: Giving Workers the Power to Improve Their Jobs and Unrig the Economy," Josh Bivens et al., Economic Policy Institute, August 2017, https://www.epi.org/publication/how-todays-unions-help-working-people-giving-workers-the-power-to-improve-their-jobs-and-unrig-the-economy/.

in the US and elsewhere in the industrialized world stopped going up, with many also falling out of the labor market. Today, as the contrasting examples of Denmark and the United States above show, any industrialized country would do well to embrace again more stakeholder-driven solutions and public investment in education. Political color or ideology should play less of a role in this debate than the notion that these solutions simply work.

Singapore is one example of how this works in Asia. In terms of openness to trade, technology, and immigration, the city-state in Southeast Asia is one of the most economically liberal countries in the world. In terms of its social policies, it is a solidly conservative country,[23] with LGBTQ rights[24] and marriage and human rights more broadly more strictly regulated than in many Western countries. But in terms of its economic policies, its Senior Minister Tharman Shanmugaratnam told us,[25] the government adopts policies that work, not ones that are ideologically driven. As an island nation that depended for its wealth on its global economic competitiveness, it had almost no choice.

Singapore started its steep economic ascent as one of the Asian Tigers, alongside Hong Kong, South Korea, and Taiwan in the 1960s. In the early stages, the island successfully bet on labor-intensive manufacturing as one of its growth poles. Manufacturing's share of GDP grew from 10 percent in 1960 to 25 percent at the end of the 1970s, in a period where GDP grew by over 6 percent per year.[26] The arrival of Japanese and other global companies looking for a cheap manufacturing hub helped many Singaporeans get decent blue-collar jobs and allowed the country to quickly develop: while its GDP per capita was a mere $500 in 1965, it exploded to $13,000 by 1990[27] (see Figure 6.1).

---

[23]"Singapore Society Still Largely Conservative but Becoming More Liberal on Gay Rights: IPS Survey," *The Straits Times*, May 2019, https://www.straitstimes.com/politics/singapore-society-still-largely-conservative-but-becoming-more-liberal-on-gay-rights-ips.

[24]"Singapore: Crazy Rich but Still Behind on Gay Rights," *The Diplomat*, October 2018, https://thediplomat.com/2018/10/singapore-crazy-rich-but-still-behind-on-gay-rights/.

[25]Interview with Senior Minister Tharman Shanmugaratnam by Peter Vanham, Singapore, July 2019.

[26]"Singapore's Economic Transformation," Gundy Cahyadi, Barbara Kursten, Dr. Marc Weiss, and Guang Yang, Global Urban Development, June 2004, http://www.globalurban.org/GUD%20Singapore%20MES%20Report.pdf.

[27]"An Economic History of Singapore—1965–2065," Ravi Menon, Bank for International Settlements, August 2015, https://www.bis.org/review/r150807b.htm.

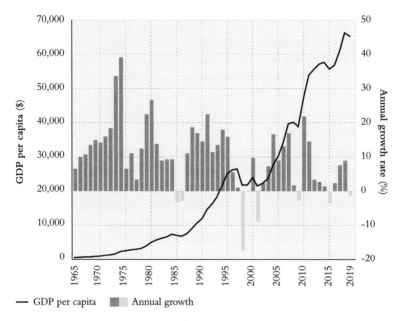

Figure 6.1 Singapore's GDP per Capita Growth (1965–2019)

Source: World Bank, Macrotrends.

But with newly developing Asian economies like China hot on its heels, Singapore already in the 1980s needed to reskill its workers, in the hopes a more service- and knowledge-oriented economy could help it move up the value chain and make the leap toward a fully developed nation status. For this purpose, Singapore invested heavily in new types of education, both for children and adults. According to a Global Urban Development report, "More training centers were geared towards the higher-skilled industries such as electronics," and a new education system was installed, "to ensure that Singapore could form a very high quality and skilled workforce out of the universities and yet at the same time, ensuring that technical training was still available to those who could not excel in the formal education system."[28] Again, the system worked. While its share of manufacturing employment dropped, the services sector in the next few decades rapidly grew, contributing a fifth to GDP in the early 1980s, but almost a third by the mid-2010s. By 2015, Singapore had a GDP per capita exceeding that of

---

[28]"Singapore's Economic Transformation," Gundy Cahyadi, Barbara Kursten, Dr. Marc Weiss, and Guang Yang, Global Urban Development, June 2004, http://www.globalurban.org/ GUD%20Singapore%20MES%20Report.pdf.

both Germany, the economic powerhouse of Europe, and the US, the wealthiest nation on earth.

While Singapore is one of the most remarkable success stories of the past half century, the Southeast Asian nation understands that they will need to continue adapting to changes in the global economy today, where new technologies and service jobs are becoming ever more important. It's why it recently set up a government-led SkillsFuture initiative. Through this system of lifelong learning, Singaporeans of any age can learn new skills to ensure they are prepared for the job market of the Fourth Industrial Revolution. Unlike in Denmark though, the system is not achieved by setting up a large state with vast social power and far-reaching programs. "We have a strong government, but not a big government," Shanmugaratnam said. One of the features of the SkillsFuture initiative, therefore, is that participants mostly have a free choice on which programs to enroll in. In a workshop organized for us by James Crabtree at the National University of Singapore, some policy thinkers made a remark that had led to some discussion in government circles. Must workers really be subsidized to learn how to become florists or cooks, for example? Currently in Singapore, the prevailing notion is that the programs may be uncommon, but they are also worth the cost. One of the features of the ongoing Fourth Industrial Revolution, the reasoning goes, is that it's hard to predict the labor market of the future. Who thought some of the most successful twentysomething professionals today would be YouTubers playing videogames or influencers making 10 second TikTok movies?

When looking at the Singaporean model, there is another important feature to note. It's been achieved by a triad of stakeholders: government, companies, and unions. Since 1965, this trifecta has had a heavy hand in all labor market and industrial policy decision-making. And it did so without major disruptions in economic activity. Strikes in Singapore are extremely rare, yet the labor market is dynamic (it is relatively easy to hire and fire), and the economy has successfully transformed itself at least twice—once in the 1960s and 1970s toward manufacturing and again in the 1980s and 1990s toward services. Such a constructive and dynamic attitude will remain important going forward, *Nikkei Asian Review* reported recently, because "Singapore will face the highest rate of job displacement resulting from technological disruption in Southeast Asia."[29] But in a sign that this coming technological disruption will not

[29]"Singapore Faces Biggest Reskilling Challenge in Southeast Asia," Justina Lee, *Nikkei Asian Review*, December 2018, https://asia.nikkei.com/Economy/Singapore-faces-biggest-reskilling-challenge-in-Southeast-Asia.

devastate Singapore's society and economy, a survey by accounting firm PwC found that "over 90% of the Singaporean respondents said, they will take any opportunity given by their employers to better understand or use technology."[30] It shows the triple challenge for economies like the US and Western Europe. Governments and companies must invest more in continuous retraining of workers, unions must be stronger but have a cooperative approach to business and government, and workers themselves should be positive and flexible about future economic challenges they and their country face.

A Changing Business Landscape

Tim Wu was still in elementary school in 1980, when he was one of the first of his class to get a personal computer: the Apple II. The now iconic computer propelled creators Steve Jobs and Steve Wozniak to stardom and heralded a new era in technology. But for Tim and his brother, the Apple II was first and foremost an exciting way to get acquainted with a new technology. "My brother and I loved Apple, we were obsessed with it," Wu told us.[31] The two preteens would make it their hobby to get the computers chips out, reprogram them, and put them back in. A couple of years later, when computer networks were first introduced, they would set up a dial-up modem, connect to other computers, and create their own networks. Those formative years made the Wus lifelong nerds for technology. Tim's brother eventually went on to work as a programmer for Microsoft, and Tim had an (unpaid) stint at Google. There too, Wu was still very excited. "I was a real believer," he said. "There was a lot of hope with what Google was trying to do. There was a feeling that we could transcend all dilemmas."

Today, though now Columbia Law Professor Wu still uses an Apple laptop, iPhone, and Google services every day, he is no longer a fan of the companies they have become. With market valuations that hover around or even well over $1 trillion,[32] the companies that once fit

---

[30]"PwC's Hopes and Fears Survey," p. 4, PwC, September 2019, https://www.pwc.com/sg/en/publications/assets/new-world-new-skills-2020.pdf.

[31]Interview with Tim Wu by Peter Vanham, New York, October 2019.

[32]"The 100 Largest Companies by Market Capitalization in 2020," Statista, consulted in October 2020, https://www.statista.com/statistics/263264/top-companies-in-the-world-by-market-capitalization.

into a garage are America's largest publicly traded companies. Apple's personal computers stopped being its top-selling products a long ago, ceding that place to the iPhone. And while it still makes the lion's share of its revenues from selling a sleek line of hardware, including the iWatch, iPad, and iPhone, its copyrighted and well-protected software products and its pioneering App Store now form the beating heart of its ecosystem. Google (now under parent company Alphabet) went from being the leading search provider to a sprawling imperium active in everything from ad sales to shopping, entertainment, and cloud computing. And while many of the early IT companies faded away as time went by, Alphabet, Apple, Microsoft, Facebook, and Amazon consolidated their leading positions, to become the corporate giants of our era.

"The turning point came when these big guys didn't go away, or got too big," Wu said. "It was when they got into too many markets." It was advice he gave to Google when he was still friendly with them. "You have this incredible thing," he told them, "but you need to be careful with adjacent markets." Wu was trying to be Google's friend, he said, but wanted to keep it out of what he called "morally dubious practices." The advice fell on deaf ears. The result, he said, is that today the top five Big Tech companies more resemble monopolists like telecom provider AT&T in the 1980s than the upstarts they were not too long ago. They buy or copy competitors to protect their markets, he said, act as both a platform and seller, and favor their own products on their stores. And as with the monopolists of every previous industrial revolution, Wu argues, they stifle the economy and competition while doing so and concentrate wealth and power in the hands of a few, rather than the many. For that reason, Wu claims, these "Big Tech" companies should face one of two tough measures: to be regulated like a natural monopoly or to be broken up.

Wu is far from the only one in America who is likening the situation of Big Tech to the monopolists of previous eras. When I visited US Senator Elizabeth Warren in Washington, DC, at the end of 2018, she was already contemplating a similar stance against the market leaders in many of America's industries, including technology, the pharmaceutical sector, and finance. Wu's colleague at Columbia Law School Lina Khan in 2016 wrote a seminal paper (while at Yale), taking a similar stance: "Amazon's Antitrust Paradox."[33] Economists such as Gabriel Zucman, Emmanuel Saez, Kenneth Rogoff, and Nobel Prize winners Paul Krugman and Joseph Stiglitz have also stated Big Tech

---

[33]Amazon's Antitrust Paradox, Lina M. Kahn, The Yale Law Journal, January 2017

has "too much power"[34] or needs to be more strictly regulated. Leading journalists including Nicholas Thompson, the editor in chief of *Wired*, and Rana Foroohar, associate editor of the *Financial Times*, favor antitrust action against Big Tech too. And even some co-founders of the tech giants that have now come under regulatory scrutiny, including Apple's Steve Wozniak[35] and Facebook's Chris Hughes, have said they favor more strict regulation. To Wu, it is the only right attitude. "I always liked the Wozniak Apple," he said. "They did amazing things."

But just as there are those like Wu, Warren, and Wozniak who believe Big Tech's monopolies or monopsonies (a variation of a monopoly in which there is only one buyer in a market) need to be regulated more, there are those who believe such actions would prove counterproductive. They point to the fact that many Big Tech services are free or that the prices they offer are the lowest and best in the market (think Amazon). In either case, they say, the best way to deal with these large technology firms is not to break them up or regulate them. Those actions would hurt some of the most innovative companies of the past years and thereby, the innovative power of the US economy. Some also point to an ongoing war for tech hegemony, mostly between the US and China, where excessive restrictions on US companies could make them lose this fight.

I had the opportunity to meet all the leaders of these Big Tech companies over the last years and to follow many of them closely in their journey toward success. For example, I visited Mark Zuckerberg in a warehouse in Palo Alto, when he had just 18 employees, and designated Jack Ma a World Economic Forum "Young Global Leader" when he had just started Alibaba. I am convinced that they, after an initial period of feeling perhaps a bit like Alice in Wonderland, have become increasingly aware of the enormous impact they have on individuals' lives and

---

[34]"Big Tech Has Too Much Monopoly Power—It's Right to Take It On," Kenneth Rogoff, *The Guardian*, April 2019, https://www.theguardian.com/technology/2019/apr/02/big-tech-monopoly-power-elizabeth-warren-technology; Quote: "Here are titles of some recent articles: Paul Krugman's "Monopoly Capitalism Is Killing US Economy," Joseph Stiglitz's "America Has a Monopoly Problem—and It's Huge," and Kenneth Rogoff's "Big Tech Is a Big Problem"; "The Rise of Corporate Monopoly Power," Zia Qureshi, Brookings, May 2019, https://www.brookings.edu/blog/up-front/2019/05/21/the-rise-of-corporate-market-power/.

[35]"Steve Wozniak Says Apple Should've Split Up a Long Time Ago, Big Tech Is Too Big," Bloomberg, August 2019, https://www.bloomberg.com/news/videos/2019-08-27/steve-wozniak-says-apple-should-ve-split-up-a-long-time-ago-big-tech-is-too-big-video.

identities. And I see among them an increasing readiness to work constructively on responses to the legitimate concerns of society, including regarding data ownership, algorithms, face recognition, and so on. They know it is in their own long-term interest not to neglect these concerns, as they could otherwise be subject to regulations that further harm their future growth.

Who in the end is right in this debate? Are Big Tech and other dominant firms in today's economy helping or hurting workers and consumers? Should we update our competition policies to make them fit for the digital economy? And have we entered a new Gilded Age because of Big Tech, or will we rather enter an innovation winter if we curtail the most successful firms of our age? Looking at economic history through the industrial revolutions lens can help answer these important questions.

Pre-Industrial Revolutions

Before the dawn of the modern era, economies around the world were mostly stagnant. The most significant change in human lifestyle had occurred some 10,000 years ago, when hunter-gatherers settled and became farmers. That change was significant in two ways. Farming led to a stable supply of food and even a regular surplus for the first time,[36] and a non-nomadic way of life allowed people to stock food and domesticate animals, providing further sources of nutrition, including meat and milk products. Aided by further technological breakthroughs, such as the development of the plough, the wheel, pottery, and iron tools, this era consisted of a true agricultural revolution. It had major political, economic, and societal consequences.

Socially, the new sedentary lifestyle allowed for the development of villages, cities, societies, and even early empires. Politically, these societies started to see hierarchies for the first time, as the food surplus allowed certain classes of people to live off the foods produced by others. And economically, early trading and specialization led to a modest increase in overall wealth. Almost invariably, the emerging civilizations that ensued

---

[36]Some scholars do dispute this notion. Yuval Noah Harari, for example, is much less upbeat about the impact of the agricultural revolution on the quality and quantity of food supply on people.

consisted of a top class of warriors and spiritual leaders, a middle class of merchants, traders, and specialized workers (making pottery, clothes, and other products), and a large base class of serfs and farmers, who produced foods for themselves and others, most often in a system of subservience to the top classes. It is an early pattern we'll see throughout history: technological breakthroughs lead to a significant increase in wealth, but that surplus almost always gets unevenly distributed and even monopolized by a small group of people at the top of society.

The following millennia saw many changes in political and societal structure, as well as various periods of innovation. On the Eurasian landmass, from China over India and the Arab world to Europe, breakthroughs occurred during medieval times in printing, finance, and accounting, as well as navigation, warfare, and transportation. As we saw in previous chapters, these technological advances spurred on various waves of intercontinental trade and led to a further increase in the lifestyle of peoples, particularly in the top classes. It was the time of the Persian, Ottoman, Mongol, and Ming empires.

In Europe, which lagged the Eurasian trend, the Renaissance and early modern period finally saw a true scientific revolution. It led to great changes in society and politics, including the dominance of European powers in the global economy, the Reformation in European Christianity, and the Peace of Westphalia in European politics. And, with the aid of the compass, sail ships, firepower, and other applications of this scientific revolution, European powers also established a number of global trading empires, epitomized by the gigantic East India Companies we wrote about in the previous chapters. But even with these advances in technology and wealth, the vast majority of people in Europe by the end of the 18th century were still active in farming, their lives having changed little from that of their forebears many centuries ago.

The First Industrial Revolution

This all changed with the arrival of the so-called First Industrial Revolution, primarily in Great Britain. By the 1760s, James Watt and his steam engine were poised to revolutionize industry. Progress was irregular at first, but by the early 19th century Britain's entrepreneurs were well on their way to becoming the world's most successful. In a matter of decades, British steam trains, ships, and machinery took over the world, and Great Britain became the most powerful empire in the world. Entire industries got completely transformed, most notably agriculture and textile manufacturing. Instead of being powered by man or horse, they were now powered by machines, allowing for a multiple increase in yields in agriculture and an even greater multiplier in manufacturing. The British economy—measured in output of final goods—started to grow by several percentage points per year, rather than the 0.1 or 0.2 percent, which was the norm in previous centuries. The population grew rapidly. And while there were many more mouths to feed, fewer people (and horses) were needed in the agricultural sector. By the end of the 19th century, more than half of the population had therefore moved to industrial cities like London, Manchester, or Liverpool, and a majority of them was active in the factories.

The ones who benefited most from this First Industrial Revolution were Britain's capitalist entrepreneurs. Capitalism was nothing new. It had existed in Europe at least since Venetian merchants pooled their risk of shipping in the medieval Mediterranean trade—but was now mainly used to fund factories and their machines, rather than trade. Those who had enough capital at hand—often large landowners, successful merchants, and members of aristocratic families—could invest in new technologies and start successful companies. With a world market now at their disposal, they pocketed huge profits. And as the labor needed to operate machines was not as specialized as that needed to manufacture goods by hand, these early industrialists had a bargaining power over workers, which led to exploitative situations (and that was only in Britain, the wealthiest country of the time; the countries whose craft manufacturing was decimated, such as India and China, were much worse off, as there were virtually no winners).

As the 19th century progressed, the technologies of the First Industrial Revolution also spread to other countries, mainly in continental Europe (most notably Belgium, France, and Germany) and Britain's former colony across the North Atlantic Ocean, the United States. The technological transformation coincided with a political, economic, and social transformation here too. By the end of the 1800s, the plight of ordinary workers had become so problematic in England, Belgium, France, and Germany, that some members of the new leading classes decried the excesses. *Les Misérables* was written, highlighting the exploitative conditions in which regular Frenchmen had to work. German émigrés Karl Marx and Friedrich Engels wrote newspaper articles and even books about the fate of the proletariat in industrial England, which was all but positive. And Charles Dickens, writing a few decades earlier, most famously wrote it was not just the "best of times," but also the "worst of times," the "season of Darkness," and the "winter of despair."[37] Was it the result of industrialization or globalization? In truth it was probably both. As we saw in the previous chapter, workers started to unite against the injustices they faced and demanded political rights, better wages and working circumstances, and even an overthrow of the new societal hierarchy, in which industrialists had replaced kings and priests at the top of society and factory workers had replaced serfs and other small farmers at the bottom.

In America, too, the first Industrial Revolution led to an untenable situation. The technological advances in transport, finance, and energy led to the formation of oligopolies and monopolies: companies with the most capital and initial resources could best afford to deploy the latest technology at the greatest scale, offer the best services, and in turn win a higher market share, make the most profit, and outcompete or buy up other companies. In the transportation sector, for example, it led to a dominant position for the railroad companies connecting the Midwest to New York, controlled by Cornelius Vanderbilt, a tycoon also active in shipping. In the energy sector, it allowed the astute John D. Rockefeller to come from almost nothing to build the world's largest oil company, Standard Oil, and later also created the first business trust (Standard Oil today lives on in ExxonMobil, still America's largest oil company). In the steel industry, it enabled the Scottish-born American Andrew Carnegie to create the forerunner of U.S. Steel, which later became the monopolist of steel production in the US. In coal production, it led to Henry Frick establishing the Frick Coke Company, which controlled 80 percent of the coal output in Pennsylvania,[38] and taking the helm at several other conglomerates of the time. And in banking, it created a situation where magnates like Andrew Mellon, of BNY-Mellon fame, and John Pierpont Morgan, founder of what is today JPMorgan Chase, could build some of the largest financial firms America had ever seen.

Today, we know many of these industrial tycoons for their societal contributions, which include Rockefeller Center, Carnegie Hall, and many philanthropic organizations, which are still active today. But at the end of the 1880s, they were best known for their opulent wealth and often questionable business practices. While their wealth in today's terms would exceed that of even Bill Gates and Jeff Bezos, that of the man and

---

[37] A Tale of Two Cities, Charles Dickens, Chapman & Hall, 1859.

[38] "The Emma Goldman Papers," Henry Clay Frick et al., University of California Press, 2003, https://www.lib.berkeley.edu/goldman/PublicationsoftheEmmaGoldmanPapers/sample biographiesfromthedirectoryofindividuals.html.

woman in the street was often non-existent. Extreme poverty was the norm in the tenement houses of big cities like New York, Philadelphia, Pittsburgh, and Chicago. Worker wages were low and bargaining power absent in the face of the trusts' economic power. The contrast between rich and poor living standards was so shocking that Mark Twain and Charles Dudley Warner in 1873 wrote a satirical book about it, which became a nickname for the era: *The Gilded Age: A Tale of Today*. By the early 1900s, the situation also led to the first era of "populism" in American politics. The People's Party in 1892 became the first third party to win electoral seats in the presidential election, coming up for the rights of "rural and urban labor," and against the "moral, political and material ruin" the then-leading class had allegedly brought about. In 1896 the candidate of this original Populist Party even became the Democratic National Convention's official presidential candidate, though he (William Jennings Bryan) did not win the presidential election—he lost to Republican William McKinley.

This First Industrial Revolution brought about incredible gains in wealth in those countries leading it but also incredible suffering among the poor in industrialized nations. But it was also bad news for those living in countries which fell behind in the Industrial Revolution, including the Asian countries that had until then led the world in GDP: China, Japan, and India. There, the entire political systems collapsed, and chaos or colonization followed. In America and Western Europe though, when the popular backlash grew so great that it was impossible to ignore, action was taken to root out the excesses of wealth and put a limit to the suffering of the working class. In Europe, from the UK to Germany, socialist parties were elected to government after universal suffrage was introduced in a series of reforms from the 1870s to the 1920s. Conservative and Christian-Democratic parties also adopted more socially conscious measures. Otto von Bismarck's government in Germany, for example, which had a conservative bent, implemented nevertheless a series of social reforms in the 1880s, which were the kernel of the social security Western Europe knows today.

In America, by contrast, the focus in those early years was less on providing social security and more on enforcing antitrust. (The Social Security program wouldn't arrive until 1935, on the back of the Great Depression,[39] which left tens of millions without jobs, food, and homes.) By 1890 it dawned on lawmakers they needed to address the hurtful

---

[39]"Historical Background and Development Of Social Security," Social Security Administration, https://www.ssa.gov/history/briefhistory3.html.

actions of the robber barons, which corrupted politics and monopolized entire industrial sectors. The first antitrust law was passed that year
and was amended several times in subsequent years. In 1914, two more
important laws were passed, including one which created the Federal
Trade Commission. Together, these laws had to make sure the trusts
of men like Rockefeller could no longer create de facto monopolies,
either by buying up all their competitors or by colluding with them
on prices. The most famous breakup that followed was that of Standard
Oil in 1911, which "controlled over 90 percent of the refined oil in the
United States"[40] by the turn of the century. The company was split up
into 34 different parts, some of which today survive as brands or separate companies, including ExxonMobil (once separated as Exxon and
Mobil), Chevron, and Amoco. Other industries also faced regulatory
scrutiny. Monopoly power was bad for innovation, regulators believed,
it was bad for consumers, and it was bad for competition. It needed to
be stopped.

The Second Industrial Revolution

As so often in economic and political history, the actions taken by governments in the industrialized world proved mostly successful in solving
the problems of the present and the past but not so much in solving
those of the future. A Second Industrial Revolution had taken place,
and the technologies it spawned, the internal combustion engine and
electricity, led to a new set of products, such as cars, planes and electric networks, and the telephone. In time, they would come to create,
reshape, and dominate industries, much as the technologies of the First
Industrial Revolution had done before them. But geopolitical friction
in 1914 interrupted the economic dynamics of the industrialized world.
In the First and Second World Wars, technology was seen as more of a
destructive power than an economic driver. The First World War was the
last one in which horses were strategically deployed. The Second World
War was the first in which tanks and planes dominated the battlefield.
Tens of millions of people died, many of them through tools of the latest
technologies.

By 1945, a new world emerged, and this time, technology would go
on to play a much more universally positive role in the West, especially

---

[40]"Standard Ogre," *The Economist*, December 1999, https://www.economist.com/business/
1999/12/23/standard-ogre.

for blue-collar workers and the middle class, economist Carl Frey pointed out in his book *The Technology Trap*. The automobile on both sides of the Atlantic quickly became a mass market means of transportation, afford- able as much for the ordinary worker as for the upper class. Electricity became standard in every home, and its applications included the washing machine, air conditioner, and refrigerator. They made life easier, healthier, and cleaner for everyone and greatly helped to emancipate women. And the industries that electricity and transportation helped create opened many middle-class job opportunities, even for medium- and low-skilled workers. Factory machines this time were complementary to workers, relieving them from heavy physical duty while still requiring them in great numbers. And drivers, telephone operators, secretaries, and cashiers all were in high demand in an economy that increasingly held the mid- dle between one based on manufacturing and one based on services.

This explosion of widespread wealth, which was accompanied by a baby boom, allowed countries to further strengthen their social security systems and education, health care and housing policies. In America, President Lyndon Johnson announced a Great Society program.[41] It aimed at eliminating poverty and racial issues through initiatives such as the War on Poverty, introduced health programs such as Medicare and Medicaid, and mandated the building of many new schools and colleges, as well as the establishing of grants and a Teacher Corps. In Europe, the welfare state was introduced, with often universal free health care, free education, and state-subsidized housing.

All the while, antitrust action remained on the political agenda. In America, the newly emerged telecom industry had consolidated to such an extent, that by the 1960s, the Bell Company (now AT&T) was a de facto monopoly. Using the antitrust legislation put in place after the First Industrial Revolution, it too was broken up, lowering prices and improving service drastically in the decades after and unleashing a new wave of innovation, which ultimately led to mobile telephony. In Europe, countries chose a more direct form of regulation, setting up electricity and telecom providers as state-owned monopolies. This too ensured any profits beyond market rate would ultimately benefit soci- ety, albeit indirectly. But this stifled innovation and competition, as the state-owned enterprises over time lost their appetite for providing better service or a lower price, lacking a strong competitive incentive.

---

[41]"The Presidents of the United States of America": Lyndon B. Johnson, Frank Freidel and Hugh Sidey, White House Historical Association, 2006, https://www.whitehouse.gov/ about-the-white-house/presidents/lyndon-b-johnson/

The auto industry became competitive enough to not require anti-trust action, although now we know they used their political influence and economic power to lobby for less-than-optimal outcomes in the transportation sector, notably by favoring funding for cars and buses and their infrastructure over that for trains and trams and by delaying the introduction of electric motors. But market concentration did remain relatively low, partially because of increased international competition over time. The sector also created directly and indirectly millions of jobs. And it offered a ticket to a middle-class lifestyle for tens of millions more. Automobile manufacturers for those reasons avoided regulatory scrutiny and were among the most revered companies all over the world.

Perhaps as consequence of the much more positive role technology and companies played in this Western golden age, people's ideological views on capital versus labor and man versus machine softened significantly. Importantly, economists too touted more the positive effects of enterprises and their innovations in societal and economic development. Austrian economist Joseph Schumpeter already in the 1940s saw a world emerge in which "creative destruction"[42] led to the breakdown of old companies and their products, by new companies and their breakthrough technologies. The car replaced the horse, the plane replaced the ship, and electric household devices replaced domestic workers. Milton Friedman and his colleagues at the University of Chicago (the so-called Chicago School) went a step further. Friedman believed in the naturally positive role of business in the economic system. An invisible hand ensured that markets would always have an optimal outcome, maximizing utility for society. It meant that "there is one and only one social responsibility of business," Friedman wrote in a 1970 *New York Times* essay.[43] It is "to use its resources and engage in activities designed to increase its profits so long as it stays within the rules of the game." In the context of the Second Industrial Revolution and the largely positive role its companies played in economic and social development at the time, that was understandable. But it would prove to have more negative consequences just a few decades later, as the positive impact of business on society increasingly faded again in the Third and Fourth Industrial Revolution.

---

[42]Term coined in "Capitalism, Socialism and Democracy", Joseph Schumpeter, Harper Brothers, 1950 (first published 1942)

[43]"A Friedman Doctrine—The Social Responsibility Of Business Is to Increase Its Profits," Milton Friedman, *The New York Times*, September 1970, https://www.nytimes.com/1970/09/13/archives/a-friedman-doctrine-the-social-responsibility-of-business-is-to.html.

The Third Industrial Revolution

In the 1970s and 1980s, as the antitrust case against Bell Company went through political and judiciary hoops, two small computer companies were created in Albuquerque and Cupertino garages that would go on to alter the course of economic history. Microsoft and Apple Computer initially built personal computers, like the one Tim Wu got from his parents. But as the 1980s progressed, the companies became increasingly famous for their software, including MS-DOS, Windows, and Mac OS. And in the 1990s Microsoft and Apple helped bring the Internet into the office and living room. Along the way, the personal computer transformed from an expensive and bulky niche device to the most important tool of workers in the modern economy. This revolution, which brought the world information technology (IT) and the Internet, and all the applications and industries that went hand in hand with it, came to be known as the Third Industrial Revolution.

The Third Industrial Revolution greatly enhanced the productivity of white-collar workers. They could process much more information much faster and instantaneously coordinate with co-workers anywhere, at the touch of their fingertips. And it helped to unleash the greatest wave of globalization in history: manufacturing could be decoupled from back-office, a company headquarters from its global value chain. This IT and Internet revolution is what allowed countries such as China, Indonesia, Vietnam, and Mexico to integrate in the world economy, helping hundreds of millions of people enter the global middle class.

Its net effect on a global scale was undoubtedly positive. In the First and Second Industrial Revolutions, wealth was accumulated at the top and in the middle of Western industrialized nations. In this Third Industrial Revolution, emerging markets finally got a fair share of the pie. Economists Christoph Lakner and Branko Milanovic showed the effect in their well-known "elephant" graph.[44] It illustrated that from 1988, as the IT revolution was in full swing, until 2008, when the Internet had shaken up the world's supply chains, the global middle class benefited, as did the 1 percent in industrialized nations. But the Western middle class paid a price. Due to the IT revolution, their jobs could as well be done by lower-wage workers elsewhere, putting pressure on both their jobs and salaries.

---

[44]Global Income Distribution From the Fall of the Berlin Wall to the Great Recession, Christoph Lakner and Branko Milanovic, World Bank, December 2013, http://documents. worldbank.org/curated/en/914431468162277879/pdf/WPS6719.pdf

That insight can be seen in the most recent "elephant" graph, which has been last updated for the World Inequality Report 2018 (see Figure 6.2). It shows the percentage income growth (on the vertical axis) of each percent of the global population (ranked from poorest to richest, on the horizontal axis). We can see that those largely between the 10th and the 50th percentile of the income distribution (which includes many of the emerging middle classes of China, India, ASEAN and elsewhere) saw very positive income growth, of often over 100 percent. They form the "back" of the elephant. The top one percent—the global elite, including the professional classes in the West—also had a high income growth rate, with the 0.1 and 0.01 percent benefiting even more, relatively speaking. They form the tip of the elephant's trunk. These two groups were by and large beneficiaries of globalization.

Those in the 60th to 90th percentile of the global income distribution however—including many in the working and middle classes of

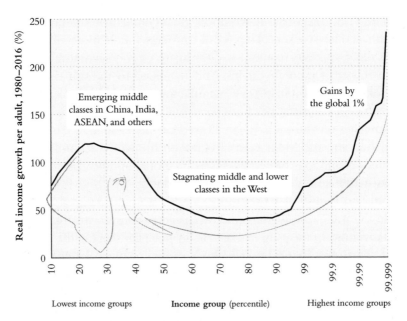

Figure 6.2 The Elephant Curve of Global Inequality and Growth

Source: World Inequality Report (2018). Inspired by Lakner and Milanovic, *World Bank Economic Review* (2015). Elephant first added by Caroline Freund[45] (Peterson Institute for International Economics).

---

[45]"Deconstructing Branko Milanovic's 'Elephant Chart': Does It Show What Everyone Thinks?" Caroline Freund, PIIE, November 2016, https://www.piie.com/blogs/realtime-economic-issues-watch/deconstructing-branko-milanovics-elephant-chart-does-it-show.

Western countries such as the US, the UK, and Western Europe—had an income growth rate that was much lower. Over the past 35 years, their average incomes grew by little over 1 percent per year, if that. Many felt no net benefit of globalization at all, and quite a few even lost their well-paid blue-collar jobs because of outsourcing to lower-income countries. And the very poorest of the poor, in the first few percentiles of the income distribution, didn't advance much either (their income growth is not shown in the graph).

But the Third Industrial Revolution had another effect. It introduced the network effect as a competitive force, locking users into networks used by a majority of others, and heightened the importance of intellectual property. Microsoft was a case in point. As personal computers conquered the office, Microsoft's Windows became the dominant operating system, Office the dominant software, and Internet Explorer the dominant web browser. That was largely thanks to its functionality and an early agreement with IBM, but Microsoft was also quick to lock consumers in to their products: it pre-installed Internet Explorer on Windows, effectively bundling the two together, and made it hard for non-Microsoft users to access files in its Office programs, or its Windows Media Player. It got the attention of US and European antitrust authorities: Was Microsoft misusing its power? On June 7, 2000, after a seven-year investigation, the US District Court in Washington, DC, reached its verdict: Yes, Microsoft had misused its monopoly power and should be broken up in two separate companies, one producing the operating system, and the other making software.[46] In 2004, the European Commission also found Microsoft guilty of anti-competitive practices, in a case related to its Windows Media Player. It ordered a fine of about 500 million euros.[47] But while Microsoft paid the European fine, the highest ever given to a company until that point, it did successfully appeal the US District Courts decision to break it up. In 2001, a new verdict was reached: Microsoft could continue to operate as one company.

According to Tim Wu, it was a turning point in the antitrust actions taken by United States and Europe. The EU Commission, emboldened by its successes, became increasingly aggressive in protecting consumer interests and combatting monopolies. In its pursuit to create a common

---

[46]US District Court for the District of Columbia - 97 F. Supp. 2d 59 (D.D.C. 2000), June 7, 2000, https://law.justia.com/cases/federal/district-courts/FSupp2/97/59/2339529/.

[47]Commission Decision of May 24, 2004 relating to a proceeding pursuant to Article 82 of the EC Treaty and Article 54 of the EEA Agreement against Microsoft Corporation, Eur-Lex, https://eur-lex.europa.eu/legal-content/EN/ALL/?uri=CELEX:32007D0053.

European market, it also opened national markets, leading to increased competition, lower prices, and better services in many industries. In the US, by contrast, market concentration kept increasing in the following years, as antitrust authorities mostly stood by the sidelines. Indeed, in the two decades since the Microsoft ruling, journalist David Leonhard observed in the *New York Times* (citing research by economist Thomas Philippon), "a few companies have grown so large that they have the power to keep prices high and wages low. It's great for those corporations—and bad for almost everyone else."[48] The resulting situation is one of factual oligopolies:

> Many Americans have a choice between only two internet providers. The airline industry is dominated by four large carriers [American, United, Delta and Southwest]. Amazon, Apple, Facebook and Google are growing ever larger. One or two hospital systems control many local markets. Home Depot and Lowe's have displaced local hardware stores. Regional pharmacy chains like Eckerd and Happy Harry's have been swallowed by national giants.[49]

It would be wrong to ascribe this evolution merely to technology or globalization, economists such as Philippon, and legal scholars such as Wu and Lina Khan also argued. Technology did of course allow these companies to continue their global growth. It created the tools for them to entrench their market positions. But it was the state which allowed this to happen. How? First, by focusing its antitrust actions in the technology sector on consumer prices, as the Chicago School had argued for a few decades earlier, it missed the broader picture of what was happening. In the case of services such as Facebook and Google, the consumer price stopped being the relevant yardstick. The consumer effectively became the product. The use of many services was free, but the flip side was that users were targeted by personalized ads. In the online ad market, then, the Big Tech firms did set the price, lacking competition. But because this market is less visible, it didn't prompt the same regulatory scrutiny. In Europe, by contrast, DG Comp, the EU competition watchdog, looked at broader market indicators, allowing it to intervene quicker. Second, having locked in consumers through the

---

[48]"Big Business Is Overcharging You $5,000 a Year," David Leonhardt, *The New York Times*, November 2019, https://www.nytimes.com/2019/11/10/opinion/big-business-consumer-prices.html.
[49]Ibidem.

network effect (as consumer, you don't want to be the only one not using a particular social network), Big Tech has also been able to put in place rules on the use of personal data that were previously unheard of. As these practices were simply non-existent in previous industrial revolutions, there was until recently no template for regulators to act against them.

As indicated, the European Commission offered an alternative way to deal with these situations. Its competition commissioner handed out more and bigger fines to monopolistic companies since the landmark Microsoft case. Google, Intel, and Qualcomm all got fined over $1 billion[50] for anti-competitive practices, with Google even given a second billion euro fine by the antitrust regulator in March 2019, for "abusing practices in online advertising."[51] The Commission also acted against cartels, including in truck manufacturing,[52] TV tubes production, foreign exchange, car repair, elevators, vitamins, and airfreight, demanding more than 26 billion euros in combined fines since the year 2000.[53] And it actively blocked mergers, ensuring large firms continue to feel competitive pressure from new entrants. In recent years, it notably stopped the mergers of Alstom and Siemens, two major rail companies, and the creation of a joint venture between steel giants Tata Steel and ThyssenKrupp. Of the 200 mergers it took a crucial second-phase decision on since 1990, 30 were blocked, 133 were deemed compatible if certain conditions were met, and only 62 mergers were given a full green light.[54] In the coming years, the *Financial Times* reported, competition commissioner plans to be even more aggressive, particularly with regards to so-called Big Tech firms: "We will be much more aware as to what [is] needed [...] in a market that has been plagued with illegal

---

[50]"The 7 Biggest Fines the EU Have Ever Imposed against Giant Companies," Ana Zarzalejos, Business Insider, July 2018, https://www.businessinsider.com/the-7-biggest-fines-the-eu-has-ever-imposed-against-giant-corporations-2018-7.

[51]Antitrust: Commission fines Google €1.49 billion for abusive practices in online advertising, European Commission, March 2019, https://ec.europa.eu/commission/presscorner/detail/en/IP_19_1770.

[52]Antitrust: Commission fines truck producers € 2.93 billion for participating in a cartel, European Commission, July 2016, https://ec.europa.eu/commission/presscorner/detail/es/IP_16_2582.

[53]Cartel Statistics, European Commission, Period 2015–2019, https://ec.europa.eu/competition/cartels/statistics/statistics.pdf.

[54]Merger Statistics, European Commission, https://ec.europa.eu/competition/mergers/statistics.pdf.

behaviour by one or more companies," she said,[55] adding that "breaking up companies [. . .] is a tool that we have available." She is right to take this assertive stance, Thomas Philippon argues, because it means "E.U. consumers are better off than American consumers today [. . .] The E.U. has adopted the U.S. [antitrust] playbook, which the U.S. itself has abandoned."[56]

Yet, even if an approach like the one adopted in Europe seems to be the right one to best protect citizens' interests, it may hurt European tech firms' competitiveness on a global level. In the case of the proposed Alstom-Siemens merger, for example, the market share of the combined firm would have been problematic in the European market, but its resulting scale would have allowed the company to more effectively compete on the global level, where it is now facing an even larger, state-backed Chinese competitor (CRRC),[57] as well as similar-sized Japanese and Canadian firms such as Hitachi and Bombardier.

Partially as a result of this increased scrutiny on the European level, European tech firms have not been able to truly break through on the global stage in recent years. Among the 10 most valuable tech companies in the world in 2020, six came from the US, and four from Asia. Could companies from Europe and other regions compete with these giants? The optimal way to create a level-playing field, of course, would be a more international policy and regulatory approach, possibly integrating antitrust measures into a deeply reformed World Trade Organization. But given the difficulties that the organization is facing, this may seem like an unlikely outcome in the short run.

The Fourth Industrial Revolution

Even as many technologies of the Third Industrial Revolution are still playing out in the market, we have entered a Fourth Industrial Revolution. As I wrote back in 2016:

---

[55]"Vestager Warns Big Tech She Will Move beyond Competition Fines," Javier Espinoza, *Financial Times*, October 2019, https://www.ft.com/content/dd3df1e8-e9ee-11e9-85f4-d00e5018f061.

[56]https://www.nytimes.com/2019/11/10/opinion/big-business-consumer-prices.html.

[57]"The Alstom-Siemens Merger and the Need for European Champions," Konstantinos Efstathiou, Bruegel Institute, March 2019, https://www.bruegel.org/2019/03/the-alstom-siemens-merger-and-the-need-for-european-champions/.

This Fourth Industrial Revolution is characterized by a fusion of technologies that is blurring the lines between the physical, digital, and biological spheres. Already, artificial intelligence is all around us, from self-driving cars and drones to virtual assistants and software that translate or invest. Impressive progress has been made in AI in recent years, driven by exponential increases in computing power and by the availability of vast amounts of data, from software used to discover new drugs to algorithms used to predict our cultural interests. Digital fabrication technologies, meanwhile, are interacting with the biological world on a daily basis. Engineers, designers, and architects are combining computational design, additive manufacturing, materials engineering, and synthetic biology to pioneer a symbiosis between microorganisms, our bodies, the products we consume, and even the buildings we inhabit.[58]

The technologies of the Fourth Industrial Revolution once again have the possibility to greatly enhance global wealth. That is because they are likely to turn into general-purpose technologies (GPTs) such as electricity and the internal combustion engine before them. The most powerful of these GPTs is likely to be artificial intelligence, or AI, according to economists such as Eric Brynjolfsson.[59] Already, major tech companies from countries such as China are using AI applications to leapfrog the leading companies from the US. Companies such as Alibaba, Baidu, and Tencent, technology entrepreneur and investor Kai-Fu Lee told us, are rapidly catching up to American AI giants such as Amazon, Facebook, Google, and Microsoft and in some instances already have superior applications. They could help China develop and its people prosper.

As in previous eras, these technologies could just as well increase inequality and social and political rifts, which could bring our existing society close to collapse. Already, companies such as Facebook are facing criticism that their algorithms are designed to sow division and have contributed to the great schism in American society, which is characterized by contentious opposition between the political left and right. This may well just be the beginning of much worse to come as people spend more time online and face ever more interactions with artificial

---

[58] *The Fourth Industrial Revolution*, Klaus Schwab, January 2016.

[59] "Unpacking the AI-Productivity Paradox," Eric Brynjolfsson, Daniel Rock and Chad Syverson, *MIT Sloan Management Review*, January 2018, https://sloanreview.mit.edu/article/unpacking-the-ai-productivity-paradox/.

intelligence (AI). Moreover, the advances in biotechnology and medical science could amplify inequality to levels never seen before, improving the lives and even bodies of wealthier humans to the point of creating a biological divide as well as a wealth divide. And technology could be applied to commit cyberwarfare too, with severe economic and social consequences.

To avoid the worst and achieve the best possible outlook, all stakeholders should remember the lessons from the past, and governments should shape inclusive policies and business practices. The challenge in regulating technological breakthroughs is often the speed of innovation. Governmental processes take time and require deep understanding of the innovations. As a frustrated chief executive once expressed to me: "Business moves in an elevator lifted by the force of creativity; government and regulatory agencies take the stairs of incremental learning." This situation poses a particular responsibility to companies in ensuring that all technological advances are well understood, not only in terms of their functionality for individual users but also what they mean for society more broadly.

This is the purpose of the World Economic Forum Centre for the Fourth Industrial Revolution in San Francisco, which was created in 2017. Its goal is to develop policy frameworks and advance collaborations that accelerate the benefits of science and technology."[60] It brings together all stakeholders that are relevant in this process, that is to say government, companies, civil society, youth, and academia. Several companies immediately signed up with the Centre as founding members, and from the start it became clear that they are open to having others help them help society. And following a wave of interest from governments from around the world, who were eager to understand the effect of new technologies and how best to regulate them, we opened sister centers in China, India, and Japan, as well as affiliate centers in Colombia, Israel, South Africa, Saudi Arabia, and the United Arab Emirates.

Going forward, we should remember that technology is never universally good or bad; all depends on how we deploy it. Every stakeholder has its part to play, from government to business to society at large. Indeed, even entrepreneurs starting out with the best intentions can end up leading companies that do more harm than good. And while innovative companies, operating in a free market, are a great motor of economic progress, an equally innovative and powerful

---

[60]Centre for the Fourth Industrial Revolution, World Economic Forum, https://www.weforum.org/centre-for-the-fourth-industrial-revolution.

government—which keeps the best interests of society in mind—is its best ally. As Mariana Mazzucato argued in her book *The Value of Everything*,[61] a strong government should not limit itself to regulation, it can also be a fundamental force of innovation and societal added value itself. Among the technologies that were initiated by government-sponsored research, are the Internet and GPS (DARPA), the world wide web (CERN), touch screen technology, and semi-conductors, all of which power some of the most innovative products of today, such as Apple's iPhone.[62]

In the end, we will have no choice than to embrace innovation and accept help from whoever is able to offer it. But we should give stronger incentives to those entrepreneurs who were once small and innovative, to not betray their own identity, and become big and monopolistic. It is only when technologies are shared widely, that they reach their full potential. And that will be more crucial than ever before in the age of AI. The ownership of data in this case will be a critical component, and we must ensure that it does not reside with monopolistic firms. That is Tim Wu's advice to the Big Tech firms he used to love, as well as the giant corporations dominating other industries. "I always liked small business," he said. "So when these companies got too big, I became an antitrust crusader."[63]

Just as important as the market structure, however, is that the value that is created is effectively shared. In previous industrial revolutions, industrial firms operated mostly in national markets. It meant that governments could intervene to ensure that value was equitably shared between all market participants. With AI, however, the picture looks different. Many companies active in Internet technology offer their services for free, meaning there is no price to regulate or tax to levy at the product level. And with almost all of the leading tech firms being American or Chinese but globally active, many national governments have not been able to tax profits either, which are often shielded through transfer pricing and IP-related exemptions. If citizens and governments everywhere want to share in the wealth creation of these companies, different regulatory and tax frameworks will need to be set up and implemented.

And then there is a final consideration: even if we get the Fourth Industrial Revolution right, there is still another global crisis we need to address as well: the ongoing climate crisis.

---

[61]Interview with Tim Wu by Peter Vanham, New York, October 2019.

[62]*The Value of Everything*, Mariana Mazzucato, Penguin, April 2019, https://www.penguin.co.uk/books/280466/the-value-of-everything/9780141980768.html.

[63] "One of the World's Most Influential Economists Is on a Mission to Save Capitalism from Itself," Eshe Nelson, Quartz, July 2019, https://qz.com/1669346/mariana-mazzucatos-plan-to-use-governments-to-save-capitalism-from-itself/.

7

People and the Planet

At places like Davos, people like to tell success stories. But their financial success has come with an unthinkable price tag. And on climate change, we have to acknowledge that we have failed. All political movements in their present form have done so. And the media has failed to create broad public awareness.[1]

These were the words from Greta Thunberg, the young Swedish climate activist, as she spoke in Davos at our Annual Meeting in January 2019. Thunberg had become known for her School Strike for Climate a few months earlier, shaking up the debate about what has increasingly become known as the global climate crisis. In Davos, she used the platform to give the world a hard wake-up call on the actions needed to avert catastrophe. "Adults keep saying: 'We owe it to the young people to give them hope,'" she said at a special press conference. "But I don't want your hope. I don't want you to be hopeful. I want you to panic. I want you to feel the fear I feel every day. And then I want you to act. I want you to act as you would in a crisis. I want you to act as if our house is on fire. Because it is."[2] After decades of scientific warnings and government discussions, how did a teenager become the world's most notable voice on climate change?

---

[1]Greta Thunberg, World Economic Forum Annual Meeting, held in Davos, Switzerland, January 2019. An edited version of this speech can be found in under the title, "Our house is on fire': Greta Thunberg, 16, Urges Leaders to Act on Climate," *The Guardian*, January 2019, https://www.theguardian.com/environment/2019/jan/25/our-house-is-on-fire-greta-thunberg16-urges-leaders-to-act-on-climate.
[2]"Ibidem".

Thunberg, born on January 3, 2003, first learned of climate change in 2011, when she was still in primary school. Despite her young age, she already realized there was a gap "in what several climate experts were saying, and the actions that were being taken in society."[3] It made her both anxious and sad. It preoccupied her to the point that she couldn't stop worrying about it. Why was no one taking action? Why were we letting our natural environment degrade? These were questions she pondered all the time. She did what she could do to help. She convinced her parents to become vegan and even stop flying—a significant change for her mother, who until then had traveled all around Europe as a prominent opera singer.

It turned out that Thunberg's single-mindedness was of a particular kind. She was diagnosed with a form of autism marked by "restricted and repetitive patterns of behaviors or interests."[4] But she would not let that get in the way of her advocacy. "I have Asperger's and that means I'm sometimes a bit different from the norm," she wrote to her critics.[5] "But," she also said, "given the right circumstances, being different is a superpower." From her perspective, worrying about climate change was something everyone else should do much more, because the problem was real. Maybe others were distracted by the more immediate day-to-day problems in front of them, but she was not. She saw it as her duty to make sure others understood the urgency just as fully.

By summer of 2018 Thunberg had taken her advocacy a step further. As Swedish parliamentary elections were approaching, she wrote an essay for a Swedish newspaper, asking for more attention for climate change and suggesting she and others would strike for climate until the elections. Her call to action fell on deaf ears. Thunberg decided to go forward by herself. One day in late August 2018, she skipped school, and went instead to Swedish parliament in Stockholm. Standing in the square outside, she held a self-made sign that simply read " *Skolstrejk för Klimatet*," or "School Strike for Climate."

It was an odd sight, but it quickly gained attention. After Thunberg posted a photo of her strike on Twitter and Instagram, "other

[3]"School Strike for Climate—Save the World by Changing the Rules," Greta Thunberg, TEDxStockholm, December 2018, https://www.youtube.com/watch?v=EAmmUIEs N9A&t=1m46s.

[4]Asperger Syndrome, National Autistic Society, United Kingdom, https://www.autism.org.uk/about/what-is/asperger.aspx.

[5]Greta Thunberg, Twitter, August 2019, https://twitter.com/GretaThunberg/status/1167916636394754049.

social media accounts amplified her cause," according to later research by *Wired*.[6] A couple of influential environmentalists shared her online posts, the magazine wrote, and by the next morning, Thunberg had her first follower, fellow 15-year old Mayson Persson. Another half-dozen people joined by midday. A few days later, 30 or so more participated. Within a month, Thunberg's strike had become a national sensation. And by the autumn of 2018, tens of thousands of school students all around Europe showed up for Thunberg's Fridays for Climate, skipping school to strike instead.

By that time, the Intergovernmental Panel on Climate Change (IPCC), the UN body for assessing the science related to climate change, had also put out a special report that added to the youngsters' sense of urgency. It warned that "limiting global warming to 1.5°C would require rapid, far-reaching and unprecedented changes in all aspects of society."[7] Unless those changes were made, climate change risked becoming an unstoppable force. "And," the report's authors also said, "we are already seeing the consequences of 1°C of global warming through more extreme weather, rising sea levels and diminishing Arctic sea ice." The striking youngsters needed no further incentives to further ramp up their campaign. In the months that followed, their protests swelled to hundreds of thousands of participants, everywhere from Brussels to Berlin, and from Canberra to Vancouver.

Thunberg at Davos

The autumn of 2018 was also the time when I became aware of Thunberg's actions, and I immediately decided to invite her to our Annual Meeting in Davos. Her advocacy has raised the issue to a level beyond that possible through normal political and academic appeals. It was both important and urgent, I realized, and hers was not a lone voice. For 50 years, the remarkable economic progress the world had made had been happening at the expense of the long-term livability of the earth. As mentioned in Chapter 2, that had been the message from the Club of Rome in the early 1970s, whose

---

[6]"Greta Thunberg: How One Teenager Became the Voice of the Planet," Amelia Tait, *Wired*, June 2019, https://www.wired.co.uk/article/greta-thunberg-climate-crisis.

[7]"Summary for Policymakers of IPCC Special Report on Global Warming of 1.5°C, Approved by Governments," IPCC, October 2018, https://www.ipcc.ch/site/assets/uploads/sites/2/2019/05/pr_181008_P48_spm_en.pdf.

president Aurelio Peccei had come to Davos. He had warned participants already in 1973 that we had reached the limits of growth. "The earth's interlocking resources—the global system of nature in which we all live—cannot support present rates of economic and population growth much beyond the year 2100, if that long, even with advanced technology,"[8] he said. Looking back, it proved to be a remarkably prescient message.

As an organization, the World Economic Forum had never stopped putting the topic on the agenda of our meetings, but it wasn't enough. There were successes: The first steps to organize the 1992 UN Earth Summit in Rio de Janeiro were taken at an Informal Gathering of World Economic Leaders (IGWEL),[9] a small group of top political and business leaders that meets every year at the World Economic Forum. Starting in the late 1990s, the Annual Meeting in Davos also became a safe space for business and civil society to meet, even as public animosity between environmental activists and multinationals grew. And in the run-up to the 2015 UN Climate Change Conference in Paris (COP21), a large group of CEOs from the world's largest companies did their part to pave the way for the Paris Agreement. In an open letter, they committed to "taking voluntary actions to reduce environmental and carbon footprints, setting targets to reduce our own greenhouse gas emissions and/or energy consumption while also collaborating in supply chains and at sectoral levels."[10] The message they sent, essentially, was that they wouldn't stand in the way of any political agreement; to the contrary, they wanted to support it. Despite these efforts, it was impossible to disagree with Thunberg at Davos, when she said that we, political, business, and societal leaders, have failed in combatting climate change.

Why did this happen? And how can we mobilize the world to turn this situation around? To answer those questions, it is important to reinterpret the global economic development story of the past two hundred years. It is during this period that the greenhouse gases that are now doing irreparable harm to the environment were emitted. And it is during this time that environmental concerns lost out to short-term priorities that now seem less important. It is only when we understand this

[8]"The Limits to Growth," The Club of Rome, 1972, https://www.clubofrome.org/report/the-limits-to-growth/.

[9]"A Partner in Shaping History," World Economic Forum, p. 55, http://www3.weforum.org/docs/WEF_First40Years_Book_2010.pdf.

[10]"These 79 CEOs believe in global climate action", World Economic Forum, November 2015, https://www.weforum.org/agenda/2015/11/open-letter-from-ceos-to-world-leaders-urging-climate-action/.

underlying logic of why this happened, I believe, that we can alter the dynamic of the economic system going forward.

We cannot go back in time and ask our predecessors why they so enthusiastically pursued the economic activities that caused climate change, but it is not hard to guess. Global greenhouse gas emissions picked up right about when the First Industrial Revolution took off, as can be seen from a data visualization by *Our World in Data*[11] (Figure 7.1). Greenhouse gases are gases such as carbon dioxide and methane, which absorb and release infrared radiation. They are created by burning fossil fuels and collect in the earth's atmosphere. In the 150 years following the

Annual total CO_2 emissions, by world region

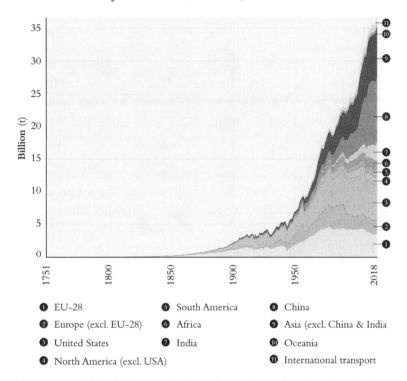

❶ EU-28	❺ South America	❽ China
❷ Europe (excl. EU-28)	❻ Africa	❾ Asia (excl. China & India)
❸ United States	❼ India	❿ Oceania
❹ North America (excl. USA)		⓫ International transport

Figure 7.1 Global CO_2 Emissions since the Industrial Revolution

Source: Our World in Data; Carbon Dioxide Information Analysis Center (CDIAC); Global Carbon Project (GCP).

Note: 'Statitistical differences' included in the GCP dataset is not included here.

OurWorldInData.org/co2-and-other-greenhouse-gas-emissions • CC BY

---

[11]"Global Emissions Have Not Yet Peaked," *Our World in Data*, August 2020, https:// ourworldindata.org/co2-and-other-greenhouse-gas-emissions#global-emissions-have-not-yet-peaked.

start of the First Industrial Revolution, the engines that powered trains, ships, and factories in North America and Europe, the most industrialized regions in the world, were almost exclusively running on coal and other fossil fuels we now know are responsible for the so-called greenhouse effect, which occurs when greenhouse gases in the atmosphere capture radiant heat from the sun, trapping it in the atmosphere, where it heats the earth's surface. There were environmental concerns then, too, mostly about the immediate health effects of air spewed from smokestacks. It was to escape their heavily polluted air, in fact, that people first started coming to alpine towns such as Davos. They believed that the healthier mountain air there could cure them from diseases such as tuberculosis, which were a primary cause of death in 1800s' and 1900s' Europe.[12] But as late as 1988, the idea that man-made pollution was causing global warming was so exceptional as to be front-page news in *The New York Times*.[13]

From then on, the fight against climate change did gain momentum. In 1989–1991, we saw the Soviet Union collapse and the Cold War come to an end, creating an opportunity for truly global cooperation for the first time in history. At the Rio Earth Summit in 1992, climate change dominated the international agenda for the first time ever. It was there that the United Nations Framework Convention on Climate Change (UNFCCC) was signed, aiming to stabilize greenhouse gas concentrations "at a level that would prevent dangerous anthropogenic interference with the climate system."[14] Another three years later, the first UN Climate Change Conference of the Parties (COP) took place in Berlin, and in 1997 the Kyoto Protocol was signed at the third COP in Japan. It obliged 35 developed countries—most of Europe, the United States, Canada, Japan, Russia, Australia, and New Zealand—to reduce their emissions compared to 1990 levels and took effect in 2008. Though Canada and the United States dropped out, the other participating countries did manage to reduce their emissions. But their collective efforts weren't enough to buck the larger trend. Total global emissions kept on rising in the 2010s and up to today. A second round

[12] "A Breath of Fresh Air from an Alpine Village," Swissinfo, https://www.swissinfo.ch/eng/tuberculosis-and-davos_a-breath-of-fresh-air-for-an-alpine-village/41896580.

[13] "Global Warming Has Begun, Expert Tells Senate," *The New York Times*, June 1988, https://www.nytimes.com/1988/06/24/us/global-warming-has-begun-expert-tells-senate.html.

[14] "What Is the UNFCCC," United Nations Climate Change, https://unfccc.int/process-and-meetings/the-convention/what-is-the-united-nations-framework-convention-on-climate-change.

of commitments in the Kyoto Protocol, and a new more comprehensive agreement in Paris in 2015, could not prevent this.

Why is that? If we know what the detrimental consequences of climate change are, why are we still paralyzed in our actions to fight them? An important answer lies in what has been happening in those 150+ countries that were not included in the Kyoto Protocol. Labeled emerging markets, the list includes countries such as India and China (see Chapter 3). Between 1990 and 2020, China experienced the greatest economic miracle in history but is now also the single largest emitter of greenhouse gases. Indonesia, the island archipelago that is heavily affected by climate change, has understandably chosen the path of industrialization in recent decades as well. Additionally, countries such as Ethiopia, which suffered from starvation and extreme poverty in the 1980s,[15] now have one of the most exciting growth trajectories in the world. It is in these countries, rather than the industrialized nations, that we can find a large part of the answer as to why it has been so incredibly hard to combat climate change, in spite of the importance and urgency of doing so.

This can be seen first and foremost in the data. As mentioned before, the Kyoto protocol did actually lead to results for those countries who signed or ratified it. Collectively, Europe (including Russia) and North America saw their carbon dioxide (CO_2) emissions decrease from about 13 billion tons in 1990 to 10.8 billion tons in 2017, a decrease of over 15 percent. But the rest of the world, including major emerging markets such as China and India, and other industrializing nations such as Indonesia and Ethiopia, saw its CO_2 emissions explode from about 9 billion tons in 1990 to some 24 billion in 2017, an increase of over 150 percent. As a result, total global emissions went up significantly between 1990 and 2017, from below 25 billion tons to over 36 billion.

From an emissions perspective, this evolution is highly problematic, but from a human development perspective, it reflects a miraculous development. All over the world, people who for generations lived in poverty, have in these past 30 years entered an emerging middle class, thanks to the economic growth their country experienced. They were excluded from modern inventions such as electricity and the internal combustion engine in all their forms—light, laundry machines, refrigerators, air conditioning, cars, and motorcycles—and are now discovering their wonders. That is the other side of the emissions coin. And to get to a sustainable solution

---

[15]"Global Extreme Poverty," Our World in Data, https://ourworldindata.org/extreme-poverty.

to climate change, one that includes all those newly industrialized nations, this other side of the coin will need to be taken into account.

To understand that point of view, one need only go somewhere like Ethiopia and speak to stakeholders in the country's economy and government. It reveals the central conundrum of the combat against climate change. The same force that helps people escape from poverty and lead a decent life is the one that is destroying the livability of our planet for future generations. The emissions that lead to climate change are not just the result of a selfish generation of industrialists or Western baby boomers. They are the consequence of the human desire to create a better future for oneself.

I work in a city on a lake in Switzerland, Geneva. Consider the story of Awasa, another city on a lake shore, but in Ethiopia. It is undergoing a similar transformation to the one European and American cities underwent more than a century ago and that Chinese cities such as Shenzhen underwent just a few decades ago. Awasa until recently was a remote city in Ethiopia's interior, hard to reach by either car or plane. Highways, as in so many other African countries, were either nonexistent or in such rudimentary shape that the best car to get to them was a rugged four-wheel drive. Awasa itself was a commercial center but mostly for basic agricultural fare, produced locally and sold locally. Its main attraction, as well as the main source of water, were the picturesque Rift Valley lakes. The outside world rarely came to Awasa and vice versa. Political and ethnic unrest were not unknown. Violence has flared up several times in the past 30 years, including in 2002 when more than a 100 people were killed in a protest over regional independence.

To a certain extent, Awasa's rural legacy lingers today. Carts with produce pulled by donkeys remain the most common vehicles seen in and around the city. But in a few important ways, Awasa is no longer a regional backwater, it is a thriving industrial center. A few kilometers outside the city, an unexpected construction site is now the main attraction: the Hawassa Industrial Park, home to over a dozen multinational firms producing textiles, clothing, and other industrially produced goods. Thousands of workers commute in and out of this industrial park every day for work. They machine manufacture all kinds of shorts, shirts, and sweaters for Western clothing brands, produce long rolls of textile, or, surprisingly perhaps, make and pack diapers for the local Ethiopian market, which is experiencing a continuing baby boom.

Getting to Awasa is no longer as hard. A newly paved road leads to the industrial park, and soon a brand-new multi-lane highway will connect it to Addis Ababa and beyond. A small, state-of-the-art regional airport is being built, replacing the rickety barracks that currently serves to welcome arriving passengers. And the Ethiopian Railway Company is operating a rail connection between Awasa, the outskirts of capital Addis Ababa, and neighboring Djibouti, Ethiopia's access to the ocean. All of these new projects should allow Hawassa to plug itself into the national, continental, and global economy, creating further job and development opportunities for tens of thousands of local workers. And those investments are already paying off. In the fiscal year ending 2019, Hawassa and other industrial parks posted a record $140 million in exports, the Ethiopian Investment Commission announced, providing jobs for over 70,000 people.[16] It is a notable success story. The flagship industrial park opened just three years ago and others yet more recently.

For the Ethiopians who live and work there, the park is life changing. The tale of Senait Sorsa, a local general manager at Everest Apparel company in the industrial zone, is a case in point.[17] Sorsa came to Awasa for college, as one of a growing number of Ethiopians leaving the countryside for the city. After completing a degree in accounting, she set up as an independent accountant, and for over a decade gathered experience at several smaller companies in the region. But when an Asian garment company, Everest, moved into the industrial park and came looking for a local manager, Sorsa did not hesitate to pursue the opportunity. She spoke English, which allowed her to communicate with the Chinese general manager. She had management experience from her previous stints at smaller companies. And, as a local, she had a natural affinity with the workforce. Her hiring represented a win–win for Everest: they found a manager with a high cultural quotient and financial expertise. And Sorsa got the chance to work for a multinational company and develop further professionally.

Industrialization in Awasa was good news for many other local workers too. Everest employs 2,300 workers in the Hawassa industrial park. The vast majority are hired locally, either from Awasa or from neighboring regions, and some 95 percent are women (their minimum age, Sorsa was quick to point out, is 18). "Most of them were unemployed before, or they worked in the household for their family," Sorsa said.

---

[16]"Ethiopia Secures Over $140 Million USD Export Revenue from Industrial Parks," Ethiopian Investment Commission, October 2019, http://www.investethiopia.gov.et/index.php/information-center/news-and-events/868-ethiopia-secures-over-$-140-million-usd-export-revenue-from-industrial-parks.html.

[17]Testimony based on an interview with Senait Sorsa by Peter Vanham, Awasa, Ethiopia, September 2019.

"They usually went to primary and middle school, though many didn't finish high school. But to work as a garment worker, that is fine."[18] The workers get up to three months on-the-job training and can then quickly compete with workers anywhere in the world. Walking around the factory, you can see how the dynamic works: some production lines working with a higher pace, some with a slightly lower one. At the end of every line, a scoreboard shows how many items of a specific piece of clothing the team has made, comparing it to previous weeks to show progress. At lunch time, the workers gather in a separate room for lunch, and at 5:00, a bus brings them to the center of Awasa. The work is not easy, nor is it especially fulfilling, but it is a massive change from what most were used to before. It brings a more stable income, a chance to work in the real economy instead of the shadow economy, and small but real opportunities for personal development. It is industrialization at work. It is how countries around the world have gone from rural and agricultural societies to urban and industrialized ones. It is a process full of trial and error, growing pains, and trade-offs, but to this day, it is still the most successful development model the world has ever known.

Ethiopia and its people are already reaping the rewards of its industrialization policy. For the past 15 years, Ethiopia's GDP growth averaged 10 percent annually,[19] which sent its GDP skyrocketing from less than $15 billion in 2003 to over $60 billion in 2018.[20] In percentual growth terms, it made Ethiopia the star performer in the "emerging markets" universe, with growth rates that China last reached in the early 2000s. For the people of Ethiopia, most of whom were still living at, or below, the poverty line around the turn of the millennium, that rapid economic growth has been a blessing. The per capita GDP almost tripled, going from barely more than 50¢ per day in 2003, to almost $2 per day today,[21] measured in "constant" US dollars. It is a jump that may seem tiny in real terms, but in so-called purchasing power parity, the average Ethiopian is no longer living in extreme poverty. Measured by what one can buy, GDP per capita in Ethiopia in 2018 reached more than $2,000, where it was barely $500 in 2003, when the economic boom began.

---

[18]"Interview with Senait Sorsa by Peter Vanham, Awasa, Ethiopia, September 2019".

[19]"GDP Growth (annual %), Ethiopia," World Bank, https://data.worldbank.org/indicator/NY.GDP.MKTP.KD.ZG?locations=ET.

[20]"GDP, Constant 2010 US$, Ethiopia," World Bank, https://data.worldbank.org/indicator/NY.GDP.MKTP.KD?locations=ET.

[21]"GDP per Capita, Constant 2010 $, Ethiopia," World Bank, https://data.worldbank.org/indicator/NY.GDP.PCAP.KD?locations=ET.

But like everywhere else, Ethiopia has paid an environmental price for its development. Almost in lockstep with its economic growth, CO_2 emissions in Ethiopia tripled from 2002 to 2017. Relatively speaking, Ethiopia's 13 million tons of CO_2 emissions in 2017 were still tiny—a rounding error almost in the 36-billion-ton global total—but the trend is undeniable: as the country grew richer, it started to pollute more as well. This is not to say Ethiopia and other emerging markets did not strive for green development or that its people did not share concerns over global warming. Already in 2011, the Ethiopian government presented its green economy strategy, which aimed at making Ethiopia a middle-income country by 2025 in a climate-resilient green economy. One part of the plan was to tackle deforestation, a serious problem in a country where "forest cover fell from 35% of total land area in the early 20th century to a little above 4% by the 2000s," according to the United Nations.[22] Following this strategy, Ethiopia in 2019 managed to rally millions of citizens to plant 350 million trees in one day.[23] Another part of the government's green development plan was to focus on renewable and/or clean sources of energy to expand its nearly non-existent energy supply. Today, the IEA reports, still only half of Ethiopia's population has access to electricity, but "great progress has been made over the past two decades."[24] Hydro, biofuel, wind, and solar capacity have more than doubled since 1990, and they make up about 90 percent of the country's energy supply. But fossil fuel energy supply more than quadrupled as well, jumping from less than 5 percent of the total energy supply in 1990 to double that in 2017. It shows that, even today, there is no magic formula for poor countries to industrialize *and* keep their carbon footprint in check. Development, an increased standard of living, and a greater carbon footprint still walk in lockstep.

This is the central conundrum in the global fight against climate change, and it is almost certain to get worse before it gets better. This is not (only) the consequence of market failures or a lack of corporate or government leadership. It is a consequence of human nature and our innate desire not just to survive but thrive. It makes weighing climate considerations against a better lifestyle a non-choice for many people

[22]"Deforestation, Did Ethiopia Plant 350 Million Trees in One Day?" BBC, August 2019, https://www.bbc.com/news/world-africa-49266983.

[23]"Ethiopia Plants over 350 Million Trees in a Day, Setting New World Record," UNEP, August 2019, https://www.unenvironment.org/news-and-stories/story/ethiopia-plants-over-350-million-trees-day-setting-new-world-record.

[24]"Ethiopia," IEA, https://www.iea.org/countries/Ethiopia.

with precarious incomes, even if the latter hurts the environment more. If you don't have electricity, a stable income, or even food on the table, worries about climate change—however life-threatening in the long run—simply don't make the shortlist.

This explains, for example, why people who live close to the coast in Jakarta, Indonesia, get on with their daily activities, even as their homes are rapidly sinking. A sea wall—literally, a meters-high concrete bastion—had to be built there to stop the rising waters from submerging entire communities. A local mosque was lost to the tide there and abandoned, leading to a rather dystopian view from the rooftop of a house overlooking the sea wall and the inundated mosque.[25]

In France, it also helps explain why the so-called Yellow Vest movement caused havoc in Paris and dozens of other French cities in a picket that ran over the course of 2018–19, ending government plans to implement a green tax on fuels. Their slogan? "*Fin du mois, fin du monde: même combat.*"[26] In English: "End of the month, end of the world: same struggle." On paper, the fuel tax proposed by the French government would have led to better environmental outcomes. It would have incentivized other means of transport in France over private use of cars. In practice, it disenfranchised a rural population that already felt locked out of education, work, and wealth opportunities in the cities.

And it explains, finally, why island nations such as Palau, Nauru, and Trinidad and Tobago, to name just a few, are at once most at risk from climate change through rising sea levels, extreme weather phenomena, and rising temperatures and among the highest per capita emitters of CO_2 in the world.[27] Left out of the Kyoto Protocol because of its developing nation status, Palau in 2015 did commit to reducing its energy consumption by 30 percent by 2020.[28] It was also one of the first to ratify the Paris Agreement. But person for person, Palauans still rank among the worst polluters in the world, as their island is largely dependent on

---

[25]"Indonesia's leader says sinking Jakarta needs giant sea wall, Associated Press, July 2019, https://apnews.com/article/8409fd8291ce43509bd3165b609de98c.

[26]"Fin du mois, fin du monde : même combat?", France Culture, November 2019, https://www.franceculture.fr/emissions/linvite-des-matins/fin-du-mois-fin-du-monde-meme-combat.

[27]"Per Capita Emissions, Navigating the Numbers: Greenhouse Gas Data and International Climate Policy," World Resources Institute, http://pdf.wri.org/navigating_numbers_chapter4.pdf.

[28]"Palau Climate Change Policy for Climate and Disaster Resilient Low Emissions Development," Government of Palau, 2015, p.22-23, https://www.pacificclimatechange.net/sites/default/files/documents/PalauCCPolicy_WebVersion-FinanceCorrections_HighQualityUPDATED%2011182015Compressed.pdf.

fossil fuels to generate electricity. Such is the conundrum of the fight against climate change.

■ ■ ■

Before we think of solutions, it is necessary to first ask, "Can we even be hopeful?" If human beings are so innately motivated to seek a better lifestyle, and if in the course of the past 200 years that has meant increasing one's carbon footprint, are more sustainable climate policies even feasible?

The answer partially depends on four key megatrends, which to varying degrees are shaped by society in its entirety and by influential individuals within it.

The first of these is urbanization. Until the 1960s, the UN calculated, roughly two-thirds of world population lived in rural areas.[29] As most of these people lived in developing countries, their access to electricity, roads, and other sources of energy consumption was limited, as was their carbon footprint. But a change was already underway, and it would transform the global landscape in the next 50 years completely. By 2007, half of the world lived in cities. Today, it is over 55 percent and still rising. The trend was notable everywhere in the world, but the most important transformation took place in Asia. Megacities of up to 20 million people grew almost from villages, especially in China and India, which together account for about half of the world's megacities. Wuhan, a city of 11 million, had barely registered on the global consciousness before a virus outbreak in 2020 brought it to the world's attention. In 1950, Wuhan had been three towns whose combined population barely numbered a million.

The urbanization trend shows no signs of abating. By 2050, the UN says, the reversal will be complete. Two-thirds of the global population will live in cities and megacities,[30] and only a third will remain in rural areas.

At first sight, this trend may worry those concerned about climate change. Some of the newest or most sophisticated cities, such as Doha, Abu Dhabi, Hong Kong, and Singapore, are also ones with the largest carbon footprint per capita.[31] And storied American cities such as Detroit, Cleveland, Pittsburgh, or Los Angeles have pioneered the notion that in a city, car is king, leading to an urban design seemingly anathema

---

[29]"Urbanization," Our World in Data, November 2019, https://ourworldindata.org/urbanization.

[30]"68% of the World Population Projected to Live in Urban Areas by 2050, Says UN," UN Department of Economic and Social Affairs, May 2018, https://www.un.org/development/desa/en/news/population/2018-revision-of-world-urbanization-prospects.html.

[31]"Global Gridded Model of Carbon Footprints (GGMCF)," http://citycarbonfootprints.info/.

to one optimized for sustainable transportation and living. But there is an important silver lining to cities driving a large share of a population's carbon emissions, Daniel Moran, a Norwegian environmental economist, told NASA's Earth Observatory:[32] "This means concerted action by a small number of local mayors and governments has the potential to significantly reduce national total carbon footprints." Moving to an entirely electric fleet of taxis and public transportation, for example, as Shenzhen recently did in China, makes a major difference in a city with a population of over 10 million. Curtailing private transportation significantly, as Singapore did by levying a steep surcharge on the purchase of cars, and by enforcing a 0% growth on the number of car permits (known as Certificates of Entitlement) also makes a big difference.[33]

The second megatrend is demographic change. For much of recent history, strong global population growth meant that carbon emissions, *ceteris paribus*, were in an upward spiral as well. Indeed, the exponential increase in carbon emissions from 5 billion tons of CO_2 per year in 1950 to 35 billion tons per year in 2017 happened concurrently with a global population explosion from 2.5 billion people in 1950, to almost 8 billion today.[34] The baby boom in the 1950s and 1960s in the Western world, was followed by an even greater baby boom in the developing world. In this more populous world, a growing GDP per capita meant that global CO_2 emissions got a double boost, one from people's more energy-dependent lifestyle and one from there being more people achieving such a lifestyle. Even if people had started curbing their emissions much earlier, global emissions would have kept rising through population growth alone.

But here too there is a silver lining. While world population is forecasted to keep rising until 2050, its rate of change is decelerating by the day. Already, large swaths of Europe, including Italy, Germany, and Russia, are experiencing a demographic bust in terms of their native populations. In 2018, for example, Russia's total population dropped for the first time in a decade,[35] and the UN forecasts that its

---

[32]"Sizing Up the Carbon Footprint of Cities," NASA Earth Observatory, April 2019, https://earthobservatory.nasa.gov/images/144807/sizing-up-the-carbon-footprint-of-cities.

[33]"Why a Car Is an Extravagance in Singapore," CNN, October 2017, https://edition.cnn.com/2017/10/31/asia/singapore-cars/index.html.

[34]"World Population Growth," Our World in Data, May 2019, https://ourworldindata.org/world-population-growth

[35]"Russia's Natural Population Decline to Hit 11-Year Record in 2019," *The Moscow Times*, https://www.themoscowtimes.com/2019/12/13/russias-natural-population-decline-hit-11-year-record-2019-a68612.

population could halve by 2100. The picture in East Asia looks similar. Japan's demographic decline has been widely reported, and China's one-child policy has given way to lower birth rates by now richer citizens. Young Chinese families show no signs of wanting two or more children per couple, meaning that China's population is set to decline well before the turn of the century. Even India, which will soon overtake China as the world's most populous country, has seen its fertility rate fall dramatically in recent decades. While women averaged almost 6 births in 1960,[36] that fell to just over two in 2019. If this continues, India too will see its population decline at some point in the future. Only on the African continent, fertility rates are over two, indicating population growth. While this projected global demographic bust comes with its own challenges, it means that the fight against climate change can benefit.

The third megatrend is technological progress. This too is a double-edged sword. It was precisely technological progress that initiated degradation of the environment in the first place. Until the early 1800s and the spread of the First Industrial Revolution, humanity's impact on its surroundings was profound but reversible. As industrialization took hold, however, we started to rapidly consume some of the world's most precious natural resources, the stored energy of oil and coal, and later also rare earth minerals and even gases such as helium. At the same time, the footprint of human activities became ever greater. It was this industrialization that led to the *Anthropocene*—a label indicating human responsibility for planetary changes in climate and biodiversity. The subsequent second and third waves of industrialization—which brought the world the internal combustion engine, cars, planes, and computers—made the human footprint on the environment only worse, even as it increased the quality of life for billions of people.

The Fourth Industrial Revolution, which started recently, and brought us innovations such as the Internet of Things, 5G, artificial intelligence, and cryptocurrencies, is so far adding to the ever-expanding human footprint on the environment. Electricity required to produce Bitcoin, one of the most popular cryptocurrencies, leads to annual carbon emissions of 22 to 23 megatons of CO_2, scientists calculated.[37] That

---

[36]"Fertility Rate, Total (Births per Woman)—India," World Bank, https://data.worldbank.org/indicator/SP.DYN.TFRT.IN?locations=IN.

[37]"The Carbon Footprint of Bitcoin," Christian Stoll, Lena Klaaßen, Ulrich Gallersdörfer, *Joule*, July 2019, https://www.cell.com/joule/fulltext/S2542-4351(19)30255-7.

figure is comparable to the emissions of countries such as Jordan or Sri Lanka. And while connected devices make our energy infrastructure smart, that doesn't automatically mean it turns green as well. For that, consumers and producers need to make conscious choices for a green energy supply and efficient energy use.

Nevertheless, if we are to be successful in our efforts to curb climate change, scientific and business innovations will play a major role. The electric engine, long thought to be economically unviable and less performant than the internal combustion engine, is rapidly becoming cheaper and better than its fossil-fueled equivalent. Advances in battery technology mean that the widespread deployment of wind, water, and solar energy is coming within reach as well. Used for the right purposes, computers and other smart devices can help save energy and resources, rather than consume more of them.

But the fastest and most important action we can take in this regard is to eliminate coal and other fossil fuels from the energy mix. We are not there yet. Dozens of new coal plants are in fact still opening every year in emerging markets, primarily China and India. But change is underway. Increasingly, large institutional investors in the US and Europe are turning away from companies that operate coal plants. They are pressured by activists and clients that demand it from them, or simply following rational concerns that fossil fuel plants will eventually become stranded assets, as former Bank of England governor Mark Carney has warned.[38] And entrepreneurs and governments in India and China are starting to take action toward a carbon-light future as well, attracted by the improving affordability of cleantech versus fossil-fuel technologies. In this regard, the World Economic Forum is taking action as well. Ahead of our Annual Meeting in Davos in 2020, Brian Moynihan, chair of the international business council, Feike Sybesma, co-chair of the Alliance of CEO Climate Leaders, and I invited participants to join the "Net-Zero Challenge,"[39] committing to achieving greenhouse gas emissions by 2050 or sooner. Many business leaders responded positively.

The final megatrend is us—or rather, our changing societal preferences. It is the trend to amplify or end all other trends. For most of

---

[38] "Firms Must Justify Investment in Fossil Fuels, Warns Mark Carney," Andrew Sparrow, *The Guardian*, December 2019, https://www.theguardian.com/business/2019/dec/30/firms-must-justify-investment-in-fossil-fuels-warns-mark-carney.

[39] "The Net-Zero Challenge: Fast-Forward to Decisive Climate Action," World Economic Forum, January 2020, https://www.weforum.org/reports/the-net-zero-challenge-fast-forward-to-decisive-climate-action.

the modern era, humans have displayed a preference for wanting more, delivered better and faster. Starting from the standard of living many people in the West had until even the late 19th century, it is only normal that people yearned for a better life, with greater wealth transferred into greater consumption. To a large degree, as indicated previously, this desire is still prevalent—and rightly so—in many developing countries today. One only needs to visit the bustling cities of Vietnam, India, China, or Indonesia to understand the profound human desire to get ahead, day by day, year by year, generation by generation.

But in the so-called developed world today, a systemic shift in societal preferences is underway. Understanding the harmful side effects of living an energy-abundant lifestyle, many are starting to turn their backs on the habits and products they once aspired to. Wealth is being transferred into health.

The number of people flying between German cities, for example, in November 2019 fell 12 percent from a year earlier, Bloomberg reported.[40] Meanwhile, Deutsche Bahn (DB), Germany's train operator, saw its rider number peak.[41] It was believed to be a consequence of the *flygskam* or "flight shame" that the popular movement against climate change had mainstreamed. In other places, people are increasingly considering again using public transportation, bicycles, or simply walking to get to destinations, turning away from the car. Cities such as London, Madrid, and Mexico City are restricting the use of cars,[42] a policy choice not only based on congestion considerations but on the increasing belief among residents that cities are for people, not cars. Even in the United States, the country that epitomizes car culture, where owning a car is a rite of passage to adulthood, as one writer put it, millennials are increasingly opting out of car ownership.

All these evolutions were underway well before the COVID crisis. Then, forced lockdowns of cities brought about a mini revolution in mobility. As World Economic Forum urban mobility specialist Sandra Caballero and Urban Radar CEO Philippe Rapin wrote during the

---

[40]"German Air Travel Slump Points to Spread of Flight Shame," William Wilkes and Richard Weiss, Bloomberg, December 2019, https://www.bloomberg.com/news/articles/2019-12-19/german-air-travel-slump-points-to-spread-of-flight-shame?sref=61mHmpU4.

[41]"How Greta Thunberg and 'Flygskam' Are Shaking the Global Airline Industry," Nicole Lyn Pesce, MarketWatch, December 2019, https://www.marketwatch.com/story/flygskam-is-the-swedish-travel-trend-that-could-shake-the-global-airline-industry-2019-06-20.

[42]"This Is What Peak Car Looks Like," Keith Naughton and David Welch, *Bloomberg Businessweek*, February 2019, https://www.bloomberg.com/news/features/2019-02-28/this-is-what-peak-car-looks-like.

crisis:[43] "After COVID-19 lockdowns, roads emptied and transit agencies either completely stopped service or drastically reduced service, allowing pedestrians and cyclists to take back streets and sidewalks." Cities from Oakland to Bogota and from Sydney to Paris, and even the city we live in, Geneva, Switzerland, built new bike lanes allowing people to commute in more eco- and public health–friendly ways. The comeback of trains was accelerated in Europe as well during the COVID crisis, with new sleeper train connections planned between cities as far apart as Barcelona, Spain, and Amsterdam, the Netherlands. And in the fall of 2020, Germany's transport minister Andreas Scheuer even made a proposal to his European peers to establish a new Trans Europe Express network,[44] to replace an older version that had ceased to play any meaningful role in international passenger transport.

The explanation for these changing habits, it should be clear, is increased consciousness among Western populations that the fight against climate change is a personal as well as a structural matter. The younger generations—millennials and Gen Zers, most significantly—act on this realization with their wallets, their brains, and their feet. They increasingly invest only in ESG-compliant[45] firms, who make concrete commitments to net-zero activities. They choose products and solutions that hurt the environment less, rather than more, and they opt for study and work careers that could be a part of the solution, rather than the problem. This shift in attitude is affecting all layers of society. It made Microsoft commit to offsetting not just its current and future CO_2 emissions, for example, but those of the past as well. It made Marc Benioff, co-CEO of Salesforce and a member the World Economic Forum's board of trustees, declare at our 2020 Annual Meeting that "Capitalism, as we know it, is dead," suggesting instead companies adhere to the stakeholder model and a better stewardship of the environment. And it made Larry Fink, the CEO of BlackRock, tell CEOs and clients that "every government, company, and shareholder must confront climate change" and that his

---

[43]"COVID-19 Made Cities More Bike-Friendly—Here's How to Keep Them That Way," Sandra Caballero and Philippe Rapin, World Economic Forum Agenda, June 2020, https://www.weforum.org/agenda/2020/06/covid-19-made-cities-more-bike-friendly-here-s-how-to-keep-them-that-way/.

[44]"Germany Calls for a New Trans Europe Express TEE 2.0 Network," *International Railway Journal*, September 2020, https://www.railjournal.com/passenger/main-line/germany-calls-for-a-new-trans-europe-express-tee-2-0-network/.

[45]ESG stands for environmental, social, and governance.

firm is in the process of "removing, from its actively managed portfolios, stocks and bonds of companies that get more than 25% of their revenue from thermal coal production."

At the World Economic Forum, we see and act on this change in attitude as well. Our events are becoming ever greener. We offer incentives for participants to reach us by rail, rather than plane, and have made commitments to offset carbon emissions. We also rely on reusable materials and local sourcing for food and drink. Such efforts are largely the result of our own convictions and a desire to align our actions with our words. But they are also enabled by this broader shift in societal preferences, which is led by the younger generations. They make it clear that no government, company, or even organization can continue business as usual when a climate emergency is unfolding.

Ultimately, these four megatrends should give us hope that the climate crisis is one we can still solve and that related planetary crises, such as the loss of biodiversity, the decline in natural resources, and various forms of pollution, can be reversed as well. But as young activities such as Greta Thunberg warn, we do need to accelerate action. Take the most pressing issue, climate change. Slowing, let alone stopping, it is a challenge that can only be met if every stakeholder on the planet—not just national governments—works toward that goal. We cannot rely on one group of stakeholders alone. After many delays and debates, governments from over 170 countries managed to commit to a joint goal in the Paris Climate Agreement: to limit global warming to 1.5 °C. But they are lagging in the implementation of their respective climate plans—if they even have them. A part of the reason for this is that climate change, despite its urgency, still isn't a top priority for many voters. Another reason is that governments don't have all the knowledge or power to act alone. The ball is thus in the camp of other stakeholders as well: companies, first of all, investors, and individuals as well as civil society at large.

In theory, the core assignment they—and we—have is simple: Decrease emissions of CO_2, methane, and other greenhouse gases as soon as possible and as drastically as possible. The adage "follow the money" in climate matters becomes "follow the emissions." That naturally leads to the single biggest source of emissions, energy production. It is here that reduction efforts by any stakeholder should focus on: change the energy mix from fossil fuels to renewables, and many current emissions down the line will disappear automatically. If investors ban coal plants from their portfolios, companies and consumers switch to renewable energy sources, and manufacturers and other companies do the same, gigatons of CO_2 emissions will be avoided straightaway. That is the first and most important contribution any stakeholder can make.

Of course, there are many obstacles to do so in practice. As we saw above, coal, oil, and gas are often still cheaper in the short run than other sources of energy. Many developing economies are still relying on these fossil fuels to become developed and industrialized, as they provide the least expensive road to success in this regard, and even industrialized economies find it hard to ditch them. In the United States, for example, new fossil fuel plants and infrastructure projects are still being considered and executed. Companies and citizens that reside in these countries would have to go beyond and sometimes against the policies favored by their governments. And the population of many of the largest oil- and gas-producing countries have in a way become addicted to cheap energy provided by oil and gas as well.

Besides altering the sources of energy production, a second major method to reduce greenhouse gas emissions is the worldwide implementation of carbon pricing and "cap-and-trade" mechanisms. By putting a price on emissions or by putting a cap on the total emissions an industry or company can emit and trade those emission rights on the market, as cap-and-trade schemes do, individual actors get a cost-based incentive to reduce their carbon intensity. Indeed, producing, moving around, or doing other economic activities in more energy-efficient ways becomes more profitable when the financial price of emissions is higher.

This isn't a theoretical consideration. The European Union has been operating its EU Emissions Trading System (EU ETS) since 2005.[46] According to the EU, it limits emissions from more than 11,000 heavy energy-using installations (power stations and industrial plants) and airlines operating between these countries, and covers "around 45% of the EU's greenhouse gas emissions." And according to researchers of the National Academy of Sciences in the US, the scheme has been a modest success,[47] leading to cumulative emissions of about 1.2 billion tons CO_2 from 2008 to 2016 or roughly 3.8 percent relative to total emissions. The European cap-and-trade system is the largest of its kind but far from the only one. Countries such as Australia and South Korea, and states such

---

[46]"EU Emissions Trading System (EU ETS)," European Commission, https://ec.europa.eu/clima/policies/ets_en.

[47]"The European Union Emissions Trading System Reduced CO_2 Emissions Despite Low Prices," Patrick Bayer and Michaël Aklin, *PNAS Proceedings of the National Academy of Sciences of the United States of America*, April 2020, https://www.pnas.org/content/117/16/8804.

as California and Quebec also have their own versions of the system. In many other places, more straightforward carbon prices or carbon taxes have been introduced.

These mechanisms—changing the energy mix and incentivizing energy efficiency—are two of the most powerful initiatives to curb emissions, as they directly affect the largest emitters of greenhouse gases: energy producers and major industrial companies. But individual, enlightened businesses and civil society groups can in fact also make a difference, even when they have to go against the current. At the World Economic Forum, a group of so-called CEO Climate Leaders[48] has over the years committed to ever more far-reaching voluntary action by their companies. They do so because they understand there is no point to being a free rider in the short run, when at the end of the ride, everyone loses. So how can they help? One study we made with consulting firm Boston Consulting Group found that their actions should center on three domains:[49]

1. Reduce the greenhouse gas intensity of own operations and that of activities in the supply chain. Often reductions can be made by simply using energy more efficiently;
2. Refocus investments in other companies, to include only those that are clean, and apply internal carbon prices to reveal the true cost of certain operations; and
3. Innovate business models, by transforming the existing one and pursuing new green opportunities.

One company that provides an excellent example of this is global shipping giant A.P. Møller-Mærsk, a case study we'll look at in more detail in Chapter 9. On greenhouse intensity of its operations, Mærsk is experimenting with more efficient ways to keep its food containers refrigerated and using ships that use less fuel and more wind power. In its own portfolio, Mærsk also divested its oil division, focusing instead on its core shipping business. And it is also pursuing a new business model, by expanding its activities from moving goods only from port to port to providing door-to-door solutions. It will allow Mærsk to keep growing,

---

[48]Alliance of CEO Climate Leaders, World Economic Forum, https://www.weforum.org/projects/alliance-of-ceo-climate-leaders.

[49]"The Net-Zero Challenge: Fast-Forward to Decisive Climate Action," World Economic Forum and Boston Consulting Group, January 2020, http://www3.weforum.org/docs/WEF_The_Net_Zero_Challenge.pdf.

while optimizing more of the total emissions associated with transport. If a company such as Mærsk, which has been very active both in fossil fuel production, distribution, and consumption, can make a green turna-round, surely the vast majority of other companies can, as well.

In this regard, we must remain optimistic. It is an area where we share the analysis of Greta Thunberg, as she spoke at Davos:

> Yes, we are failing, but there is still time to turn everything around. We can still fix this. We still have everything in our own hands. The main solution is so simple that even a small child can understand it. We have to stop the emissions of greenhouse gases. And either we do that, or we don't. We all have a choice: we can create transformational action that will safeguard the future living conditions for humankind, or we can continue with our business as usual and fail. It is up to you and me.[50]

But we must be aware that time is running out. The accumulation of harmful emissions in the atmosphere is like the water that fills a bathtub with only a small drainage. At one point, when the tub is almost full, it won't suffice to close the faucet slowly. The tub will overflow unless no water is added at all. The same is true for climate change. The world is in fact very close to the tipping point where even drastic efforts won't stop the situation from spinning out of control. In a way, the only positive sign from 2020 may have been that moment was delayed, as emissions came to a near standstill in many places for a few months. As we try and move to a better post-pandemic world, we'll need to achieve similar results despite being in an economy that is fully up and running again.

---

[50]Greta Thunberg, World Economic Forum Annual Meeting, held in Davos, Switzerland, January 2019. An edited version of this speech can be found under the title "'Our house is on fire': Greta Thunberg, 16, Urges Leaders to Act on Climate," *The Guardian*, January 2019, https://www.theguardian.com/environment/2019/jan/25/our-house-is-on-fire-greta-thunberg16-urges-leaders-to-act-on-climate.

PART III
STAKEHOLDER CAPITALISM

8

Concept

Given the downsides of our global economic system, it is clear we must reform it. But how?

The world currently knows two prevailing and competing economic systems: shareholder capitalism, which is dominant in the United States and in many other countries in the West, and state capitalism, which is championed by China and is gaining popularity in many other emerging markets. Both have led to tremendous economic progress over the past few decades. They left us with a world that is more prosperous than ever before. But each has equally brought about major social, economic, and environmental downsides. They led to rising inequalities of income, wealth, and opportunity; increased tensions between the haves and the have-nots; and above all, a mass degradation of the environment. Given the shortcomings of both of these systems, we believe we need a new, better global system: stakeholder capitalism. In this system, the interests of all stakeholders in the economy and society are taken on board, companies optimize for more than just short-term profits, and governments are the guardians of equality of opportunity, a level-playing field in competition, and a fair contribution of and distribution to all stakeholders with regards to the sustainability and inclusivity of the system. But how can we achieve this? What does it look like in practice? And where did the current two systems go wrong?

Let us start with the last question first and take a closer look at the two prevailing systems of today. Consider first shareholder capitalism. It is the form of capitalism in which the interests of one stakeholder, the shareholder, dominate over all others. Companies operate

171

with the sole purpose of maximizing profits and returning the highest possible dividends to shareholders. As I wrote in a contribution to *TIME Magazine*:[1]

> Shareholder capitalism first gained ground in the United States in the 1970s, and expanded its influence globally in the following decades. Its rise was not without merit. During its heyday, hundreds of millions of people around the world prospered, as profit-seeking companies unlocked new markets and created new jobs. But that wasn't the whole story. Advocates of shareholder capitalism, including Milton Friedman and the Chicago School [of economists], neglected the fact that a publicly listed corporation is not just a profit-seeking entity but also a social organism. Together with financial-industry pressures to boost short-term results, the single-minded focus on profits caused shareholder capitalism to become increasingly disconnected from the real economy.

That is the force we have seen at work in the past few decades. Moreover, as companies increasingly became global, the power of unions evaporated, and the ability of national governments to act as an arbiter declined. It led to a situation where shareholders became not just preeminent nationally but dominant globally, and many other stakeholders—employees, communities, suppliers, governments, and the environment—lost out as a consequence.

In recent decades, another form of capitalism emerged as an alternative: state capitalism. It, too, is a capitalist model, if we follow the definition that a system is capitalist when "private actors own and control property in accord with their interests, and demand and supply freely set prices in markets in a way that can serve the best interests of society."[2] In China, to take the most notable example,[3] the private sector now produces more than 60 percent of GDP. Despite this, the state is considered the most important stakeholder and retains power over individual shareholders. The government achieves its dominant role in at least three ways. First, it keeps a strong hand in the distribution of both resources and opportunities. Second, it can intervene in virtually any industry. And third, it can direct the economy by means of large-scale infrastructure, research and development, and education, health care, or housing projects. Theoretically at least, it solves a major shortcoming of shareholder

---

[1]"What Kind of Capitalism Do We Want?", Klaus Schwab, TIME Magazine, December 2019, https://time.com/5742066/klaus-schwab-stakeholder-capitalism-davos/.

[2]"What is Capitalism," Sarwat Jahan and Ahmed Saber Mahmud, *Finance & Development*, International Monetary Fund, June 2015, https://www.imf.org/external/pubs/ft/fandd/2015/06/basics.htm.

[3]China describes this system as "socialism with Chinese characteristics for a new era."

capitalism because there are mechanisms in place to ensure that private and short-term interests do not overtake broader societal interests. This system allowed Singapore, China, Vietnam, and more recently countries such as Ethiopia, to build a strong and growing economy, while keeping, if needed, private corporate interests in check. In fact, were it not for state capitalism, large parts of the developing world may not have seen a major growth spurt at all. But as economists such as Branko Milanovic (in his book *Capitalism, Alone*) have argued, state capitalism too has its fundamental flaws. Most importantly, given the hegemony of the state, corruption is a constant threat. Favoritism can play a role in distributing contracts, and the application of the law can become arbitrary, given the lack of checks and balances. When those at the top of the state assess an economic trend wrongly, the vast resources they control risk getting misallocated. It creates an issue that is almost the mirror image of that in shareholder capitalism.

In both shareholder and state capitalism, the dominance of one stakeholder over the others is the system's greatest flaw. In shareholder capitalism, shareholders' aims are often the singular focus; in state capitalism, the government wields too much power.

I therefore advocate for a third system, which can be defined as stakeholder capitalism. It is capitalism in the traditional definition of the word: individuals and private companies make up the largest share of the economy. This is, I believe, a requirement for a sustainable economic system: private individuals and companies must be able to innovate and compete freely, as it unleashes the creative energy and work ethic of most people in society. The economic activities of such private actors must also be protected and guided, to ensure the overall direction of economic development is beneficial to society, and no actor can free-ride on the efforts of others. This is the kind of capitalism we ought to endorse. But stakeholder capitalism does fundamentally differ from the other forms of capitalism we saw, in a way that overcomes much of their shortcomings. First, all those who have a stake in the economy can influence decision-making, and the metrics optimized for in economic activities bake in broader societal interests. Moreover, a system of checks and balances exists, so that no one stakeholder can become or remain overly dominant. Both government and companies, the main players in any capitalist system, thus optimize for a broader objective than profits: the health and wealth of societies overall, as well as that of the planet and that of future generations. It makes stakeholder capitalism the preferred economic system and the one we ought to implement going forward.

The History of the Stakeholder Concept

I first described the ideas behind the stakeholder concept 50 years ago, when I was a young business academic who had studied both the United States and Europe. In Germany and Switzerland at the time, respectively the countries I came from and worked in, it was quite natural for a company and its CEO to consider not just shareholders and their expectations of profits but all stakeholders of a company. It was something I saw in the way my father ran a company in Ravensburg called Escher Wyss. He consulted with employees on the shop floor, respected their input in decision making, and paid them competitive wages that compared reasonably to his own. The company was also deeply embedded in the town of Ravensburg, with which it had a symbiotic relationship. Escher Wyss thrived when Ravensburg did and vice versa. This mutual benefit was common in the post-war decades, when it became clear that one person or entity could only do well if the whole community and economy functioned. My father's experience was thus representative for what happened both in Europe and—albeit to a lesser extent—the United States. There was a strong linkage between companies and their community. In Germany, as I indicated, it led to the representation of employees on the board, a tradition that continues today. As sourcing, production, and selling took place mostly locally or at least regionally, there was a connection with suppliers and clients as well. This fostered a strong sense that local companies were embedded in their surroundings, and from that grew a mutual respect between companies and local institutions such as government, schools, and health organizations. It led to a constellation of stakeholders that I visualized in my 1971 book *Modern Company Management in Mechanical Engineering* (Figure 8.1).[4]

In subsequent years, the stakeholder concept was adopted most prominently in the social democracies of Northern and Western Europe, including Sweden, Denmark, Finland, the Netherlands, Belgium, and Germany. It led there, among other effects, to a tripartite system of collective labor negotiations including company management, employees, and government. And it contributed to the welfare state in which companies and employees paid their fair share of taxes to fund public education, health care, and social security. This system did adapt as decades

---

[4]*Modern Company Management in Mechanical Engineering*, Klaus Schwab, Hein Kroos, Verein Deutscher Maschinenbau-Anstalten, 1971, http://www3.weforum.org/docs/WEF_KSC_CompanyStrategy_Presentation_2014.pdf.

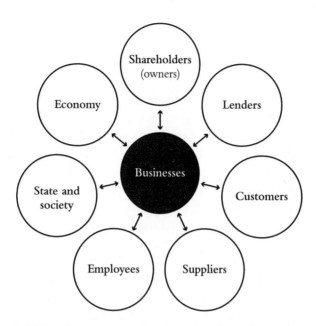

Figure 8.1 The Company at the Center Point of Its Stakeholders

Source: Redrawn from Schwab, Modern Company Management in
Mechanical Engineering, 1971.

went by, and it lives on to various degrees in these countries. But as a
global organizing principle for business, the stakeholder concept com-
peted head-on with Friedman's notion that "the business of business is
business"—and it ultimately lost out. Shareholder capitalism became the
norm across the West as companies globalized, loosening their ties with
local communities and national governments, and focusing instead on
maximizing short-term profits for shareholders in competitive global
markets. At the same time, labor unions, governments, and other civil
society stakeholders lost a lot of their power and influence, further weakening the fabric in which a stakeholder model could prosper. It meant
that even in those countries that did adhere to the stakeholder concept as a governance principle, other actors got weaker, as companies,
and specifically those who prospered in the Third and Fourth Industrial
Revolutions, got stronger.

The Stakeholder Model Today

Today, the stakeholder concept is ready for a comeback, albeit in an
updated, more comprehensive form. While it is unreasonable to expect

that the constellation of stakeholders will again be exactly what it was in the 1970s, when a company still operated largely within national boundaries, a modified version, which I will define as *21st century stakeholder capitalism*, or simply *stakeholder capitalism*, can ensure capitalist societies can survive and thrive in the current era, characterized by climate change, globalization, and digitization. So what does it look like, and how does it differ from the stakeholder management my father's generation intuitively implemented in the 1960s and 1970s?

The most important characteristic of the stakeholder model today is that the stakes of our system are now more clearly global. Economies, societies, and the environment are more closely linked to each other now than 50 years ago. The model we present here is therefore fundamentally global in nature, and the two primary stakeholders are as well.

This is true first and foremost for the *planet*. The planet's health, we now know, is dependent not just on individual or national decisions but on the sum of decisions made by actors from around the world. If we are to safeguard the planet for future generations, every stakeholder will therefore need to take responsibility for its part in it. What was once seen as externalities in national economic policy making and individual corporate decision-making will now need to be incorporated or internalized in the operations of every government, company, community, and individual. The planet, in other words, is the central stakeholder in the global economic system, and its health should be optimized in the decisions made by all other stakeholders.

Nowhere has this become more apparent than in the reality of planetary climate change, the extreme weather events it has brought about, and the ancillary effects that come with it. One recent example makes the case in point: the recent plague of locusts in Africa and the Middle East, sometimes nicknamed "Locust-19".[5] This phenomenon, whereby trillions of insects are swarming across continents, is thought to have come about because of the extremely wet year 2019 in this part of the world.[6] As a consequence of the wet weather, swarms of locusts could breed and spread all over East Africa, as well as parts of the Arabian Peninsula and South Asia, and threaten the food supply in each of those regions.

---

[5]"'Locust-19' set to ravage crops across east Africa", David Pilling and Emiko Terazono, Financial Times, April 2020, https://www.ft.com/content/b93293d4-3d73-42bc-b8b7-2d3e7939490e.

[6]"The Locust Plague in East Africa Is Sending Us a Message, And It's Not Good News," Carly Casella, Science Alert, July 2020, https://www.sciencealert.com/the-locust-plagues-in-east-africa-are-sending-us-a-message-and-it-s-not-a-good-one.

The same interconnectedness can be observed for the *people* who live on the planet. Whereas previously, countries and companies could optimize their economic system individually, without accounting for the side effects their decisions may have had on societies outside of their scope, the deep connectedness of the global economy makes it impossible to do so anymore. The well-being of people in one society affects that of those in another, and it is incumbent on all of us as global citizens to optimize the well-being of all. Failing to do so will inevitably come back to haunt us.

One place where this can be observed is in the global streams of migration. People who are left out economically or politically in one part of the world will seek to improve their lives in parts of the world that are better off. In 2020, the "world is on the move as never before,"[7] with an estimated 350 million people, or 3.4 percent of global population, living outside of their country of birth, Bloomberg estimates. This is despite an increasing tendency in many parts of the world to stem migration and, of course, the COVID-19 pandemic. If migration wasn't enough of a reminder of the interconnectedness, COVID-19 provided the ultimate proof. When the SARS-CoV-2 virus spread around the planet, it devastated the livelihoods of hundreds of millions of people and led to death or severe illness for many millions. With the exception of a few island nations, no border closure was stringent enough to prevent the spread of the disease.

The extensive spread of Internet technology also makes people around the world more aware than ever of the fortunes of people elsewhere. This draws attention to global equity, making it an important objective, perhaps for the first time in history. Indeed, people are social animals, and their absolute well-being is less important than their relative well-being. During most of world history, the reference point that most people had was a local one. In the Industrial Revolution, it become a national one. In the post–world war decades, the reference point widened to become the West for those in the influence sphere of the United States and the East for those in the influence sphere of the Soviet Union. Since the dawn of the Fourth Industrial Revolution, however, and the connective technologies it provided, people's reference point has become that of their most advanced peers anywhere in the world, whether it is China, the United States, or Europe. Global equity thus has become a notion to be considered for the first time in history.

[7]"The World is On the Move as Never Before," Bloomberg, October 2019, https://www.bloomberg.com/graphics/2019-how-migration-is-changing-our-world/.

Wherever you are in the world, there is thus an increased consensus that the well-being of people—wherever they live—and the planet as a whole matter to all of us. These two elements are natural stakeholders, with *people* being simply all human individuals and *planet* being the natural environment we all share. It leads to a new stakeholder model where those two are at the center (Figure 8.2).

Four key stakeholders can optimize the well-being of people and the planet. They are:

1. Governments (of countries, states, and local communities, consisting of representatives of the people and having the legal authority in a region or place);
2. Civil society (in its broadest sense, from unions to NGOs, from schools and universities to action groups, and from religious organizations to sports clubs);
3. Companies (constituting the private sector, whether freelancers, micro enterprises, small and medium-sized enterprises, or large multinational companies); and
4. The International Community (consisting of international organizations such as the UN, the World Trade Organization, or the OECD, as well as regional organizations such as the European Union or ASEAN).

It is important to remember what or who comprise each of these stakeholder groups because this explains their interest in the public good. Indeed, even though they are recognized as social and/or legal organisms, all these stakeholders crucially consist of people and make use of the planet. It is no surprise then, that they should want to optimize the well-being of all of us as well as that of the environment. But equally, it should be clear they have specific objectives that make them distinct organisms in the first place. Governments, notably, focus on creating

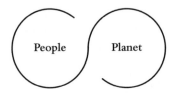

Figure 8.2 The Simplified Stakeholder Model, with People and Planet at the Center

Source: Klaus Schwab and Peter Vanham, 2020.

the greatest possibly *prosperity* for the greatest number of people. Civil society exists to advance the interest of its constituents and to give a meaning or *purpose* to its members. Companies obviously aim to generate an economic surplus, measurable in *profits*. And the overarching goal for the international community is to preserve *peace*. Finally, it is important to note that all these stakeholders are interconnected, too. Companies operate in the regulatory framework that governments provide for them. Civil society exerts pressure on governments and companies and contributes to their overall resilience. Finally, international organizations ensure consideration is given to consequences in one part of the world of the decisions made in another.[8]

It leads to the *stakeholder model* as we know it today (see Figure 8.3), valid anywhere in the world. When the well-being of people and planet are at the center of business, the four remaining key groups of stakeholders contribute to their betterment. These stakeholders each have their own primary objectives:

- companies pursue profits and seek long-term value creation;
- civil society's primary aim is each organization's purpose or mission;
- governments pursue equitable prosperity; and
- the international community works toward peace.

In a stakeholder model, all of these groups and their goals are interconnected. One cannot succeed if the others fail.

---

[8]This interconnectedness, as we've seen, has been a reality forever. But it is nevertheless amplified and intensified for these stakeholders by the technological progress of recent decades and therefore deserves particular attention in the new stakeholder model. Just as modern technology connected people around the world, it also enabled global commerce for companies, and competition between nations. Indeed, despite indicators of the contrary and policies to stem the trend, the world is more globalized than ever. To be fair, global physical trade between multinational companies is growing at a slower pace than the global economy overall since about a decade ago, and governmental trade protectionism is again on the rise. But digital trade is rising at a rapid pace still, trumping the slowdown in globalization—or "slowbalisation," as *The Economist* called it—trend in physical trade. The consequences can be felt among all stakeholder groups. As a result of this digital globalization, for example, a handful of Big Tech companies dominate global markets, with some of them worth more than $1 trillion. It explains in part why global corporate inequality and global market concentration are at their highest point ever. And it helps explain why, despite a trend toward declining global income inequality (thanks to the rise of China), the concentration of wealth among individuals in the world is higher than ever. (Oxfam International reported that in 2019, the world's 2,000 richest people own more wealth than the poorest 4.6 billion people in the world, and the wealth of the world's richest men derives from the Big Tech companies they founded.)

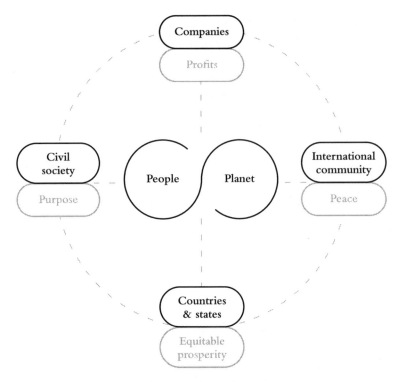

Figure 8.3 People and Planet at the Center of the Global Stakeholder Model

Source: Redrawn from Klaus Schwab and Peter Vanham, 2020.

The model is simple, but it immediately reveals why shareholder primacy and state capitalism lead to suboptimal outcomes: they focus on the more granular and exclusive objectives of profits or prosperity in a particular company or country rather than the well-being of all people and the planet as a whole. By contrast, in the stakeholder model, neither of the more granular objectives is set aside, but the interconnectivity and the overarching well-being of people and the planet are central, ensuring a more harmonious outcome over time.

Principles and Beliefs Underlying the Stakeholder Model

Having identified this global stakeholder model, we can now look at how it applies in a more confined context, such as that of a particular country or community. Going from a global to a local perspective is a crucial element for the stakeholder model's success. Indeed, although the stakes of the economic system are more global than ever, the implementation of any approach will mostly be done at a more local level. Communities are locally embedded, and people know and trust those they live and work in close proximity to. It increases their sense of solidarity and their willingness to buy into projects that benefit the whole, rather than the individual.

Consider just for once the alternative: a global government regulates multinational companies in global markets, and people gather in a global democracy and global unions. It is an unrealistic and undesirable goal, as it increases the distance between individuals and the immediate social ecosystems they are part of. It also decreases their feeling of commitment to the people and environment closest to them. Though 20th century neoliberalists once may have seen such a global model as a Utopian ideal (as Quinn Slobodian asserted in his book *Globalists, The End of Empire and the Birth of Neoliberalism*), it would inevitably end in the political disenfranchisement of local communities. When the center of power is too far removed from people's everyday realities, neither political governance nor economic decision-making would have popular support.

Subsidiarity

A primary principle for the implementation of stakeholder capitalism is therefore that of *subsidiarity*. It is not an untested or purely theoretical principle. Applied most famously in the governance of the European Union,[9] the subsidiarity principle has also been used in the Swiss Federation, the UAE, Micronesia, and other federal states around the world. It asserts that decisions should be taken at the most granular level possible, closest to where they will have their most noticeable effects.[10] It determines, in other words, that local stakeholders should be able to decide for themselves, except when it is not feasible or effective for them to do so.

It should immediately become clear how this principle applies to the global challenges of our economic system today. Consider first the climate crisis. It makes sense to coordinate this challenge first on the

---

[9]"Fact Sheets on the European Union: The Principle of Subsidiarity," European Parliament, http://www.europarl.europa.eu/factsheets/en/sheet/7/subsidiaritatsprinzip.

[10]"Subsidiarity," Cambridge Dictionary, https://dictionary.cambridge.org/dictionary/english/subsidiarity.

global level. Attempting to address it first at any lower level would be ineffective: only if everyone around the world moves into the same direction will climate action have any noticeable effect. And, relying on local action in absence of coordination would also expose everyone involved to a free-rider effect. Indeed, communities that would opt out of a climate agreement would benefit twice: once from enjoying the climate improvements that result from other' efforts and again from sustaining their desired way of life, regardless of how much pollution they produce.

The second level of action and decision making supported by subsidiarity is the national level. Consider again climate action. Each country contributes to climate change in specific ways. For example, reducing factory emissions would negatively affect China more than others, as it has more factories than any country in the world. Similarly, a limit on auto travel would have a significant effect on the United States, where cars are a primary mode of transportation. Taking a different approach, such as limiting air travel, would affect certain groups of people more than others. Subsidiarity supports a national or local level of decision-making for countries to determine which path will work best for them to effectively address the global goal.

This is why a UN framework such as the Paris Agreement from 2017 is a good idea. No single country is responsible for (significantly) more than a quarter of global CO_2 emissions,[11] but global emissions must fall by more than half to avert a climate disaster. It means that no country or region—not the US, not China, and not the European Union—could curb global emissions by their own efforts. But it also means that no country has the incentive to reduce their emissions unless they know others would do the same; it wouldn't make a major difference on a global scale, and it may hurt economic development or prosperity in the short run. The only way out of this Catch-22, then, is to cooperate on a global scale. Yet, given the very different economic structures of each country, it would make no sense for a global governance body to decide *how* each country should reduce its emissions, once country-specific goals are set.

The same is true on a company level, where no company would be able or willing individually to reduce its emissions, *ceteris paribus*, given the competitive handicap it would initially entail. But once an industry arbitrator (for example, the European Union) sets goals for each industry and

[11]"Chart of the Day: These Countries Create Most of the World's CO2 Emissions," World Economic Forum, June 2019, https://www.weforum.org/agenda/2019/06/chart-of-the-day-these-countries-create-most-of-the-world-s-co2-emissions/.

defines emission rights for each company, those companies should be able to decide *how* they reduce their emissions to the desired optimum (for example, they could either produce in a less energy-consuming way or buy emission rights from other companies). These two examples are not taken from thin air; the Paris Agreement in fact incorporated the subsidiarity principle in much the same way as described above. And the European Union, with its Green New Deal and emissions cap-and-trade scheme for companies, applies the same principle as well. The groundwork for both plans was prepared in part at meetings of the World Economic Forum, and they exemplify how stakeholder capitalism can work if it adheres to the subsidiarity principle.

A similar logic applies to matters of technology governance, competition, and global taxation. Many companies today operate globally, whether in the digital sphere or the physical sphere, but they are mostly regulated by national governments. It is this imbalance, where companies can develop technology and IP in one country, gain the lion's share of their revenues in a second, pay taxes in a third, compete at low-cost in a fourth, and evade rules on collective labor agreements in a fifth, that has led to an uneven playing field. It has often eroded tax bases, weakened institutions and trust in them, created a lopsided marketplace, and reduced employment and entrepreneurship opportunities.

Again, the response should not be to create a global governance hegemon but to coordinate actions among regulators so that the level playing field can be evened within the confines of each jurisdiction. The efforts by the OECD to coordinate a tax on the revenues of digital companies, to ensure tax contributions are made in each country a company is active in, regardless from where the corporate headquarters are or the IP is based, are a good example of this principle in action.

With the subsidiarity principle in mind, the confines within which stakeholder capitalism should operate are now clear. It is a system wherein certain trends and stakes are global (climate change, digital globalization, global inequality, and market concentration) but where the best organizing principle is that of subsidiarity. The resulting stakeholder model is one where on the one hand, each company or organization individually is still at the center of the obligations to its stakeholders, as in the original model. But on the other hand, companies, governments, NGOs, next generations, and others are recognized as stakeholders of our common global future and well-being. The economic system we build to shape these realities must thus be both locally embedded and globally coherent.

It leads us to the next question: Which beliefs should underpin stakeholder capitalism?

Value Creation and Sharing

The set of beliefs that underpin the stakeholder model remains largely unchanged from when it was first conceived. They are those that led to the construction of the welfare state in Western Europe in the post–world war era, the Great Society in the United States, and the Chinese Dream[12] in modern China. The most important of them is that a society will do best when all of its people thrive, rather than a small subset among them. For example, the Great Society, President Lyndon B. Johnson said, is "a place where every child can find knowledge to enrich his mind and enlarge his talent [and] where the city of man serves not only the needs of the body and the demands of commerce but the desire for beauty and the hunger for community."[13] And in the case of the Chinese Dream, the idea of great rejuvenation of the Chinese Nation "is a dream of the whole nation, as well as of every individual,"[12] according to President Xi Jinping.

Embedded in this belief is thus a second one, namely that value in society is not only or primarily created by companies and their (most) productive employees but also by educators, scientists, cultural actors, government institutions, and above all, society and the natural environment itself—in other words: by all stakeholders. This may sound like a straightforward perspective, seen as self-evident by most people. But as Mariana Mazzucato wrote in her book *The Value of Everything*, this view did not inform how the global economic system functioned in the last few decades. Rather, she says, the dominant belief in the recent past has been that value is created mostly by and in companies, and within that, to a large degree by financial institutions (and, we would add, by technology companies, in recent years).

That different view on value creation, and the practices that went along with it, Mazzucato asserted, created a system in which value extraction became normalized, as many of the most productive members of the economic system, including those active state-funded scientific

---

[12]"Connotations of Chinese Dream," *China Daily*, March 2014, https://www.chinadaily.com.cn/china/2014npcandcppcc/2014-03/05/content_17324203.htm.

[13]"The Speech that Launched the Great Society," The Conversation, January 2015, https://theconversation.com/the-speech-that-launched-the-great-society-35836.

research, education, and social services, were undervalued. It also led to a financialization of the economic system, in which revenues and profits were confounded with true value creation. And it created a cult around CEOs and tech start-up founders, in which private innovations generated more praise and protection than the fundamental breakthroughs achieved through public funding and institutions.[14]

While we don't agree in full with Mazzucato's assessment, it is clear that the contributions made by other stakeholders in our economic system have been undervalued and that the equilibrium of the stakeholder economy needs to be restored. To do so, stakeholder capitalism must ensure that:

- all stakeholders get the seat at the table of decision-making that concerns them;
- the appropriate measurement systems exist to calculate any stakeholder's true value creation or destruction, not just in financial terms but also in achieving of environment, social, and governance (ESG) objectives; and
- the necessary checks and balances exist so that each stakeholder compensates what it takes from society and that it receives a share of the total pie commensurate with its contributions, both locally and globally.

Let us now look at these three requirements in detail.

Stakeholder Capitalism in Practice

A Seat at the Table

To give meaning to the stakeholder model as an organizing principle, we must first make sure every stakeholder gets a seat at each table that concerns her. We know that this an objective worth pursuing and that it often is lacking, as can be seen from the social, economic, and political imbalances that persist in our societies. On the economic front, for example, there is a highly positive correlation between strong stakeholder representation on the one hand, and low inequality and commensurate wages, for example, on the other. One

---

[14]For commentary, see "Who Creates a Nation's Economic Value?" Martin Wolf, *Financial Times*, April 2018, https://www.ft.com/content/e00099f0-3c19-11e8-b9f9-de94fa33a81e.

striking visual representation, which we saw in Chapter 6, comes from the United States, where the Economic Policy Institute plotted union membership against income inequality over the past 100 years. It showed that income inequality was high when organized labor was absent and that it dropped during the golden age of American organized labor, roughly between 1940 and 1980, as union membership surged. Finally, when union membership started falling again, inequality increased again, hitting an all-time high in the mid-2010s. And, as we have seen earlier in the case of Denmark, in those countries where union representation remained strong, income inequality remained low as well, even in the context of today's globalized and technology-driven economy.

To the extent that a drop in union participation, or the lack of representation of all layers in society in decision-making, is a consequence of conscious policy choices, governments would do well to revert to more inclusive policies going forward. Not doing so leads to detrimental outcomes for all in the long run. The fact that worker wages haven't gone up in a commensurate way in the United States for decades led to a less cohesive and resilient society, which was ill-prepared for once-in-a-century events such as COVID-19 or the disruption of the Fourth Industrial Revolution. And it may have been at least partially the result of exclusive social and political policy choices as well, as was brought to the fore by the Black Lives Matter movement in the United States. After decades of facing discriminatory government policies and actions, many rose up to decry this situation. The lessons from countries such as Malaysia, where inclusive policies have been a focal point for policymakers, shows that a more inclusive approach to government could have and can still avoid such unequal outcomes.

Similarly, where other stakeholders lack a seat at the table because of individual corporate governance decisions, boards would do well to actively pursue a more representative selection of members. Making sure management teams, corporate boards, governments, and other leadership committees reflect better the setup of society in its entirety is a recipe for more holistic decision-making and ultimately, better and more performant organizations. There is a far way to go on this front. Leadership committees continue to be monocultural in gender, job, and educational background and other factors such as race, sexual orientation, and age. Each company, each community, and each government should decide which actions and criteria fit their situation best, but the general idea that decision-making organizations must be more representative and diverse is an almost universal objective. Realizing it would lead to healthier and more balanced organizations, achieving outcomes that are ultimately better for societies.

To get stakeholders at the table, we cannot solely rely on the patterns of the past. The reality in which organizations operate has in some instances fundamentally changed. For example, more workers now work remotely or under freelance contracts than ever before in modern history, making it harder to assemble them. In the case of gig economy workers like those driving or delivering for Uber, Grab, or Didi, the workers no longer physically work in the same place. They may not even know one another, and they likely have different interests and goals. This makes it harder for them to organize and agree on a common agenda to advocate for. Traditional, factory- or office-based unions may not be the answer, as people move around jobs more often than they used to, are often not even physically working in the same space as co-workers, and companies are likewise more geographically mobile than in the past, but the principle must remain the same. Those who work for platforms or companies must have a say in the way these companies operate, how they treat their workers, and what responsibility they take toward society. There have been real-life experiments to assemble these stakeholders, such as when Rideshare Drivers United, a Californian advocacy group for drivers of Uber and Lyft, called for a global strike in May 2019, ahead of Uber's planned IPO. They encouraged drivers to shut off their mobile apps to make their case for more pay and better protections.[15] But despite attracting a lot of media and political attention[16] and leading to a one-off financial settlement for some drivers ahead of the IPO,[17] the strike mostly revealed how hard it will be to replicate the influence taxi unions once had, as the structural demands of the drivers were not met. It showed how difficult it is to ensure the gig economy respects the rights of its workers. In a further development, in November 2020, California voted on a Proposition that would designate gig economy workers as employees, but after a campaign labeled

[15]"The Worldwide Uber Strike Is a Key Test for the Gig Economy," Alexia Fernandez Campbell, Vox, May 219, https://www.vox.com/2019/5/8/18535367/uber-drivers-strike-2019-cities.

[16]"Uber Pre IPO, 8th May, 2019 Global Strike Results," RideShare Drivers United, May 2019, https://ridesharedriversunited.com/uber-pre-ipo-8th-may-2019-global-strike-results/.

[17]"Worker or Independent Contractor? Uber Settles Driver Claims Before Disappointing IPO," *Forbes*, May 2019, https://www.forbes.com/sites/kellyphillipserb/2019/05/13/worker-or-independent-contractor-uber-settles-driver-claims-before-disappointing-ipo/#7a157b93f39f.

as the "most expensive initiative in the state's history", the proposal was rejected, suggesting a resolution that works for all stakeholders has not yet been found.[18]

In stakeholder capitalism, the same level of representation in companies should also apply to political representation. Representation-based governments and political parties all over the world face an existential crisis. Even as societal discontent increases, voter turnout and party membership declines. In Europe, for example, the traditional political parties that shaped democracy are facing a triple crisis. Over the last few decades, parties such as the Christian Democrats, Liberals, and Social Democrats saw their membership decrease. Fewer voters of all political opinions showed up to vote in elections and, of those who did, fewer voted for a traditional party.[19] Similarly, in most countries in Latin America—with the exception of Colombia—voter turnout for elections has dropped over time, even in countries such as Brazil and Costa Rica, where voting is mandatory.[20] And in the United States, which has seen a surge in social unrest in recent years, turnout for presidential elections has been declining over time. From a high of about 70 percent in the 1950s and 1960s, it sunk to a low in the late 1990s; in the 2016 presidential election turnout was about 55 percent.[21] (The 2018 mid-term elections, though, were a notable exception to that downward trend, attracting the highest voter turnout in half a century). Even in one-party political systems such as China, age and gender representation are acknowledged issues. Until at least 2016, according to the Communist Party of China's Central Committee, "the age, culture, and distribution of the existing party members have not been well adapted to the needs of the party's great mission in the new era and new stage." At that point, there were "few first-line party members and youth party members, and the proportion of women party members [was]

---

[18]"Uber and Lyft Drivers in California Will Remain Contractors", Kate Conger, The New York Times, November 2020, https://www.nytimes.com/2020/11/04/technology/california-uber-lyft-prop-22.html.

[19]"Are Political Parties in Trouble?" Patrick Liddiard, Wilson Center, December 2018, https://www.wilsoncenter.org/sites/default/files/media/documents/publication/happ_liddiard_are_political_parties_in_trouble_december_2018.pdf.

[20]"A Deep Dive into Voter Turnout in Latin America," Holly Sunderland, Americas Society / Council of the Americas, June 2018, https://www.as-coa.org/articles/chart-deep-dive-voter-turnout-latin-america.

[21]"Historical Reported Voting Rates, Table A.1," United States Census Bureau, https://www.census.gov/data/tables/time-series/demo/voting-and-registration/voting-historical-time-series.html.

low.[22]" Since then, the share of women and millennials in the party has risen, but it remains below their demographic representation.[23]

Such representation issues will need to be resolved if we want to get the stakeholder model right. There is only so much value to getting the key stakeholders to talk to each other and take each other's objectives into account, when they themselves are not representative of the groups of people they are meant to represent.[24] History is filled with examples of heads of governments, companies, and religious organizations bonding together for their mutual benefit. But almost without fault, society as a whole or important groups of minority stakeholders have suffered when they were not properly accounted for in those alliances. We will look in more detail on how to get this right in the coming chapters.

Going Beyond GDP and Profits

Once all stakeholders have a seat at the table, corporations, organizations, and governments must move away from the fetishization of profits or related metrics, such as gross domestic product (GDP). The single-minded pursuit of profit should be replaced with more holistic measures of value creation. As we have discussed, companies did not always optimize for profits and shareholder dividends alone, and GDP wasn't always a holy grail for governments. As shareholder capitalism gained ground in the last decades of the 20th century, profits and GDP became the be-all and end-all. In today's world, we must end the singular focus on these short-term financial measures and complement them with ones that provide a fuller picture of how people and the planet are faring. As I wrote in an earlier op-ed,[25] our goals should be "achieving the United Nations Sustainable Development Goals (SDGs) by 2030; delivering on the Paris climate agreement over the next 30 years; and reforming our global

---

[22]"How to Correctly Understand the General Requirements of Recruiting Party Members?" Communist Party, April 2016, http://fuwu.12371.cn/2016/04/22/ARTI1461286650793416.shtml.

[23]"Recruitment Trends in the Chinese Communist Party," Neil Thomas, Macro Polo, July 2020, https://macropolo.org/analysis/members-only-recruitment-trends-in-the-chinese-communist-party/.

[24]This is why for a number of years, the World Economic Forum has made additional efforts to ensure every stakeholder is represented in its meetings, whether it is the voice of youth, cultural leaders, civil society, or academia.

[25]"Ending Short-Termism by Keeping Score," Klaus Schwab, Project Syndicate, October 2019, https://www.weforum.org/agenda/2019/10/how-we-can-end-short-termism-by-keeping-score/.

economic system to make it fit for the next 50 years and beyond." These are the additional objectives we should optimize for in the next decade.

For countries that wish to go beyond GDP, a number of alternatives already exist. The World Economic Forum's Global Competitiveness Index, and its Inclusive Development Index, for example, track a broad variety of environmental, social, and governance indicators, beyond the economic ones. The OECD similarly has a Better Life Index,[26] in which it measures and ranks countries in a number of well-being areas, from education, health and housing, income, and jobs, to work-life balance, life satisfaction, and care for the environment. As we'll see in later chapters, some countries, including New Zealand, have already made their own dashboard, in which they keep track of the progress they make on a number of key well-being indicators for their citizens. (We explore some examples of these metrics later in this chapter.)

Interestingly, the World Economic Forum's Competitiveness Report shows that countries that optimize for sustainable and inclusive development alongside economic competitiveness often end up as the most competitive as well. It is thus possible to do well economically, ecologically, and socially at the same time, *provided* the right policy choices are made. This is, for example, the case in the Nordic countries, which we discussed in Chapter 6. But why? On creating a more sustainable and green economy, the 2019 report found, "highly competitive economies are better placed to foster the emergence of new technologies in all sectors, including potential breakthrough technologies in green inventions, because they provide a more conducive innovation ecosystem."[27] In addition, "countries that possess better human capital, better infrastructure and greater innovation capability are, on average, more likely to adopt a greener energy mix."[28] To put it more simply still, if you have a society in which all people are well educated and environmentally conscious, you have a higher chance that the society as a whole will make choices that make the economy more prosperous *and* more sustainable in the long run. The other explanation for the correlation is that economic competitiveness ultimately depends on the planet's resource function and a society's human capital, whether those are accounted for in GDP or not. Countries that truly only account for GDP will run into a wall sooner or later, as you can only ignore investments in education,

[26]"Better Life Index," OECD, http://www.oecdbetterlifeindex.org/#/11111111111.

[27]The Global Competitiveness Report 2019, World Economic Forum, p. 27, http://www3.weforum.org/docs/WEF_TheGlobalCompetitivenessReport2019.pdf.

[28]Ibidem.

training, and care for the planet for so long before they start to affect the economic production function.

In addition to the tools provided by indices on competitiveness and inclusiveness, the world also desperately needs to walk to a different drum than that provided by GDP. Some complementary measures already exist, and others are on the way. "One quick fix is to adopt a measure like median income per capita, which better reflects the economic conditions real people face," I wrote in a 2019 op-ed. "A more ambitious measure is Natural Capital,[29] based on a country's ecosystems, fish stocks, minerals, and other natural assets. Because this balance sheet would also need to include human capital, we could incorporate all of the relevant elements in one composite scorecard.[30] And a third, concrete option is to include the Climate Action Tracker in the dashboard of governments, as it shows each country's progress toward meeting its national commitments under the Paris agreement."[31] Some of these proposals are developed by the Wealth Project, a group consisting of economists including Diane Coyle and Mariana Mazzucato,[32] who have long expressed their concern of the dominance of GDP.

Companies, too, should expand their horizon beyond the profit-and-loss statement—and they are increasingly willing to do so. Ahead of the 50th Annual Meeting in Davos, I presented companies with a "Davos Manifesto 2020," which describes "The Universal Purpose of a Company in the Fourth Industrial Revolution."[33]

A. **The purpose of a company is to engage all its stakeholders in shared and sustained value creation**. In creating such value, a company serves not only its shareholders, but all its stakeholders—employees, customers, suppliers, local communities and society at large. The best way to understand and harmonize the divergent interests of all stakeholders is through a shared commitment to policies and decisions that strengthen the long-term prosperity of a company.

---

[29]"What Is Natural Capital?" World Forum on Natural Capital, https://naturalcapitalforum.com/about/.

[30]https://www.weforum.org/reports/the-inclusive-development-index-2018.

[31]https://climateactiontracker.org/.

[32]"Changing how we measure economic progress, The Wealth Project, https://www.wealth-economics.org/about/.

[33]"Davos Manifesto 2020," Klaus Schwab, World Economic Forum, December 2019, https://www.weforum.org/agenda/2019/12/davos-manifesto-2020-the-universal-purpose-of-a-company-in-the-fourth-industrial-revolution/.

i. A company serves its **customers** by providing a value proposition that best meets their needs. It accepts and supports fair competition and a level playing field. It has zero tolerance for corruption. It keeps the digital ecosystem in which it operates reliable and trustworthy. It makes customers fully aware of the functionality of its products and services, including adverse implications or negative externalities.

ii. A company treats its **people** with dignity and respect. It honours diversity and strives for continuous improvements in working conditions and employee well-being. In a world of rapid change, a company fosters continued employability through ongoing upskilling and reskilling.

iii. A company considers its **suppliers** as true partners in value creation. It provides a fair chance to new market entrants. It integrates respect for human rights into the entire supply chain.

iv. A company serves **society at large** through its activities, supports the communities in which it works, and pays its fair share of taxes. It ensures the safe, ethical and efficient use of data. It acts as a steward of the environmental and material universe for future generations. It consciously protects our biosphere and champions a circular, shared and regenerative economy. It continuously expands the frontiers of knowledge, innovation and technology to improve people's well-being.

v. A company provides its **shareholders** with a return on investment that takes into account the incurred entrepreneurial risks and the need for continuous innovation and sustained investments. It responsibly manages near-term, medium-term and long-term value creation in pursuit of sustainable shareholder returns that do not sacrifice the future for the present.

B. A company is more than an economic unit generating wealth. It fulfils human and societal aspirations as part of the broader social system. Performance must be measured not only on the return to shareholders, but also on how it achieves its environmental, social and good governance objectives. Executive remuneration should reflect stakeholder responsibility.

C. A company that has a multinational scope of activities not only serves all those stakeholders who are directly engaged, but **acts itself as a stakeholder—together with governments and civil society— of our global future.** Corporate global citizenship requires a company to harness its core competencies, its entrepreneurship, skills and relevant resources in collaborative efforts with other companies and stakeholders to improve the state of the world.

It is worthwhile examining a few of the specific metrics by which a company can measure its performance toward its stakeholders. The manifesto specifically mentions accepting a level playing field in competition, showing zero tolerance for corruption, striving for improvements in working conditions and employee well-being, supporting the communities in which it is active, paying one's fair share of taxes, and reflecting stakeholder responsibility in executive remuneration. Taken together, these requirements make for a corporate governance that is very different from one where short-term financial success is paramount.[34] If every company individually commits to these goals and addresses the underlying issues, many of the excesses of shareholder capitalism will be rooted out automatically.

But in a world where management often happens by numbers, this corporate stakeholder responsibility must also be measured, and goals must be quantified. On this front, there is good news. In September 2020, the International Business Council of the World Economic Forum—comprising 140 of the largest global companies—presented the "Stakeholder Capitalism Metrics." They are a core set of metrics and disclosures on the non-financial aspects of business performance, including variables such as greenhouse gas emissions, diversity, employee health and well-being, and other factors that are generally framed as ESG topics.[35] Once implemented, they should make it easier for executives to optimize for more than just profits and for other stakeholders, such as employees, clients, and governments, to judge the performance of stakeholder-oriented companies. In that way, they are a major step toward making stakeholder capitalism a reality on the ground. You can read more about the metrics in the following chapter and in the conclusion to this book.

Check and Balances, and Robust Institutions

Finally, a stakeholder model must include the necessary checks and balances and must have robust and independent institutions, as power imbalances are likely to arise. In principle, each stakeholder contributes what it can in stakeholder capitalism and receives what it needs, to achieve

---

[34] And, I should add, these elements also make the 2020 Davos Manifesto differ from the 2019 U.S. Business Roundtable's Statement on the Purpose of a Corporation. It lists a similar set of stakeholders, to which a company should commit delivering value to. But it stops short of mentioning a level playing field in competition, paying fair taxes, or executive remuneration. Source: https://www.businessroundtable.org/business-roundtable-redefines-the-purpose-of-a-corporation-to-promote-an-economy-that-serves-all-americans.

[35] "Measuring Stakeholder Capitalism: World's Largest Companies Support Developing Core Set of Universal ESG Disclosures," World Economic Forum, January 2020, https://www.weforum.org/press/2020/01/measuring-stakeholder-capitalism-world-s-largest-companies-support-developing-core-set-of-universal-esg-disclosures/.

the most successful societal outcomes. But given the natural tendency of the existing capitalist models to favor the interests of large companies and wealthy individuals (shareholder capitalism) and political insiders (state capitalism), it is of utmost importance that governments and companies—the two stakeholders with most power and influence in the current economic system—agree to be held accountable by each other and other stakeholders. This is where the role of democratic accountability, division of powers, and the role of international organizations come into play. They are the checks and balances our system needs.

Of course, we must confront the reality that democracies are fracturing at the base (see Chapter 4) and that the efficacy of and support for our international institutions is weakening. It is thus needed to first strengthen the trust in government from the ground up and only then to strengthen the mandate of decision-makers from top to bottom. It will ensure the checks and balances of the system can function again. How can we do this?

As I wrote in another 2019 op-ed,[36] "rather than focusing on the pinnacle of the global-governance pyramid, we should be tending to the fractures in its base." One country that did an interesting experiment in this regard is Ireland. "For decades, abortion was political kryptonite for Irish policymakers. But then Ireland tried a socio-political experiment that is fit for our age of division: it convened a citizens' assembly to devise abortion legislation that a broad base of voters could support. The Irish assembly selected 99 citizens (and one chairperson) at random to convene a body that was "broadly representative of society as reflected in the census, including age, gender, social class, regional spread." As such, it achieved a much wider diversity of views than one finds in the established political system. The public closely followed the proceedings of citizens' assembly, creating a unique sense of broad-based political participation. People cared deeply about the topic being discussed, but they also learned to appreciate the views held by those they disagreed with. Ultimately, the assembly issued recommendations, including legalizing abortion, which were then put to the public in the form of a referendum. Many of its proposals are now law.

If we want to overcome political divisions elsewhere in the world, we should champion these and other novel kinds of stakeholder engagement in government:

> By design, deliberative gatherings of ordinary citizens—whose primary task is to reach agreement, rather than get re-elected—can bypass

[36]"A Better World Starts at Home," Klaus Schwab, Project Syndicate, December 2019, https://www.project-syndicate.org/onpoint/citizen-assemblies-to-end-polarization-by-klaus-schwab-2019-12.

political antagonism and move toward pragmatic solutions to specific issues. Although they cannot replace democratically elected legislatures, they should supplement them when needed.[37]

Similar stakeholder approaches also helped elected leaders confront major challenges in other cases:

In France, the "yellow vest" protesters ("*gilets jaunes*") softened their tone once President Emmanuel Macron organized a "Grand Debate" for citizens to engage directly in town hall–style meetings across the country. In Belgium, a gathering of stakeholders in Antwerp produced a resolution to settle disagreements over a major infrastructure project after decades of inaction. And in Gdansk, Poland, a citizen assembly achieved what Tin Gazivoda of the Open Society Initiative for Europe described as "binding changes in city policy on flood mitigation, air pollution, civic engagement, and the treatment of LGBT people."[38]

It must be stressed, once again, that the way in which democracies adopt the stakeholder model in political decision-making is theirs alone to decide. The resulting methods may look very different in each country, and that is okay. In Switzerland, a long history of direct democracy has meant that people get to vote in referenda on all kinds of political and economic issues, from proposals on curbing immigration to reinstating the gold standard and from public housing projects to the opening hours of a local airport. But while this system may sound ideal, it may not work for everyone. In Belgium, for example, ideological, religious, and language differences run right through the middle of society. Implementing referenda in the past led to scarring results there, which did more to separate citizens than unite them and led to the eventual abandonment of the system. It is now experimenting with more consensus-seeking stakeholder participation, such as mediated conversations between various interest groups and gatherings of randomly selected citizens, to increase the sense of participation in the democracy.

Similarly, the organization of democracy itself should respect local customs and traditions and be shaped by a country's citizens themselves, not outsiders. A good example comes from Afghanistan, where political participation has traditionally been organized very differently than in Western democracies. In his book *Destiny Disrupted*, Afghan-American

---

[37]"ibidem".
[38]"ibidem".

writer Tamim Ansary pointed out that the American-imposed democracy in his country in practice meant a continuation of a much more tribal political system, as communities reverted to voting for candidates whose families had played a leading social and economic role in their town for generations. If the goal was to put a democratic layer on top of the existing societal and political structure, the effort was successful. But if the goal was to increase the direct participation of citizens in decision-making, it would have been a better idea to let communities decide for themselves which system was better suited for that.

Finally, it is important that domestic public institutions, which play a key role in the stakeholder model, are and remain robust. For a few decades after World War II, new generations in the West grew up with the idea that strong public institutions were a given, that they had a well-defined role, and that they would always play that role. In the Western view on global economic development, developing economies also had to build such strong public institutions, as they were believed to be as a cornerstone to a well-functioning society and economy.

But in recent years, many societies experienced an erosion of trust in their own institutions and a decline in their effectiveness and ability to act as an objective arbiter. In the US, for example, a decline in public trust in institutions went hand in hand with a perceived decline in their performance.[39] On the other hand, in the Scandinavian countries, Switzerland, and Singapore, and even in larger countries such as Indonesia, China, and India, citizens do still strongly trust public institutions, which is one crucial building block to keep them more robust. Seen from the stakeholder perspective, public institutions have a central role to play, so it is important to act to make them both strong and competent (again).

Another step we must take is to strengthen the mandate of international institutions. The need for this is obvious: as information, technology, money, people, and viruses flow around the world, and climate change affects all people and countries, the need for coordination of these issues on a global level is higher than ever. Moreover, with companies growing more global, their ability to optimize their obligations and maximize their influence creates an imbalance in their relationship to national governments. Representative international organizations such as the United Nations and its committees, arbiters such as the European

---

[39]"Key Findings about Americans' Declining Trust in Government and Each Other," Pew Research Center, July 2019, https://www.pewresearch.org/fact-tank/2019/07/22/key-findings-about-americans-declining-trust-in-government-and-each-other/.

Court of Justice or the Appellate Judges of the World Trade Organization, and regulators such as the European Commission or the Universal
Postal Union will and must continue to play an important role in global
governance.

But as we have seen, these supranational institutions operate at a level
that is unnatural for many individual stakeholders to relate to—they are
simply too remote and impersonal for most people. Their response then,
must be to implement decision-making processes that include all of their
stakeholders (usually sovereign governments) and understand the global
trends they face and regulate, thus creating a higher societal buy-in for
their mandate. Too often, international organizations have fallen short of
these requirements in the past.

First, the organizations created at the end of Second World War were
representative of the winners of that war but are no longer representative
of the world today. This lack of representation is apparent from top to
bottom in the administration of these institutions and often in its voting
procedures as well. For evidence, one needs to look no further than the
International Monetary Fund and the World Bank, whose voting rights
still favor Western nations and whose leadership has traditionally gone to
a European and American, respectively, even as emerging markets elsewhere rose to prominence. Moreover, international organizations have
been representative for most of their history of only one type of stakeholder—national governments—whereas a large and increasing part of
global challenges has a much greater plethora of stakeholders.

Second, the understanding of international organizations of the
trends in the global economy is often late or lacking. Two examples suffice to make this point. To this day, for example, no international organization has an agreed metric for the global digital economy, despite it
clearly being of major importance both economically and socially. (The
best estimate comes from consulting firm McKinsey's Global Institute, a
private institution.) And, to take another example, the Universal Postal[40]
Union until 2019 unknowingly contributed to unfair international
competition and a rise in emissions coming from international shipping.
It had set outdated rules on sending packages between countries of varying economic income status. In practice, it meant that sending a package
from China to the US often cost significantly less than sending the same
package from one street corner to another within a US town.

---

[40]"Digital globalization: The new era of global flows", McKinsey Global Institute, February 2016, and "Globalization in Transition: the future of trade and value chains", McKinsey
Global Institute, January 2019.

The good news is that these shortcomings can be set straight. And when that happens, the global checks and balances on our economic system improve. To revert to the previous examples, the OECD is currently working on a uniform definition and measurement system for digital trade.[41] The Universal Postal Union at the end of 2019 took the initiative to reform its postal rates.[42] And the Paris Agreement, as we showed earlier, was to a large extent a multi-stakeholder effort. The private sector, NGOs, and representatives of various other stakeholders prepare and shape the discussions in Paris, making it easier for the represented governments to ultimately agree on a compromise.

Finally, let us consider how the decision-making process among stakeholders can function. It is easy to imagine this becoming a hodgepodge if no clear processes and guidelines exist. For example, if a government, organization, or company first has to get the sign-off from all its stakeholders before it can make a decision, how can they still effectively steer their organization? It may well be that the interests of various stakeholders diverge in the short term. It is also not far-fetched to see a scenario in which the most vocal stakeholder would try to monopolize or block decision-making, leading to a standstill or lopsided outcomes.

The solution, I believe, lies in separating the consultative process from the decision-making one. In the consultative stage, all stakeholders should be included, and their concerns should be heard. In the decision-making stage, by contrast, only those mandated to make decisions should be able to do so, which means in the case of companies, respectively the board or the executive management.

In the short run, that may still mean that difficult choices need to be made, which benefit one stakeholder or its concerns more than another. But, basing the decisions on the preceding consultative process should lead in the long run to better decisions and outcomes for all.

This then is stakeholder capitalism. In the coming chapters we will discuss how the model applies to some of the key stakeholders individually and the key issues we identified in previous chapters, such as climate change, market concentration and economic inequality, and debt left for the next generations.

---

[41]"The impact of digitalisation on trade", OECD, https://www.oecd.org/trade/topics/digital-trade/.

[42]"5 things to know about Option V", Universal Postal Union, October 2019, https://www.upu.int/en/Publications/Factsheets-backgrounders/5-things-to-know-about-Option-V.

9

Companies

When former SAP co-CEO Jim Snabe—a member of the World Economic Forum's Board of Trustees—joined shipping giant A.P. Møller-Mærsk in 2016, the Danish multinational was getting ready for a major transformation. The 112-year-old company had had a hugely successful run in the years before he joined but had in recent years suffered from challenging market conditions in both the shipping and the oil industry. As a consequence the revenue had declined from $60 billion to $30 billion, and the conglomerate was making a loss. Looking ahead, it needed to make sure it evolved with the times and remained relevant for another 100 years. Its transportation services gave people access to markets and goods from all over the world, increasing their standards of living, and creating millions of jobs in all markets, participating in global trade along the way. But the company also contributed greatly to greenhouse gas emissions and enabled a global economic system in which inequality and increased market concentration were the order of the day. Could Snabe help the company become a champion of the stakeholder capitalist model he thought was necessary for companies to thrive?

As with every behemoth, Mærsk was once a small start-up, looking to capitalize on new opportunities in a changing world. The company was founded in 1904 in the small Danish coastal town of Svendborg by a young man, A.P. Møller, and his father, Peter Mærsk-Møller, to bring goods in and out of the tiny Baltic port. Over the course of the next 100 years, it grew from being the owner and operator of a second-hand

steamer to the largest shipping company in the world and the pride of
Denmark's economy. The conglomerate was active in everything from
oil exploration to transportation, from freight forwarding to rescue
operations, and from container manufacturing to the shipping of goods
to over 120 countries in the world. It counted for about 15 percent of
global sea freight,[1] making it the largest such company in the world.

From one perspective, the company was a wonder of globalization
and successive industrial revolutions. In Qingdao, China, the company
produced refrigerated containers. In the North Sea it drilled for oil.
In the Suez Canal, its gigantic *Mærsk Mc-Kinney Møller* ship impressed
onlookers with its capacity of 18,000 containers (to this day, it is one of
the largest ships in the world). And around the globe, Mærsk's reefers,
container ships, and tankers crisscrossed the seven seas. From Guayaquil
to Novorossiysk, from Sydney to Charleston, and from Busan to Mon-
tevideo, there was not a port in the world without a Mærsk vessel. It
helped lower the cost of goods and improve the connectedness of people, supply chains, and companies the world over.

From another perspective, Mærsk also represented much of what was
wrong with the global economy. Its exploration and drilling activities could
only be profitable if more oil was found, drilled, transported, and used.
The global shipping industry it dominated was responsible for a large and
increasing share of CO_2 emissions, which if left unchecked could reach 17
percent of the world's total CO_2 emissions by 2050.[2] And the global value
chains it enabled didn't only mean more people had access to more goods
but also that an ever-smaller group of global companies and their owners
could dominate an ever-larger share of global industries, increasing market
concentration and worsening inequalities of income and wealth.

For Snabe, though, joining the board was a kind of homecoming.
He was born in Denmark, and the company had loomed large over
his country for his entire life. The Mærsk headquarters, an enormous,
elegant glass building in the heart of Copenhagen's port area, was almost
as famous as the nearby statue celebrating Hans Christian Andersen's
"Little Mermaid" that looked out over the water, or the brightly colored
harbor houses and sailing ships that dotted the inner-city port. Mærsk's
shipyard in Odense, recently closed, had, for Snabe's entire life, been

---

[1] "Mærsk Hails Growth in Global Trade," *Financial Times*, November 2013, https://www
.ft.com/content/35b9748e-4c55-11e3-923d-00144feabdc0.

[2] "Emission Reduction Targets for International Aviation and Shipping," Director General
for Internal Studies, European Parliament, November 2015, http://www.europarl.europa
.eu/RegData/etudes/STUD/2015/569964/IPOL_STU(2015)569964_EN.pdf.

a powerful reminder of the millennium-long tradition and prowess of Danish shipbuilding. And when he joined the board, the company still contributed more than 2.5 percent to Denmark's GDP, making it the largest private company in the country and an employer of thousands.

After a long career in the software industry, culminating in the role of co-CEO at Germany's SAP, Snabe wanted to work in a company that operated in the physical world. It was a very deliberate choice. The next wave of value in the Fourth Industrial Revolution, he believed, would come from companies that mastered the physical world in a sustainable way, companies such as shipping giant Mærsk, industrial manufacturer Siemens, or car manufacturer Tesla. "If you add the latest technologies to what they do in the physical world," he told us, "these companies, can be the drivers of a more sustainable world. They can have a big impact, because without the physical world, we are nothing."[3]

■ ■ ■

In the technology sector, around the same time, it was starting to dawn on some that Big Tech was equally in need of a change of direction. Technology firms in recent years had gone from being hailed as the vanguards of progress and democratizers of information to being a part of the problem that the global economy was facing. Marc Benioff, CEO of Salesforce, and like Snabe, a member of the World Economic Forum's Board of Trustees, had said as much at Davos in 2018. "I mentioned tech in the same breath as credit default swaps, sugar, cigarettes—harmful products that companies had been allowed to peddle to customers, unconstrained by regulations," he recalled in his most recent book.[4] "Our industry had been given a regulatory pass for years, and when CEOs wouldn't take responsibility," he said, "I thought you'd have no choice but for the government to come in."

Snabe, Benioff, and others understood that their companies and industries needed to change; they needed to act more like stakeholder companies. But how could they go about it?

The notion of stakeholder capitalism, as we saw in the last chapter, has been in existence for a long time. In that sense, the easy solution would be to go back to the way businesses were run in the early days of

---

[3] Interview with Jim Snabe by Peter Vanham, August 2019.

[4] *Trailblazer: The Power of Business as the Greatest Platform for Change*, Marc Benioff, Random House, October 2019, p. 12.

"stakeholderism" that took place in the 1960s. That of course would not work. The world has drastically changed since the stakeholder model first gained ground. Societal divides, globalization, technological progress, climate change, and demographics were at entirely different stages than they are today. So how can companies implement the stakeholder concept successfully again, and contribute to improving the state of the world? Let us have a look at what happened next for these CEOs and their companies.

Mærsk

With Snabe on board, Mærsk wanted to waste no time in beginning a transformation process. The Danish business leader could build on a similar and successful experience at SAP, where he had served as co-CEO from 2010 to 2014. At the software company, he had galvanized the entire organization around a common dream, helping its clients "save scarce resources and thus contribute to a more sustainable world"[5]—and a few crucial details to make it happen. SAP had begun operating in 1972, the year after the first Davos meeting. It had used software to replace punch cards, to help managed financial resources. It had gone global expanding the scope of that resource management. What, wondered Snabe, if they could go further?[6]

> What if SAP could also help companies manage scarce resources such as energy, water or CO_2? What if SAP could leverage its considerable base of customers in nearly every industry, from raw materials to retail, to optimize scarce resources, not just for a single company, but across all companies in an entire value chain? What if SAP could help the world manage its scarce resources?
>
> In a world of increasing issues due to limited resources, the ability to help companies manage them more efficiently and the opportunity to make a positive difference in the world was much more inspiring than the company's quarterly earnings could ever be. Our line of thinking led to the decision to revisit the purpose of the company to become: "We make the world run better—and improve people's lives." It was an inspiring dream, one that was about much more than selling software to companies. It would force us to focus on acting responsibly and making a positive contribution to the world.

---

[5] "Dreams and Details", Jim Snabe and Mikael Trolle, Spintype, 2018, p. 128.
[6] *Dreams and Details*, Jim Snabe and Mikael Trolle, Spintype, 2018, pp. 128–129.

The reorientation at SAP led to a fundamental shift in overall strategy. Snabe and his colleagues decided on a few crucial points. First, if they were going to help others reduce waste, SAP had to lead by example. It therefore decided on a plan to reduce their own CO_2 emissions in absolute terms by 50 percent in the next decade, even if the company kept growing in size. Second, they had an explicitly financial goal linked to it. With its new, appealing purpose, SAP believed it should aim to grow more rapidly. The company had already set a goal to double revenue while increasing profitability, and the reorientation of their purpose gave them the motivation to achieve that goal. As Snabe recalled, "The reinvented purpose was the driving force to spark the internal inspiration needed to reinvent the company from a position of strength. We were not driven by a burning platform, but by a burning desire fuelled by a dream of making a difference."[7]

SAP's new strategy worked. Not only did it make sense to clients, it also motivated employees, who felt they were working for more than just a software company. The ambitious goal and new purpose also rallied shareholders, who saw SAP as a model company. As co-CEO, Snabe helped implement the new strategy and was there to see its initial results. Though he stepped down in 2014, he was proud to see the company achieving its twin goals in 2018, doubling revenue and halving CO_2 emissions ahead of schedule.[8,9] With that experience under its belt, he took on the challenge of transforming Mærsk.

Mærsk did have one important intangible asset: a strong core of values. "The basic principle is that people can trust us," former Chairman Arnold Mærsk Mc-Kinney Møller, and A.P.'s son, had once said. That focus on trust had helped the company build long-lasting relationships with its clients, as well as the government. Beyond that, the company was guided by five more values: "Constant Care, Humbleness, Uprightness, Our Employees, and Our Name."[10] They were officially announced when the 90-year-old Mc-Kinney Møller stepped down as chairman in 2003, but they had been present all throughout the family's leadership of

[7] Interview with Jim Snabe by Peter Vanham, August 2019.

[8] "SAP's Global Revenue from 2001 to 2018," Statista, March 2019, https://www.statista.com/statistics/263838/saps-global-revenue-since-2001/.

[9] "SAP Integrated Report: 2020 Targets Met Early," SAP, March 2018, https://news.sap.com/2018/03/sap-integrated-report-2020-targets-met-early/.

[10] "The Values Are Constant in a Complex World," Mærsk, June 2019, https://www.Mærsk.com/news/articles/2018/06/29/the-values-are-constant-in-a-complex-world.

the company. The values "carried the business for more than a century," wrote his daughter Ane Mærsk Mc-Kinney Uggla, in 2019, as vice-chairman and a fourth-generation family member.

Given Mærsk's values of uprightness and constant care, and its commitment to its employees and reputation, the need for action on two aspects had been obvious for a while. First, Mærsk's environmental footprint, the company realized, was contributing to the global problems of climate change and pollution. If it wanted to maintain a societal and environmental license to operate, that needed to change. Second, with economic activities now sprawling across the globe, often in virtually lawless seas and oceans, it had become less clear which duties it had to which communities.

Still it did want to make sure to contribute to society wherever it went. It was, after all, thanks to the industrialization of its home port of Svendborg during the Second Industrial Revolution and Denmark's strong welfare state and the social tissue of its stakeholder economy that the company had been able to grow to its current size.

Mærsk immediately turned to action. To improve its accountability toward communities and governments, early in 2017, the company participated in a working group brought together by a nonprofit aiming to "redefine the culture of accountability in business."[11] Together with like-minded firms, it committed to a set of principles for responsible tax management.[12] The principles, Mærsk said, went on to define its "basic approach to tax, its engagement with authorities and others regarding tax affairs, and its reporting to stakeholders."

The accountability commitment led to concrete outcomes. For one, Mærsk started to annually reveal its payments to governments, increasing the transparency and accountability of its public interactions. Second, it published a list of companies it fully or partially owns around the world, taking away any obfuscation as to the true extent of its activities and accounting. And third, the company made clear its ambition to be a "compliant and accountable tax payer with responsible and transparent tax practices." Its sustainability reporting started to highlight taxes paid, alongside other measures of environmental, social, and governance (ESG) issues, performance such as revenues, profits, and greenhouse gas emissions. For example, in 2019, Mærsk reported it had paid $458 million in corporate profit taxes on $5.7 billion profit, an effective tax rate of just over 8 percent. Going into 2020, it said it would "continue to engage in dialogue with stakeholders on

---

[11]"Tax Principles," Mærsk, https://www.maersk.com/about/tax-principles.

[12]"A New Bar for Responsible Tax," The B Team, https://bteam.org/assets/reports/A-New-Bar-for-Responsible-Tax.pdf.

tax matters" and "implement the B Team Responsible Tax Principles with reporting for 2020,"[13] as it wanted to be "a compliant and accountable tax-payer with responsible and transparent tax practices."

On climate change, there was even more radical business action. Over the period 2017–19, the company took drastic steps to divest some of its most profitable activities: Mærsk Drilling, Mærsk Tankers, and Mærsk Oil. These parts of the company—which as their names suggest were involved in the extraction, transportation, and exploitation of fossil fuels—were sold off or made separate entities.[14] These were big decisions, and they weighed on the company's short-term profitability. But once undertaken, they helped clear the road ahead and put Mærsk on track to become a truly purpose-driven company. After all, it was founded to move goods around the world, not to exploit the world's finite resources.

With those initial moves made, stakeholder duties could be taken to the next level. This was becoming a necessity, Snabe said, for several reasons. First, there was name and reputation. The Internet and social networks made it no longer possible for Mærsk to *say* one thing, for example, about the environment, and to *do* another. The company would quickly get called out, and Mærsk's core value of preserving its good name would be in peril. Second, there were its employees and customers. They, too, were demanding companies like Mærsk take better care of their societal responsibilities. If Mærsk didn't live up to their demands, a new generation of consumers and workers may well decide to turn its back on Mærsk. And finally, it began to dawn on investors that ESG-based companies have fewer risks. Larry Fink's 2018 letter to his shareholders was a case in point. If Mærsk wanted to keep growing and make money, a stakeholder focus would sooner or later become necessary.

Becoming a stakeholder company was also becoming a long-term opportunity. In the past, Mærsk had followed Milton Friedman's advice that the business of business was business. It originated in the pretty straightforward process of moving goods across water from point A to point B and some related activities in shipping; to this day, that was the way the company made its money. Any corporate social responsibility (CSR) projects it undertook served the purpose of creating a feel-good effect among employees or perhaps burnishing its reputation: either way, they were simply a matter of spending money. No longer. Thanks to the

---

[13]Sustainability Report 2019, Maersk, https://www.maersk.com/about/sustainability/reports

[14]2017: Sale of Mærsk Tankers, 2018: Sale of Mærsk Oil, 2019: Mærsk Drilling listed on the Copenhagen stock exchange, https://www.Mærsk.com/about/our-history/explore-our-history.

opportunities new technologies offered, a stakeholder-orientation could become about "how you make money, not how you spend it," said Snabe. Moving from shareholder primacy to stakeholder primacy was[15] "not an afterthought anymore." It could become core to business. But how?

To find out, Mærsk started "a profound conversation about purpose." "Why do we have this company? Why does it exist?" Snabe asked. "We went back in history, to the roots of the company. Then we would find out who the stakeholders are for what we did," he said.

Yet at Mærsk, the exercise didn't immediately yield a satisfactory answer. "We're a transportation company," Snabe realized. "We move boxes around. That's not a compelling purpose." But one level deeper, he did find the answer. "Why do we move boxes? Well, we connect any place in the world that produces things, to global markets. And because the cost of moving is very, very low, sellers can reach global markets at almost zero costs, but with substantial added revenues. So, we create livelihoods by moving products anywhere in the world."

Snabe gives the example of bananas to make his point. "It is better not to produce bananas in Denmark," he said, referring to the Northern European country's inhospitable climate. Moving them from where they were grown, Mærsk could create jobs, opportunities and prosperity." That was Mærsk's first contribution: to enable global trade, and thereby livelihoods. And there was a second, thanks to its refrigerated containers. "Once bananas get into our refrigerators, we lose only 0.4% of them to waste," he said. "Compare that to the average 40% loss elsewhere along the supply chain, and suddenly we reduce food waste."

It showed what Mærsk's purpose really was. Not to move boxes. Instead it was "to enable global trade and through it, prosperity, and dramatically reduce food waste." Suddenly, the company's true purpose was much broader than moving boxes, and the company's work could be linked to contributions to the U.N. Sustainable Development Goals such as Decent Work and Economic Growth (8), Responsible Consumption and Production (12), Industry, Innovation and Infrastructure (9), and Climate Action (13).

From there, it was much easier for the company to reprioritize its activities. Drilling, tankering, and selling oil clearly no longer fit its purpose, and moreover deteriorated the environment. It made sense to divest them. But trade, another aspect of the global economy that had come under scrutiny, did fit within the company's goals. In fact, it was core to it. So Mærsk chose to defend trade and expand its efforts to connect the world.

---

[15]Interview with Jim Snabe by Peter Vanham, August 2019.

To ensure that goal did not clash with care for the environment, Mærsk set aggressive goals on trade emissions: it aimed to "to decarbonize its own operations, and decouple growth in its business from CO_2 emissions," and it committed to net-zero emissions by 2050. From a 2008 baseline, it achieved 41 percent like-for-like reduction in transportation by 2018, and more aggressive goals followed. "It's not our *core* business," Snabe said, "but it is a *good* business. When we save 41% of CO_2 emissions, we save an equal amount of fuel. That's not a bad business. We earn more money because we do that."

To ensure that its trade didn't just benefit the happy few multinational companies but the livelihoods of real people around the world, Mærsk also added a number of targets on which customers it would help: it wanted to have "small and medium-sized customers account for 10% of our total revenue and 30% of our revenue from e-commerce logistics by 2025" and "help partners build capacity of 100,000 small and medium-sized enterprises, including women-operated businesses, to engage in cross-border trade by 2025."[16] In setting these goals, Mærsk explicitly endorsed the viewpoint that being a stakeholder company could be about making money, not about spending it. Would it be proven right?

The transformation of Mærsk, like that of many other companies, is still a work in progress, with many of its goals not fully achieved. By doing an exercise on purpose, by asking how it could contribute to the Sustainable Development Goals, and by committing to goals toward all its stakeholders, the company did dramatically change direction. Its employees found a new reason to "get out of bed in the morning" as Snabe said, and investors and regulators had a reason to be enthusiastic and appreciative of Mærsk in the long run, rather than to want to divest it from their portfolio or curtail it. Mærsk had acted in good faith, to bring its values to life.

■ ■ ■

Marc Benioff's to-do list for becoming a stakeholder company were very different to those of Mærsk. The Salesforce founder had built a business of the future. Technology companies brought innovations that made people's lives better and products cheaper. These companies did not adversely affect the climate like heavy industries of old, and they gave their well-paid employees some of the best perks around. At least that had become the dominant—and rosy—view.

---

[16]A.P. Moller – Mærsk, Sustainability Report 2018, February 2019, pp.18–19.

As a fourth generation San Franciscan, Benioff was convinced the sector in which he had grown up was creating problems of its own. Most fundamentally, he believed, Big Tech lacked the core values so crucial to an earlier generation of businesses such as Mærsk in Europe, or earlier entrepreneurs in the Bay Area like his father, who ran a clothing store chain called Stuart's. For companies like these, trust, reputation, and reliability were hardly marketing buzzwords. They were central to the functioning of their business.

For a new generation of tech companies, which were a product of the Fourth Industrial Revolution, the mantras were "move fast and break things"[17] and "ask for forgiveness, rather than permission."[18] Traditional values seemed pointless and outdated, when in the new world of business everything was malleable, mutable, and re-makeable.

As a business leader with roots in both his city and his industry, Benioff realized this was a problem, since from a company's values, everything else followed. Yet only a handful of other innovators and investors shared his view. For most entrepreneurs, the fact that they were creating entirely new industries and breaking conventional business practices to great success and acclaim gave them the confidence to reinterpret concepts such as corporate responsibility, governance, and the building of trust as well.

Benioff realized too that there was a problem with competition in Silicon Valley. When the Internet emerged, many entrepreneurs including himself had been given a chance to create new companies and compete for clients and market share. In recent years, markets had become concentrated in the hands of just a handful of Big Tech firms. Creation of new companies had fallen to an all-time low, and some start-ups responded to the lack of opportunities by simply wanting to get bought by one of the dominant firms. That stifled not just competition but innovation, and it created a mono-culture harmful to all kinds of fresh and diverse perspectives.

For Big Tech firms, however, acting as oligopolist or even monopolist was not just not a problem but something to strive for. Peter Thiel, co-founder of PayPal and Palantir, and an early outsider investor in Facebook, made that case powerfully in a 2014 editorial. *Wall Street Journal* editors headlined it: "Competition Is for Losers."[19] Of Google, he wrote:

---

[17] "Facebook Strategy Revealed: Move Fast And Break Things!", Henry Blodget, Business Insider, March 2010, https://www.businessinsider.com/henry-blodget-innovation-highlights-2010-2?r=US&IR=T

[18] "Want to Succeed in Life? Ask for Forgiveness, Not Permission", Bill Murphy, Inc. January 2016, https://www.inc.com/bill-murphy-jr/9-words-to-live-by-its-always-better-to-beg-forgiveness-than-ask-permission.html

[19] "Competition Is for Losers," Peter Thiel, *Wall Street Journal*, September 2014, https://www.wsj.com/articles/peter-thiel-competition-is-for-losers-1410535536.

A monopoly like Google is different. Since it doesn't have to worry about competing with anyone, it has wider latitude to care about its workers, its products and its impact on the wider world. Google's motto—"Don't be evil"—is in part a branding ploy, but it is also characteristic of a kind of business that is successful enough to take ethics seriously without jeopardizing its own existence.

In business, money is either an important thing or it is everything. Monopolists can afford to think about things other than making money; non-monopolists can't. In perfect competition, a business is so focused on today's margins that it can't possibly plan for a long-term future. Only one thing can allow a business to transcend the daily brute struggle for survival: monopoly profits.

Thiel's view was a provocative restatement of Friedman: only monopolies could pay for good corporate behavior. He teasingly challenged the belief among tech entrepreneurs that, because of their idealism and success, their technologies and products would almost automatically make the world a better place, and they must therefore be left to their own devices. But it was also a consequence of the Milton Friedman doctrine on competition. It held that market concentration and monopolies in themselves were not bad; only their likely effect in increasing consumer prices. This view on competition had become ingrained not just in the psyche of Friedman's supporters but in the antitrust agenda of the US government and in the practices passed down at leading business schools. Since Silicon Valley mostly offered its products free to consumers, surely there was no problem?

For people living in other parts of the world, the economic perspectives of Silicon Valley entrepreneurs always sounded strange. In Europe, regulators held the belief that monopolistic markets were problematic not just when there is an effect on consumer prices but also when there are other abuses of market power by the monopolist. "Requiring that buyers purchase all units of a particular product only from the dominant company" (exclusive purchasing), "setting prices at a loss-making level" (predation), or "refusing to supply input indispensable for competition in an ancillary market"[20] were problematic too. Applying those kinds of definitions even led to antitrust fines for so-called Big Tech companies such as Microsoft and Google and ongoing investigations into Apple and Amazon.[21]

---

[20] "Antitrust Procedures in Abuse of Dominance," European Commission, August 2013, https://ec.europa.eu/competition/antitrust/procedures_102_en.html.

[21] "If You Want to Know What a US Tech Crackdown May Look Like, Check Out What Europe Did," Elizabeth Schulze, CNBC, June 2019, https://www.cnbc.com/2019/06/07/how-google-facebook-amazon-and-apple-faced-eu-tech-antitrust-rules.html.

Lastly, Benioff's billions did not insulate him from what he saw as a glaringly obvious problem—growing inequality. While he and his fellow founders, investors, and employees were doing extremely well for themselves, some less well-off San Franciscans were so deprived of opportunities and income they literally started "throwing rocks at the Google bus," the private transport service that shuttled technology workers from their homes in San Francisco to the Google campus and back. Some observers, such as writer Douglas Rushkoff, who wrote *Throwing Rocks at the Google Bus: How Growth Became the Enemy of Prosperity*, realized it was just one of many signs that Big Tech's effect was to widen the divides between haves and have-nots and that if left unchecked, the situation would worsen. Others simply saw right past the issue. Even as homelessness in one of wealthiest cities in America was getting out of hand, there was no realization by most entrepreneurs that they could or should do anything about it. By 2019, San Francisco county had over 8,000 homeless people, up 17 percent from two years earlier,[22] and a far cry from the city's 2004 ambition to end homelessness in a decade.[23] This was the kind of civic slight that businesspeople like Benioff's father might have tackled head on. But when calls were made for the city's tech community to chip in, most responded with silence. It was especially egregious, given the fact that some large tech companies, including in Silicon Valley, had for years paid very little in taxes, either because of the expansion path they were on, which made them run losses instead of profits, or because of global tax optimization schemes, where profits were shuffled between subsidiary companies to game different tax regimes.

Benioff responded on all fronts. Trust in the sector was something that could only be regained in the long run, he realized. There were short-term steps he could take to create good faith. He advocated for causes he felt were good for society at large, even if they weren't necessarily good for his own standing in the industry. That, he felt, would help show he could be trusted to think of the wider implications of his company's leadership beyond just profit and growth. He pointed to the adverse if unintended consequences of new technologies, writing that "technology is no

---

[22]"Why San Francisco's Homeless Population Keeps Increasing," Associated Press, May 2019, https://www.marketwatch.com/story/the-homeless-population-in-san-francisco-is-skyrocketing-2019-05-17.

[23]"A Decade of Homelessness: Thousands in S.F. Remain in Crisis," Heather Knight, *San Francisco Chronicle*, 2014, https://www.sfchronicle.com/archive/item/A-decade-of-home-lessness-Thousands-in-S-F-30431.php.

panacea."[24] New technology had brought new pressures and dangers, he argued, and with them, new moral conundrums. And he reminded his peers that focusing on gaining trust was absolutely crucial, even if it meant lower profits in the short run. "Trust has to be your highest value in your company," he said in Davos, "and if it's not, something bad is going to happen."

In 2016, Benioff took his advocacy a step further. He started calling on European Commission antitrust chief Margarethe Vestager and other regulators to consider breaking up Big Tech companies. He believed that several among them were out to stifle competition and lock in customers, rather than creating innovation. "We've seen that companies are acquiring companies to potentially create proprietary data streams to create barriers of competition," he said,[25] "so if the US government isn't going to look at that then another government will have to." He repeated similar calls in the years following. Marc homed in on the belief that many companies were misusing data and violating privacy standards, as regulators had "fallen asleep at the wheel." It came as no surprise, then, that he used the Davos platform in 2019 to call for regulation. "When the CEOs won't take responsibility," he said, "then I think you have no choice but for the government to come in."[26]

Such calls could still be understood from the competitive landscape in the tech sector. There were possibly negative consequences for Salesforce too, if companies such as Microsoft or Facebook could buy companies such as LinkedIn or WhatsApp. But over time, Benioff's outspoken stance did inspire others to take similar steps. Fellow Big Tech leaders, such as Tim Cook of Apple, started calling for regulation of their sector, in areas where they felt they were ill-equipped to make decisions on their own. Even if subtly aimed at other competitors, it showed that technology companies had started to reflect on the societal consequences of their actions.

"Technology has the potential to keep changing the world for the better," Apple's Tim Cook wrote ahead of Davos in 2019,[27] "but it will never achieve that potential without the full faith and confidence of the

---

[24] *Trailblazer*, Marc Benioff, October 2019, pp. 12–13.

[25] "Marc Benioff Says Companies Buy Each Other for the Data, and the Government Isn't Doing Anything about It," April Glaser, Recode., November 2016, https://www.vox.com/2016/11/15/13631938/benioff-salesforce-data-government-federal-trade-commission-ftc-linkedin-microsoft.

[26] *Trailblazer*, Marc Benioff, October 2019, pp. 12–13.

[27] "You Deserve Privacy Online. Here's How You Could Actually Get It," Tim Cook, *TIME Magazine*, January 2019, https://time.com/collection/davos-2019/5502591/tim-cook-data-privacy/.

people who use it." He laid out four principles that he believed should guide legislation in the United States, which lacked rules similar to the EU's General Data Protection Regulation: minimum personal data use, the "right to know" who uses your data, the "right to access" your data, and the "right to data security," "without which trust is impossible."

In 2020 Facebook's Mark Zuckerberg joined the chorus to ask for regulation. He suggested the European Commission look at implementing tighter rules on political advertising, the portability of user data, and the oversight over tech companies like his, so regulation could "hold companies accountable when they make mistakes."[28] But importantly, he also supported new rules on taxation: "Tech companies should serve society," he wrote. "That includes at the corporate level, so we support the OECD's efforts to create fair global tax rules for the Internet ... good regulation may hurt Facebook's business in the near term but it will be better for everyone, including us, over the long term."

It is easy to be critical of such proposals, and it is not too hard to see how they are also part of a global competitive struggle. They are significant nonetheless, as they mark a new stage in the maturity of the tech sector dominating the Fourth Industrial Revolution and are a step toward a better regulation of it, too.

Ultimately, it is actions, rather than words, that make the difference in becoming a stakeholder company. For Benioff, this implied actions on at least two fronts. First, realizing that Silicon Valley, including his company, had a diversity problem, Benioff brought in an outside advisory firm to review the company's salaries and HR practices. It revealed a gender pay gap at Salesforce and led management to adjust the contracts of those paid less for similar work. And second, as he was confronted with the reality of homelessness in San Francisco, the city that he and his family had grown up in, Benioff decided to speak out in favor of a tax on large tech companies such as his own, which could help finance a structural solution for the homeless in the city. Proposition C, as the initiative was called, proposed a 0.5 percent tax on corporate revenue above $50 million[29] for companies headquartered in the city. Other tech CEOs who would be affected spoke out against the initiative. For Benioff, it was a way of giving back to the community he and his company called

[28]"Big Tech Needs More Regulation," Mark Zuckerberg, *Financial Times*, February 2020, https://www.ft.com/content/602ec7ec-4f18-11ea-95a0-43d18ec715f5.

[29]"Benioff Comes Out Strong for Homeless Initiative, although Salesforce Would Pay Big," Kevin Fagan, *San Francisco Chronicle*, October 2018, https://www.sfchronicle.com/bayarea/article/Benioff-comes-out-strong-for-homeless-initiative-13291392.php.

home. In a *New York Times* editorial,[30] he left no doubt as to the reason for his support. The time for stakeholder capitalism, he said, had come:

> Proposition C is a referendum on the role of business in our communities and, by extension, our country. The business of business is no longer merely business. Our obligation is not just to increase profits for shareholders. We must also hold ourselves accountable to a broader set of stakeholders: to our customers, our employees, the environment and the communities in which we work and live. It's time for the wealthiest businesses and business owners to step up and give back to the most vulnerable among us.

It is the actions that back up the words of leaders like Benioff and Snabe, and the companies they head, which serve as a reminder of the broader responsibility of business in the age of the Fourth Industrial Revolution. Corporations in this era should expand their horizon beyond the profit and loss statement, and the trailblazers are already doing so.

For those who are willing to choose this route, the aspects of business to focus on look a lot like those Snabe, Benioff, and others already identified:

- accepting a level playing field in competition;
- striving for improvements in working conditions and employee well-being;
- supporting the communities in which the company is active;
- looking after the environment and the long-term sustainability of their business;
- and paying one's fair share of taxes.

These are actions that are stipulated in the 2020 Davos Manifesto and the general notion of acting in the interest of all stakeholders, as our model prescribes. If every company individually commits to these goals and addresses the underlying issues, much of the excesses of shareholder capitalism will be rooted out automatically. The examples of Mærsk and Salesforce are a good proof of that assertion.

Does that mean we should leave corporate reform to the goodwill of executive leadership teams alone? No. As we know, management often happens by numbers, and this stakeholder responsibility must also be measured. As we already briefly mentioned in the previous chapter,

---

[30]"The Social Responsibility of Business," Marc Benioff, *The New York Times*, October 2018, https://www.nytimes.com/2018/10/24/opinion/business-social-responsibility-proposition-c.html.

recently a big step forward has been made on this front. The World Economic Forum's International Business Council, led by Bank of America CEO Brian Moynihan,[31] late last year presented the "Stakeholder Capitalism Metrics." They measure companies' progress toward environmental, social, and governance (ESG) goals in numbers and thereby allow them to optimize for more than just profits. More specifically:[32]

- The **Principles of governance** pillar includes metrics and disclosures on the company's stated purpose, board composition (relevant experience, gender, membership of underrepresented groups, stakeholder representation), stakeholder engagement (which topics that are material to stakeholders were identified? How were they discussed with stakeholders?), anti-corruption efforts, mechanisms to report on unethical and unlawful behavior, and risks and opportunities that affect the business processes;
- The **Planet** pillar includes metrics on climate change, such as all relevant greenhouse gas emissions (and plans to get them in line with Paris targets), land use and ecological sensitivity of business activities, and water use and withdrawal in water-stressed areas;
- The **People** pillar includes metrics on diversity and inclusion, pay equality (for each relevant group: women vs. men, minor vs. major ethnic groups, etc.), wage level (ratio of CEO compensation to median compensation, ratio of entry level wage to mandated minimum wage), and risk for incidents of child, forced of compulsory labor, health and safety (number of accidents, and explanation on how to avoid them), and training provided; and
- The **Prosperity** pillar includes metrics on employee turnover and hires, the economic contribution a company makes (positively, in form of wages of community investments, or negatively, in government aid received), financial investments and R&D expenditures, and total taxes paid (including corporate income taxes, VAT and sales taxes, property taxes, employer-paid payroll taxes, and others).

Reporting on these metrics will allow executives and boards to understand where they might need to change their approach, and it

---

[31]"We can now measure the progress of stakeholder capitalism. Here's how", Brian T. Moynihan, World Economic Forum, October 2020, https://www.weforum.org/agenda/2020/10/measure-progress-stakeholder-capitalism-brian-moynihan/

[32]Measuring Stakeholder Capitalism, White Paper, World Economic Forum, September 2020, http://www3.weforum.org/docs/WEF_IBC_Measuring_Stakeholder_Capitalism_Report_2020.pdf

will allow other stakeholders (e.g., employees, clients, supplier, investors, NGOs, and governments) to judge the performance of stakeholder-oriented companies. A widespread adoption of these Stakeholder Capitalism Metrics is realistic and could happen as soon as 2022. That is because there is a broad support for them: pioneers such as Bank of America, the Dutch firms DSM and Philips, and the companies described above, such as Mærsk and Salesforce, support them. During the consultation process on the metrics, more than two-thirds of the 140 International Business Council members—including many of the largest companies in the world—supported them too. And all major accounting firms, the so-called Big Four (Deloitte, EY, KPMG, and PwC) even helped develop the metrics. They are committed to helping the metrics become a global standard. In this way, the Stakeholder Capitalism Metrics are a major step in turning the idea of stakeholder capitalism into a practical reality.

This does not mean that companies will be put in a straitjacket or that they should get a free pass once they sign up for ESG measurement. But it can help companies who, unlike some of those mentioned in this chapter, have yet to define what being a stakeholder company means to them. It is an ever-more important task, because investors are losing their patience with companies that optimize only short-term profits. Consider in this regard Larry Fink, the founder and chief executive of BlackRock, an investment firm that managed more than $6 trillion,[33] making it the largest private asset manager in the world, and as such a major shareholder—and a voice to be reckoned with—in many of the world's biggest publicly listed companies.

A few years ago, Fink and some of his fellow investment managers started to sound the alarm on companies that were only managed with short-term financial profits in mind, rather than broader stakeholder objectives. Such a short-termist approach could do considerable harm to society, the planet, and ultimately to the investors and the companies themselves. It needed to change. That was the gist of the message Fink delivered in 2018, in his annual letter to CEOs of companies he invested in. "Society is demanding that companies, both public and private, serve a social purpose," Fink wrote in his letter. "To prosper over time, every company must not only deliver financial performance, but also show how it makes a positive contribution to society."

---

[33] "BlackRock's Message: Contribute to Society, or Risk Losing Our Support," Andrew Ross Sorkin, *New York Times*, January 2018, https://www.nytimes.com/2018/01/15/business/dealbook/blackrock-laurence-fink-letter.html.

In the profit-oriented culture of Wall Street, Fink's message was surprising to shareholders and observers alike. "It may be a watershed moment," wrote the *New York Times* columnist Andrew Ross Sorkin, "one that raises all sorts of questions about the very nature of capitalism."[34,35] But for others, it came not a moment too soon. As the *Financial Times*'s Gillian Tett noted in one of her columns,[36] even as BlackRock was championing ESG ideas in its annual letters, "environmental groups complain[ed] that the asset manager continue[d] to pour money into sectors such as fossil fuels through its mainstream investment products."

That back and forth between the asset manager (urging its stakeholders to take more action on ESG issues), and climate activists (criticizing BlackRock that it did not do enough), persisted in the months and years after Fink's landmark letter. But it did seem to lead to better outcomes over time. In 2019, Majority Action, an advocacy organization, calculated that as a shareholder, BlackRock voted in favor of corporate climate resolutions only 12 percent of the times.[37] In response, Fink's message in his 2020 letter was that BlackRock would "put sustainability at the heart of its investment process."[38] When again accused of "climate hypocrisy" shortly afterwards, BlackRock responded by "punishing more than 50 companies over their lack of progress on tackling global warming,"[39] and warned another 191 companies in which it held shares that they "risk voting action in 2021 if they do not make substantial progress."

Fink also stood by his ESG commitments when he talked to us for this book. It is not short-term profits that should matter, he said, but the long-term viability of the firm. And with such a longer term in mind, "a stakeholder capitalistic model creates greater profits," he said: "When a company is better connected in the society where they work, society

---

[34] Ibidem.

[35] One thing Fink's letter certainly did was take the wind out of the sails of those who believed that companies were legally bound to chase short-term profits, because of their "fiduciary duty" to shareholders. Here was one major shareholder who said that he saw the fiduciary duty rather in the long term, not on a quarter-by-quarter basis.

[36] "The Battle over Green Investment Is Hotting Up," Gillian Tett, *Financial Times*, December 2019, https://www.ft.com/content/bacefd80-175e-11ea-9ee4-11f260415385.

[37] "BlackRock Seeks to Regain Lost Ground in Climate Fight," Attracta Mooney and Owen Walker, *Financial Times*, January 2020, https://www.ft.com/content/36282d86-36e4-11ea-a6d3-9a26f8c3cba4.

[38] "BlackRock Accused of Climate Change Hypocrisy," Attracta Mooney, *Financial Times*, May 2020, https://www.ft.com/content/0e489444-2783-4f6e-a006-aa8126d2ff46.

[39] "BlackRock Punishes 53 Companies over Climate Inaction," Attracta Mooney, *Financial Times*, July 2020, https://www.ft.com/content/8809032d-47a1-47c3-ae88-ef3c182134c0.

wants to do more with that company."[40] The stakeholder model is better suited even from a capitalist perspective, Fink said, because "companies that are just focusing on shareholder capitalism are not fast enough." They don't see the macro-trends that will affect them in the long run, such as the changing preferences and concerns of new generations. They are blinded by the pursuit of profits and growth, without understanding their underlying drivers. And that may ultimately be the cause for their demise. Consider in this regard and in closing, the story of Enron.

■ ■ ■

Enron is an excellent example of the dangers of being singularly oriented on shareholders. The Texas-based conglomerate had started in the mid-1980s as a merger of two energy companies, Houston Natural Gas and InterNorth, two firms with origins in the exploration, production, and distribution of fossil fuels such as natural gas.[41] A review of the company's purpose along the stakeholder mindset may have led to insights on how the companies could continue to play a role in states like Texas and Omaha, where they had a major footprint in terms of personnel and GDP. It may have led to a reorientation, over time, toward renewable energy production in those states, or a reinvention as an R&D firm, specialized in energy efficiency and improving the lives of the people it supplied energy to. As we know, however, that is not what happened.

Surfing on the M&A and deregulation waves of the 1980s and 1990s, the company's new leadership instead diversified into activities with better short-term returns. It got into short-term energy trading, acting more as a financial services firm than as an energy company. It created special-purpose companies for bookkeeping reasons, hiding costs, and boosting profits. The moment it had the opportunity to do so legally, it hiked prices in the energy supply in states it controlled, leading to astronomic profits for the company but disastrous outcomes for consumers. Rather than having a long-term orientation toward its stakeholders, Enron's management thought only to inflate revenue and profits in the short run. For a number of years, it didn't only work well, it worked fantastically. Enron became a sprawling conglomerate, with revenues and profits making anyone jealous. And except to insiders, it wasn't yet clear that its success was mostly built on deception and corruption. As a consequence, Enron was named the most innovative Fortune 500 company

---

[40] Interview with Larry Fink, by Peter Vanham, November 2019.

[41] For a brief summary of the rise and fall of Enron, see: "Enron scandal", Peter Bondarenko, Encyclopedia Brittanica, February 2016, https://www.britannica.com/event/Enron-scandal.

several times. And the company attracted investors and employees eager to be part of their apparent success.

But the Enron story turned out to be a lie. Rather than becoming ever-more profitable, the company management became ever-better at hiding costs, reporting false revenues, and misleading both investors and government overseers. When the truth came out in 2001, the company had no option but to declare bankruptcy. The smoke and mirrors they had put up for 15 years turned out to be an empty box. Several of the company's top managers, including its CEO and CFO, were convicted of fraud.[42] Their singular focus on generating profits and improving shareholder value had ultimately led to the opposite. Investors were defrauded, and the company was worth only a fraction of its peak valuation.

There is however a moral to the Enron story. When the Chapter 11 bankruptcy procedure was completed, it turned out there was still a valuable part to its business left: InterNorth, one of the two original natural gas companies that had formed Enron. Specifically, InterNorth's Northern Natural Gas division, which had operated since the early 1930s and was still active in Omaha, Nebraska, proved to be very good at what it was originally intended for: supplying energy to the people of the region.

It wasn't too hard to find a buyer for it. Warren Buffet, the billionaire investor who had lived his whole life in Omaha, bought what was left of the division from its original purchaser[43] and turned it into a successful division of his own Berkshire Hathaway Energy. That company is still active today. And as reasons for its success, it points to a much more stakeholder-oriented mission. Northern Natural Gas, it says, "doesn't just deliver natural gas, they deliver solutions, tools and resources that improve the lives of their customers."[44] It is a lesson well worth remembering.

■ ■ ■

Now that we've seen what stakeholder companies and corporate leadership looks like, let us turn to the other stakeholder that play a crucial role in our economy and society.

[42]"See what happened to key players in Enron scandal", The Houston Chronicle, August 2018, https://www.houstonchronicle.com/business/article/Jeffrey-Skillings-release-to-halfway-house-13196786.php

[43]"Enron Opens Up Bidding On 12 of Its Major Assets", Kathryn Kranhold, The Wall Street Journal, August 2002, https://www.wsj.com/articles/SB1030487405721514155

[44]"A Natural Gas Transportation Leader", Northern Natural Gas, Berkshire Hathaway Energy, https://www.brkenergy.com/our-businesses/northern-natural-gas

10

Communities

New Zealand during the COVID-19 Crisis

In the early weeks of March 2020, New Zealand's Prime Minister Jacinda Ardern and her cabinet ministers faced a major dilemma. They could either implement a strict lockdown of the country to try and stop the spread of the novel coronavirus or keep the economy open in an effort to avoid a steep recession. At the outset, it seemed like a classic no-win situation; there would be losses to either New Zealand lives or livelihoods—probably both. As a remote island nation with a strong health care system, New Zealand did have a better chance than most to withstand the virus without draconian measures. But at the same time, the country was alarmed by the situation in countries such as Italy and Iran, where the uncontrolled spread of the virus had led to dramatic consequences for both public health and the economy. Which policy approach would lead to the lesser of two evils for New Zealand?

One advantage Ardern and her government had was that they could draw on some early lessons from elsewhere. The virus had first been observed in Wuhan, China, in late 2019. Once it started to spread in other parts of China, by early 2020, it quickly became clear this was an extremely contagious and possibly very deadly virus. By February, the novel coronavirus had embarked on an exponential international growth path. The rest of the world was about to realize just how severe the pandemic would turn out to be. As COVID-19 spread, first in Asian countries such as Thailand, Japan, and South Korea and then in Europe, the Middle East, and Australia, the worries in the Pacific island nation grew, and so did its government's determination to learn from others' mistakes.

Then, the virus arrived in New Zealand. On February 28, the first positive case was recorded in the country: a traveller returning from Iran. In the days following, more cases followed, including the first locally transmitted one. And by mid-March, dozens of new cases were reported each day. As the cabinet and the country's senior health experts met, the opinions were mixed. Some experts backed a lighter approach, along the lines of what Sweden ended up doing, Alice Klein reported in the *New Scientist*.[1] (In the Scandinavian country, there were no mandatory closures of shops, schools, and workplaces, but tens of thousands of people ended up catching the virus, and several thousand died). Others advocated a much more aggressive approach, with strict lockdowns, closures of nearly all economic activities, and travel bans. Such an approach, they hoped, would help flatten[2] the curve, but it wasn't uncontested. Michael Baker, an epidemiologist who backed the tougher stance, said that some of his colleagues thought his plan was too radical. "Some likened it to using a sledgehammer to kill a flea," he said.[3]

On March 21, Prime Minister Ardern made her government's decision public. They went with the "sledgehammer" plan advocated by Baker and others. Almost overnight, New Zealand's public life would come to a standstill. Every citizen would have to stay at home. Schools would be closed. All non-essential shops would be shut. The economy would

---

[1]"Why New Zealand Decided to Go for Full Elimination of the Coronavirus," Alice Klein, *New Scientist*, June 2020, https://www.newscientist.com/article/2246858-why-new-zealand-decided-to-go-for-full-elimination-of-the-coronavirus/#ixzz6T1rYuK5U.

[2]"New Zealand Isn't Just Flattening the Curve. It's Squashing It," Anna Fifield, *The Washington Post*, April 2020, https://www.washingtonpost.com/world/asia_pacific/new-zealand-isnt-just-flattening-the-curve-its-squashing-it/2020/04/07/6cab3a4a-7822-11ea-a311-ad-b1344719a9_story.html.

[3]"Why New Zealand Decided to Go for Full Elimination of the Coronavirus," Alice Klein, *New Scientist*, June 2020, https://www.newscientist.com/article/2246858-why-new-zealand-decided-to-go-for-full-elimination-of-the-coronavirus/#ixzz6T1rYuK5U.

greatly suffer. But in a speech announcing the government's actions, given a few days after the first lockdowns went into effect, Ardern didn't linger on the economic fallout. Instead, she pointed to what she believed mattered much more: "Without the measures I have just announced, up to tens of thousands of New Zealanders could die from COVID-19," she said on national television.[4] "Everything you will all give up for the next few weeks, all of the lost contact with others, all of the isolation, and difficult time entertaining children—it will literally save lives. Thousands of lives." In her opinion, she said, "the worst-case scenario is simply intolerable. It would represent the greatest loss of New Zealanders' lives in our country's history. I will not take that chance."

It was a bold move for Ardern, who just over two years earlier had become the world's youngest female leader at age 37.[5] But she did receive immediate support. Many influential leaders in the country backed the government's plan from the start, including Stephen Tindall, the founder of New Zealand's largest retailer.[6] "If we didn't shut down quickly enough, the pain was going to go on for a very long time," he told the *Washington Post* in a phone interview in early April. The businessman thought a holistic perspective was the right one, rather than one that was focused too much on the short-term or the narrow effect on his business. And compliance among the population was high too, perhaps in part thanks to the empathetic approach of their prime minister. "Be kind," she asked the population before asking her finance minister and police commissioner speak about the economic consequences and enforcement. "What we need from you, is support one another. Go home tonight and check in on your neighbours. Start a phone tree with your street. Plan how you'll keep in touch with one another. We will get through this together, but only if we stick together. Be strong and be kind."

[4] PM Jacinda Ardern's full lockdown speech, Newsroom, March 2020, https://www.newsroom.co.nz/2020/03/23/1096999/pm-jacinda-arderns-full-lockdown-speech.

[5] "The World's Youngest Female Leader Takes Over in New Zealand," *The Economist*, October 2017, https://www.economist.com/asia/2017/10/26/the-worlds-youngest-female-leader-takes-over-in-new-zealand.

[6] "New Zealand Isn't Just Flattening the Curve. It's Squashing It," Anna Fifield, *The Washington Post*, April 2020, https://www.washingtonpost.com/world/asia_pacific/new-zealand-isnt-just-flattening-the-curve-its-squashing-it/2020/04/07/6cab3a4a-7822-11ea-a311-adb1344719a9_story.html.

The swift reaction by Ardern, her government, and the people of New Zealand paid off. Within a few short weeks, new infections in the country started dropping. In May, with new recorded cases falling to less than five a day, a first easing of the lockdown measures was possible. Later that month, local transmission stopped completely. Seeing no new cases, the country ended all its internal lockdown measures in June, and by July, no new COVID-19 infection had been recorded for over two months (though some repatriated New Zealanders did test positive in quarantine). In all, the "first wave" of the COVID-19 crisis cost the lives of less than 25 New Zealanders (in a population of almost 5 million), and public life and economic activity returned to quasi normal in barely three months. The economy, of course, did suffer, with New Zealand recording its biggest quarterly drop in GDP since 1991 in the quarter ending March 2020, contracting by 1.6 percent,[7] according to analyses from Murat Ungor, an economist at Otago University. And by October 2020, the IMF estimated an economic contraction of over 6 percent for the entire year,[8] partially caused by the immediate effects of the early lockdown and partially by the overall decline in sectors such as tourism.

But for a country and a leader that had stopped fetishizing GDP growth, the short-term economic costs were a price they were willing to pay. It would pay back immediately in terms of human cost and a second time in the long run because of a faster-than-usual return to normal in economic life, it was hoped. The first already panned out; the second will become clear in a few quarters.

The choice was perhaps made easier also because it could more easily be measured in other metrics. Just over a year earlier, New Zealand had created a Living Standards Framework (LSF) dashboard with broad well-being indicators, to add to the existing measurements of GDP growth. The dashboard was meant to provide "policy advice on cross-government well-being priorities," and it was updated regularly. Looking at the COVID crisis with this broader mindset, the chosen

---

[7]"Coronavirus: New Zealand Records Biggest GDP Quarterly Fall in 29 years - Top Kiwi Economist, Newshub, July 2020, https://www.newshub.co.nz/home/money/2020/07/coronavirus-new-zealand-records-biggest-gdp-quarterly-fall-in-29-years-top-kiwi-economist.html.

[8]"World Economic Outlook," International Monetary Fund, October 2020, Chapter 1, p. 56, https://www.imf.org/en/Publications/WEO/Issues/2020/09/30/world-economic-outlook-october-2020.

Kiwi approach made a lot of sense. Yes, GDP growth may suffer in the short run, but health, safety and security, and social connections, all metrics measured in the LSF dashboard, would benefit. The LSF dashboard was not an end to itself but just one of various tools that reflected the different approach New Zealand had taken to governing. It is also an approach that fits with the principles and beliefs behind stakeholder capitalism: a society will do well if everyone does well; progress is about more than profits or GDP, everyone's contribution to society and the economy need to be valued, and both effective leadership at the top and empowerment of action at the base of society matter.

This all-encompassing, stakeholder approach pays off both in the long term and the short term, both for companies and for workers, and both in good times and in bad times. After New Zealand had been COVID-free for months, local researchers talked about why they thought the country had been so successful: "We came together as a country, in part because we believed in our political and health experts to deliver and they did," Dr Jagadish Thaker, a senior lecturer at the School of Communication, Journalism and Marketing at Massey University, told *The Guardian*[9] in July 2020. And, they also found, "almost all New Zealanders correctly understand important facts about the coronavirus," and acted accordingly, adopting frequent handwashing behaviors, and practicing social distancing.[10] It proved to be a winning strategy in the marathon that is the fight against COVID-19. When the virus eventually did reappear in August 2020, with a worker and family cluster centered around a meat-importing factory, New Zealand was ready to begin its battle all over again. With the same determination, it once again revived Prime Minister Ardern's "go hard and go early" approach, as the *New York Times* summarized it[11] and beat back a second wave in a matter of a few short weeks. Approving of her government's approach, voters in October 2020 gave Ardern a historic election victory in a COVID-free New Zealand.

■ ■ ■

[9]"New Zealand Beat Covid-19 by Trusting Leaders and Following Advice—Study," Eleanor Ainge Roy, *The Guardian*, July 2020, https://www.theguardian.com/world/2020/jul/24/new-zealand-beat-covid-19-by-trusting-leaders-and-following-advice-study.

[10]Ibidem.

[11]"New Zealand Beat the Virus Once. Can It Do It Again?" *The New York Times*, August 2020, https://www.nytimes.com/2020/08/13/world/asia/new-zealand-coronavirus-lockdown-elimination.html.

The case of New Zealand fits in a bigger picture. Around the world, the COVID crisis laid bare which countries were prepared to act against a pandemic outbreak and which ones were not. Some observers pointed out to a remarkable commonality among those governments that responded well. Those with female leaders seemed to do better. And indeed, in June 2020, researchers Supriya Garikipati (University of Liverpool) and Uma Kambhampati (University of Reading) confirmed the finding statistically,[12] arguing that female-led countries, such as Germany, Denmark, Finland, Iceland, and indeed New Zealand, did better than most in responding to the pandemic. As for the reasons why, the researchers pointed to "proactive and coordinated policy responses" adopted by female leaders as well as some traits they may share, such as risk-aversion (leading them to lock down after fewer deaths) and empathy.[13] Other academics and journalists (anecdotally) alleged female leaders are generally more inclusive, welcoming to diverse viewpoints, and accepting of science.[14]

I also see another commonality: many of the leaders who responded well to this particular crisis, took an "all of society" approach. They looked out for, and included, all stakeholders. And that[15], as we claimed previously, is not only the best recipe for success in fighting a virus but also for leading a country, city, state, or community overall. Let us, therefore, look at what a stakeholder approach to governments looks like more in general.

The Key Tasks of National Governments

The question as to how national and local governments can best fulfill their duties in the modern era has been a difficult one to answer. As we have seen, many governments in recent years responded late and inadequately to technological progress, struggled to maintain solid tax bases

---

[12]"Leading the Fight Against the Pandemic: Does Gender 'Really' Matter?" Supriya Garikipati (University of Liverpool), Uma Kambhampati (University of Reading), June 2020 https://papers.ssrn.com/sol3/papers.cfm?abstract_id=3617953.

[13]"Do Countries with Female Leaders Truly Fare Better with Covid-19?" Alexandra Ossola, Quartz, July 2020, https://qz.com/1877836/do-countries-with-female-leaders-truly-fare-better-with-covid-19/.

[14]Ibidem.

[15]The World Health Organization calls this a "whole-of-government" or "whole-of-society" approach, see: https://www.who.int/global-coordination-mechanism/dialogues/glossary-whole-of-govt-multisectoral.pdf.

and to keep inequality under control, and had an increasingly hard time regulating the free market. How can they do better?

It certainly makes no sense to return to the economic ideologies of the 20th century. On the one hand, protectionism and autarky are not sustainable strategies. As many countries found out last century, those tools lead to increased prices, slower technological progress, and poorer and less prosperous societies. It is something many countries in the former Soviet Union found out, as well as others who pursued a closed economy. But at the same time, a laissez-faire, or hands-off, economic approach is not the right answer, either. Where that strategy has been applied, inequality often went through the roof, and popular and political sentiment turned against it. Many Latin American countries, including Argentina, Brazil, Bolivia, Mexico, and Venezuela, turned from neo-liberalist governments to "21st century socialism" at some point in the 2000s or 2010s, in part because of the economic inequality that resulted of relying too much on the market. The result of these pendulum swings was often disastrous, showing that neither the neoliberal ideology nor the socialist one works well in our current era.

For governments to be most effective, they should follow a more pragmatic path. At its simplest, a government's main role in the stakeholder model is to enable *equitable prosperity*. That means a government should enable any individual actor to maximize his or her *prosperity* but do so in a way that is *equitable* for both its people and the planet. It should do so in three primary ways. First, a government should value the contributions everyone makes to society, provide equal opportunities to all, and curb any excessive inequalities as they arise. Second, it should act as an arbiter and regulator for companies operating in the free market. And third, as a guardian of future generations, it should put a stop to activities that degrade the environment.

In its first task, ensuring equal opportunities and curbing excessive inequalities, I believe a government will be most effective when it focuses on three age-old societal needs: *education, health care,* and *housing.* And, in a world where people are increasingly dependent on their online activities as well, I might add that *digital connectivity* should be a fourth core pillar. From China to the United States, these domains matter to every person in society, and they often provide a government's greatest challenges.

Consider first the three initial ones, education, health care, and housing. In China, for example, Dean Bai Chong-En of the School of

Economics and Management of Tsinghua University[16] told us that "in terms of the observed inequality, these are the most important factors."[17] As the Chinese economy gradually opened starting in the late 1970s, he said, "Not everybody had the same opportunity. Some people had better access to resources than others, and that was neither helpful for inequality nor for economic growth." Urban residents, notably, had better access to health care, social services, and education. Rural health insurance, on the other hand, did not exist until 2003, and education has been historically tied to parents' *hukou* or residence permit, with good urban schools often being out of reach for those lacking an urban hukou. Even among urbanites, some citizens had preferential access to real estate, whereas others did not. Over time, as cities developed and so-called Tier I and Tier II cities skyrocketed, those initial inequalities widened, leading to systemic inequality and a lack of opportunities for many. (Until, Bai noted, around 2010, when the Gini coefficient of China peaked, the labor share of income GDP bottomed out, and the skill premium for educated workers started declining. These were all indicators that income inequality was at its highest level ever, despite improvements in the skills of workers.)

The story of unequal access to education, health care, and housing must sound familiar to an American ear as well. Most famously, racially inspired segregation and zoning policies meant that, until the second half of the 20th century, many American cities blocked African American residents from better schools, neighborhoods, and jobs. But the private sector too played a major role in this. The most known practice in this regard was the so-called redlining,[18] where banks used racist criteria to approve or deny bank loan requests in certain areas. A part of what drives the social justice movement today is that many of those systemic inequalities never really disappeared, despite the original Civil Rights Act and subsequent legislative changes. Nor is inequality in education, health care, and housing limited to race-based discrimination. Many of the best American colleges until today have so-called *legacy preferences*, giving preferred admission to children of parents who also studied at the institution or, in some cases, gave money to it. And while US governments for decades promoted

[16]Biography Bai Chong-En, Tsinghua University, People's Republic of China, http://crm.sem.tsinghua.edu.cn/psc/CRMPRD/EMPLOYEE/CRM/s/WEBLIB_SPE_ISCT.TZ_SETSPE_ISCRIPT.FieldFormula.IScript_SpecialPages?TZ_SPE_ID=251.

[17]Interview with Bai Chong-En by Peter Vanham, Beijing, September 2019.

[18]"Redlining," Encyclopedia Britannica, https://www.britannica.com/topic/redlining.

homeownership, opaque financial innovation with mortgage-backed securities and collateralized debt obligations led to a housing crisis in 2008, pushing millions of Americans out of their houses and out of their jobs. To this day, some people have not recovered financially from that crisis. Finally, some 28 million Americans, almost 10 percent of the total, did not have health insurance in 2018[19] (the last year for which data were available at the time of writing). And for those Americans who did have one, health care costs were often much higher than elsewhere, as the per capita cost of the US health system is the highest in the OECD, and many people are required to carry a significant part through co-pays and other out-of-pocket costs. It should come as no surprise that these longstanding inequalities have led to a dual public health crisis and a deep social and economic crisis in the US, as COVID-19 spread in 2020.

But digital connectivity matters an awful lot, too. Access to Internet in this era of the Fourth Industrial Revolution is a bit like having access to oil and the combustion engine in a previous era. Immediately after the Internet became publicly available, a "digital divide" emerged between demographic groups that had access to it and those that didn't. As more and more jobs and services started to depend on digital connectivity, this caused a major shift in economic fortunes, which continues to this day. Research[20] after research[21] showed how crucial reliable, ubiquitous Internet access was during the worst of the COVID pandemic, for instance. Those that had high-quality Internet access and connected devices could more easily tele-work and thus retain their jobs and incomes. Similarly, children who had access to the Internet could continue to attend school, while those who didn't were often left to their own devices. And those who didn't dare go to doctors and hospitals could get medical advice through tele-medicine. Countries that had a high degree of smartphone penetration, such as Singapore,

---

[19]"Key Facts about the Uninsured Population," Kaiser Family Foundation, December 2019, https://www.kff.org/uninsured/issue-brief/key-facts-about-the-uninsured-population/.

[20]"53% of Americans Say the Internet Has Been Essential During the COVID-19 Outbreak," Pew Research Center, April 2020, https://www.pewresearch.org/internet/2020/04/30/53-of-americans-say-the-internet-has-been-essential-during-the-covid-19-outbreak/.

[21]"59% of US Parents with Lower Incomes Say Their Child May Face Digital Obstacles in Schoolwork," Pew Research Center, September 2020, https://www.pewresearch.org/fact-tank/2020/09/10/59-of-u-s-parents-with-lower-incomes-say-their-child-may-face-digital-obstacles-in-schoolwork/.

could more easily introduce effective test and trace strategies involving blue tooth apps.[22]

Singapore as a Model of Stakeholder Government

As the two examples above show, it is hard for a government to get its core functions right. But some, such as the Nordic nations, New Zealand, or Singapore, do manage to do significantly better than others, and their model provides lessons for (much bigger) economies too.

The most remarkable blueprint, in fact, may come from Singapore, the peninsula of 5 million at the tip of Southeast Asia. As we saw in Chapter 6, the city-state was one of the Asian Tigers, which starting in the 1960s underwent an incredible technological and economic transformation. It is now the prime tech and trade hub of Asia. To get there, their efforts to provide high-quality education, health care, and housing to all its citizens, played a crucial role That may come as a surprise to those who think of Singapore as a collection of flashy skyscrapers, reserved for the happy few among the international jet set. As Bloomberg noted in a recent article, "In the movie *Crazy Rich Asians*, the main characters move between opulent mansions and colonial-era hotels in Singapore. But the reality is the vast majority of families [in Singapore] live in modestly sized apartments built by the government."[23]

At their core, the public housing built and maintained by Singapore's Housing Development Board (HDB) is not very different from the housing projects in American or European cities. They are no-frills, mass apartment buildings, reserved for specific groups of people. Yet the Singapore version stands apart for at least three reasons. First, the apartments were from the onset designed to encourage social and ethnic mixing through the Ethnic Integration Policy. There is a quota for each of Singapore's main ethnic groups (Chinese, Indian, and Malay). This has prevented different groups from isolating themselves, a phenomenon that often occurs in cities. Mixing populations in housing has ensured a

---

[22]"Is a Successful Contact Tracing App Possible? These Countries Think So," *MIT Technology Review*, August 2020, https://www.technologyreview.com/2020/08/10/1006174/covid-contract-tracing-app-germany-ireland-success/.

[23]"Why Singapore Has One of the Highest Home Ownership Rates," Adam Majendie, Bloomberg City Lab, July 2020, https://www.bloomberg.com/news/articles/2020-07-08/behind-the-design-of-singapore-s-low-cost-housing.

social harmony,[24] according to Senior Minister Tharman Shanmugarat-nam. "Once people of different ethnic groups live together, they are not just walking the corridors and taking the same elevator up and down," he said in a 2020 government interview.[25] "The kids go to the same kindergarten, the kids go to the same primary school, because all over the world young kids go to school very near to where they live, and they grow up together."

Second, journalist Adam Majendie noted that "while many governments have focused public housing programs on the poorest members of society—often allowing the austere concrete blocks to deteriorate into urban slums—Singapore recognized that these homes represented the biggest stake its citizens had in the prosperity of the country. The HDB not only maintained its buildings and grounds carefully, but it also periodically upgraded estates with new elevators, walkways and facelifts."[26] It is something that any visitor can see with his or her own eyes. During the time I spent in Singapore over the years, I spent quite a bit of time walking around some of HDB neighborhoods, which look and feel charming and offer pleasant walkways for pedestrians. Often, they were surrounded by gentrified coffee bars, fashion outlets, and bookstores. It made for a very different experience than we might have gotten from doing a tour of a similar housing project elsewhere.

Third and finally, apartments of HDB are available for long-term lease. It allows inhabitants to build up a source of wealth, while nevertheless keeping real estate–based inequality in check. That is because the sale of HDB apartments is most often structured as a 99-year lease. It gives the "owner" a long enough window to be able to live there until old age and eventually resell and get money from their investment. But since any resale comes with the caveat that it is only for however much years are left on the lease, prices of these government-built apartments don't skyrocket in the same way private apartments do in metropolis cities such as New York, London, Hong Kong, or indeed, Singapore itself. It explains why Singapore is one of the most expensive cities in the world for real estate (ranked second in the world for its private real

---

[24]"HDB's Ethnic Integration Policy: Why It Still Matters," Singapore Government, April 2020, https://www.gov.sg/article/hdbs-ethnic-integration-policy-why-it-still-matters.

[25]Ibidem.

[26]"Why Singapore Has One of the Highest Home Ownership Rates," Adam Majendie, Bloomberg City Lab, July 2020, https://www.bloomberg.com/news/articles/2020-07-08/behind-the-design-of-singapore-s-low-cost-housing.

estate market[27]) and also one of the more affordable ones (80 percent of its citizens lives in the HDB housing the government provides at more attractive rates).

In education too, Singapore's achievements stand out. Quite simply, *The Economist* stated in 2018, "Singapore's education system is considered the best in the world."[28] That can be observed, first and foremost, in its students' performance. Randomly selected pupils hailing from the Southeast Asian peninsula consistently rank in the global top three of the Programme for International Student Assessment (PISA) ranking, which measures students' knowledge in mathematics, science, and reading. It makes Singapore the best among equals in the region. But where Singapore really excels is in the way it structures and finances its educational system. Public school teachers are paid salaries commensurate with those in the private sector. They can make career progress as master teachers, and curricula are adapted based on the latest educational research.[29] It is the result of a deliberate, long-term government strategy, valuing education as a primary means to advance as a nation. Prime Minister Lee Hsien Loong in 2020 reiterated that vision upon visiting one of the country's state primary schools, which account for the vast majority of students. "Education is one of the most important things that Singaporeans have," he said. "And it is one of the most important things that the Government pays attention to because we believe that through education, we can help our citizens gain skills, learn knowledge, become productive and useful, become good people and make a living for themselves."[30]

Singapore also has a world-class health system, which manages to deliver universal health care to all its citizens, without gobbling up too much of either the government's or the people's own budget. In the

---

[27]"Singapore Remains the 2nd Most Expensive Housing Market in the World after Hong Kong," CBRE, April 2019, https://www.cbre.com/singapore/about/media-centre/singapore-remains-the-2nd-most-expensive-housing-market-in-the-world-after-hong-kong.

[28]"What Other Countries Can Learn from Singapore's Schools," *The Economist*, August 2018, https://www.economist.com/leaders/2018/08/30/what-other-countries-can-learn-from-singapores-schools.

[29]"What Other Countries Can Learn from Singapore's Schools," *The Economist*, August 2018, https://www.economist.com/leaders/2018/08/30/what-other-countries-can-learn-from-singapores-schools.

[30]"Education System Designed to Bring Out Best in Every Student: PM," *The Straits Times*, January 2020, https://www.straitstimes.com/singapore/education-system-designed-to-bring-out-best-in-every-student-pm.

2019 Legatum Prosperity Index measuring people's health and access to health care, for example,[31] Singapore came up top, ahead of Japan, Switzerland, and South Korea. As with its education model, the strong Singaporean performance thus means its citizens stay healthy until old age and get the care they need if problems arise. But the health care system isn't just good at delivering strong outcomes; it does so very efficiently as well. Whereas in the US, health care spending makes up 17 percent of GDP and in the European Union economies spend about 10s percent of their GDP on health, in Singapore that percentage is lower than 5 percent. The reason for this excellent price/quality ratio lies in its unique blend of public and private roles and contributions. In Singapore, "the government holds the cards," Aaron E. Carroll, a professor of pediatrics, noted in his analysis of the Singapore model for *The New York Times*. "The government strictly regulates what technology is available in the country and where. It makes decisions as to what drugs and devices are covered in public facilities. [And] it sets the prices and determines what subsidies are available." The government also acts preventively, for example, in regulating food quality. But the private sector and the free market play a major role too. For one, "primary care, which is mostly at low cost, is provided mostly by the private sector," with about 80 percent of Singaporeans getting such care from general practitioners[32] (the share is flipped for hospitalizations, which mostly happens in large public hospitals). And citizens—not the government—largely pay for their own health care costs through two major programmes, journalist Ezra Klein explains.[33] One such fund is for routine health care (Medisave, which is mandatory), and one is for non-routine interventions (Medishield, which is automatically added to your payroll, but you can opt out of). Only when these two privately funded schemes don't

[31]"The Healthiest Countries to Live In," BBC, April 2020, http://www.bbc.com/travel/story/20200419-coronavirus-five-countries-with-the-best-healthcare-systems.

The Legatum index "measures the extent to which people in each country are healthy and have access to the services necessary to maintain good health, including health outcomes, healthy systems, illnesses and risk factors, and mortality rate."

[32]"What Can the US Health System Learn From Singapore?" Aaron E. Carroll, *The New York Times*, April 2019, https://www.nytimes.com/2019/04/22/upshot/singapore-health-system-lessons.html.

[33]"Is Singapore's 'Miracle' Health Care System the Answer for America?" Ezra Klein, Vox, April 2017, https://www.vox.com/policy-and-politics/2017/4/25/15356118/singapore-health-care-system-explained.

suffice, the government steps in with Medifund, a payer of last resort. In this way, the Singapore model is the opposite of what you would find in, say, the United States: "[The United States has] a largely publicly financed private delivery system," Carroll explained. "Singapore has a largely privately financed public delivery system."[34]

Finally, digital connectivity has been a focus of Singaporean policies as well. Already one of the world's best digitally connected countries, the city-state in 2019 rolled out its "Smart Nation strategy"[35] across key sectors such as education, health care, housing, and transport. In doing so, the government wanted to make sure its citizens and businesses could get even more value out of their digital connectivity and skills. It quickly led to successes. The Healthy365 app, for instance, was downloaded by almost half the population, giving health tips and tricks and keeping track of users' health activities. MyInfo Business and GoBusiness allowed thousands of businesses to more easily fill in government papers and apply for business licenses. And the Moments of Life app allowed tens of thousands of families to do anything from birth registration to finding new jobs or gaining new skills online.[36] Each individual application or service may seem like a minor improvement, but they all together add up to make Singapore and its people one of the most digitally savvy economies in the world.

Taken together, the approach of the Singaporean government toward education, health care, housing, and connectivity is a pragmatic one. Realizing the importance of these three policy areas, and its own crucial role in providing them, Singapore takes decisive actions to ensure its population benefits from quality access to education, health care, and housing. But it steers clear from doing so in an ideological way, or by seeing itself as the primary stakeholder. "Singapore believes in strong government, not big government," Senior Minister Tharman told us in an interview.

That is not to say the Singapore model is flawless, of course. The COVID-19 pandemic revealed some painful shortcomings in the Lion

---

[34]"What Can the US Health System Learn From Singapore?" Aaron E. Carroll, *The New York Times*, April 2019, https://www.nytimes.com/2019/04/22/upshot/singapore-health-system-lessons.html.

[35]"Smart Nation: The Way Forward," Government of Singapore, November 2018, https://www.smartnation.gov.sg/docs/default-source/default-document-library/smart-nation-strategy_nov2018.pdf?sfvrsn=3f5c2af8_2.

[36]"Transforming Singapore Through Technology," Smart Nation Singapore, accessed October 2020, https://www.smartnation.gov.sg/why-Smart-Nation/transforming-singapore.

City model. Initially, Singapore seemed to have a firm grip on the spread of COVID, a remarkable feat for an international city so closely connected to other hotspots of the pandemic. The government acted swiftly, putting in place a national test, trace, and treat strategy, and curtailing public life and (international) travel. But despite these early successes, the city-state did face a major outbreak, located initially in the city's migrant dormitories and spreading from there. It put the spotlights on this oft-forgotten part of the population, which unlike the majority of Singaporean nationals or international expats operated in large part outside of the formal system, and was more restricted in its access to the social services the country provided. Stefania Palma, a *Financial Times* journalist based in Singapore, pointed out that critics of the government approach saw in it a "testament to the 'invisibility' of Singapore's low-wage migrants" but also noted the authorities "started to move" in response to the migrant dormitories COVID outbreak. "New standards, including a 10-people-per-room limit, will ensure that dorms are more resilient to public health risks including pandemics," she wrote in June 2020.[37]

In addition, Singapore's electoral model is very different from that of many other democracies. The ruling People's Action Party has led single-party governments continuously since Singapore's independence in 1965. Other parties do participate in the country's general elections, organized every five years, and in 2020 even won close to 40 percent of the vote. But these opposition parties have so far failed to win a significant number of seats or lead major government ministries. As a result, *Nikkei Asian Review* reported, "Singapore ranked 75th in the Economist Intelligence Unit's global democracy index for 2019, behind regional peers Malaysia (43rd), Indonesia (64th), and Thailand (68th). The city-state performed especially poorly in the category of "electoral process and pluralism."[38]

Finally, the precise approach Singapore follows may not be replicable in the same way elsewhere: many larger, less densely populated, or poorer countries would not be able to provide the same services if they tried.

---

[37]"Surge in Covid Cases Shows Up Singapore's Blind Spots over Migrant Workers," Stefania Palma, *Financial Times*, June 2020, https://www.ft.com/content/0fdb770a-a57a-11ea-92e2-cbd9b7e28ee6.

[38]"Singapore's 'democratic dawn'? Parties Adapt to New Landscape," *Nikkei Asian Review*, July 2020, https://asia.nikkei.com/Spotlight/Asia-Insight/Singapore-s-democratic-dawn-Parties-adapt-to-new-landscape.

But the pragmatic, stakeholder-led philosophy that guides Singaporean policymaking, like that of New Zealand or Denmark, is nevertheless one that merits to be looked at by others.

New Zealand and the Move Away from GDP

If focusing on policy areas including education, health care, and housing are one key success factor of a stakeholder government, New Zealand's government shows that there is another one: moving away from narrowly targeting GDP growth and focusing instead on a larger dashboard of metrics.

As we've seen, to this date, most governments around the world, and many leading international organizations, still use gross domestic product (GDP) as the primary variable to measure the success of a given economy. But we also know GDP was never meant to be a measure of well-being. In the late 1930s, when GDP started its ascent, it was used primarily to estimate the war-time production capacity of a country—no luxury with the Second World War around the corner. Since then, however, not only the inventor of the metric, Simon Kuznets, but many other economists, including Mariana Mazzucato, Diane Coyle, and Nobel Prize winner Joseph Stiglitz, pointed out some of the fundamental flaws of GDP.[39]

While organizations such as our own as well as the OECD have worked on a more comprehensive set of metrics, New Zealand is one of the first countries to implement the idea of going beyond GDP in practice. It is worthwhile to look at its Living Standards Framework (Figure 10.1) in a bit more detail.

Conceptually, the Living Standards Framework is meant to provide it with "a shared understanding of what helps achieve higher living standards to support intergenerational well-being." Seen from this perspective, well-being is not measured (solely) by GDP but by the country's four capitals":[40]

---

[39]It is not hard to understand some of its drawbacks: GDP goes up when oil or coal is produced and consumed, but it goes down when people switch from using a car to a bicycle or public transportation (assuming a car is more expensive). GDP also goes up when banks post financial profits, but it remains stagnant when digital innovations get introduced that make our lives easier.

[40]"The Treasury's Living Standards Framework," New Zealand Government, December 2019, https://treasury.govt.nz/sites/default/files/2019-12/lsf-dashboard-update-dec19.pdf.

- **Natural capital**, consisting of "all aspects of the natural environment that support life and human activity," which include "land, soil, water, plants and animals, minerals and energy resources";
- **Human capital**, or the "capabilities and capacities of people to engage in work, study, recreation, and social activities," including "skills, knowledge, physical and mental health";
- **Social capital**, which are the "norms, rules and institutions that influence the way in which people live and work together and experience a sense of belonging." They include "trust, reciprocity, the rule of law, cultural and community identity, traditions and customs, common values and interests"; and
- **Financial and physical** capital, most closely associated with GDP, as it includes "financial and human-made (produced) physical assets, usually closely associated with supporting material living conditions." These include "factories, equipment, houses, roads, buildings, hospitals, and financial securities."

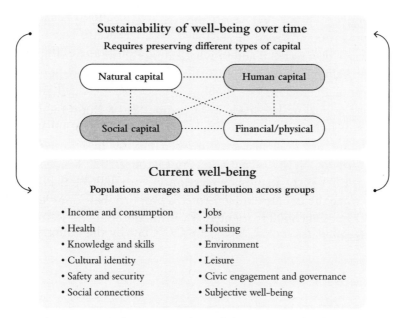

Figure 10.1 A Representation of the New Zealand Living Standards Framework

Source: Redrawn from New Zealand Treasury, "The Relationship between the Sustainable Development Goals and the Living Standards Framework (DP 18/06)," July 26, 2018, https://treasury.govt.nz/publications/dp/dp-18-06-html.

Taken together, these four types of capital determine the well-being of the people, the country as a whole, and their future generations. And to measure where the country stands on these types of capital, the framework is complemented by a dashboard, which shows New Zealand's performance on 12 current and future well-being domains. These include civic engagement, cultural identity, the environment, health, housing, income and consumption, jobs and earnings, knowledge and skills, time use, safety and security, social connections, and subjective well-being.

It should be immediately clear that these domains are closely linked to our own definition of what constitutes equitable prosperity. Three indicators concern education, health care, and housing (knowledge and skills, health, and housing); two others are more refined and personalized versions of GDP (jobs and earnings, and income and consumption); and the others concern either the well-being of the planet or elements of personal well-being that are either subjective or part of a societal dynamic. Finally, it should be noted, the framework also recognizes there is a risk and resilience element to their prosperity, which comes into play "in the face of change, shocks, and unexpected events." Unfortunately, however, the dashboard has not yet found an adequate metric to measure this resilience. (The COVID crisis, though, seems to have been a litmus test the government passed successfully.)

It is early days to tell if and to what extent this framework and dashboard are helping New Zealand in managing the well-being of their country and its citizens. The dashboard was only activated late 2018, with a first annual update made in December 2019. But if the COVID crisis is any indication, the holistic approach New Zealand is taking to well-being and resilience are a marked success. In a clear signal of popular support, New Zealand voters in October 2020 handed Jacinda Ardern and her party a landslide election victory and the first absolute majority since the country implemented a proportional voting system in 1996.[41] Other stakeholder-oriented governments could do well to learn from its lessons.

---

[41]"New Zealand's Ardern Wins 2nd Term in Election Landslide," Associated Press, October 2020, https://apnews.com/article/virus-outbreak-new-zealand-mosque-attacks-auckland-elections-new-zealand-b1ab788954f23f948d8b6c3258c02634.

Civil Society and the International Community

The final group that has a central place in the stakeholder model is civil society. In recent years, organizations such as worker unions, NGOs, and organized civil rights groups have struggled to maintain the membership base and influence they had in the 20th century. But the emergence of a host of new issues shows that no society can properly function without them, and other stakeholders would do well to accept and support them.

Take as first example the role new worker and consumer groups play in the Fourth Industrial Revolution. In previous industrial revolutions, workers over time developed the traditional employee-employer relationship we know today, and they often bargained collectively about their pay and working conditions, aided by powerful unions. But this relationship is on the wane. Legislative reforms and increased globalization provided a first hit to the traditional power of unions. And the gig economy that resulted from the Fourth Industrial Revolution in most places did away with unions, collective bargaining, and the traditional employment relationships as we've known them for decades almost entirely.

In some regions, this *tabula rasa* has had positive outcomes. In Indonesia, for example, where my colleague drove around in scooters and cars of the ride-hailing companies Grab and Go-Jek on a country visit, drivers were mostly enthusiastic about the opportunities gig work provided to them. Many had previously been agricultural workers or had worked odd jobs in the city. Not having a traditional employment contract wasn't a barrier or inconvenience; it was what they were used to. In fact, the technology ride-sharing companies used gave them more transparency and choice, not less, in terms of their work and pay. And even some drivers who had previously worked in factories expressed their satisfaction about switching to be a gig economy worker. One of them told us that as a Grab car driver, he earned on average four times the monthly salary of his factory days.

This experience isn't unique to the Asian archipelago or merely anecdotal. Around the world, designers, drivers, handymen, and many other professionals have found new work opportunities and higher pay thanks to platform companies ranging from Upwork to TaskRabbit and Fiverr and from Didi to Grab or Lyft. In countries such as Serbia, Pakistan, or Ukraine, having the ability to enter a freelance contract with the aid of an online platform has proven a popular alternative to finding work in the traditional employment market.

But in many other cases, the emergence of the gig economy has been less kind to workers. In the US, for example, the rise of ride-hailing companies has meant that hundreds of thousands of workers don't have the legal protections and financial benefits that traditional employment used to provide them with. In New York City, for example, the largest US market for personal transport, the average Uber or Lyft driver by the end of 2018 had hourly net earnings of $11.9, far below the $15 the city set later that year as state minimum wage[42] (the earnings were later raised to be in compliance with the new minimum wage). And during the 2020 COVID crisis, Aziz Bah of the Independent Drivers Guild, a newly created union for platform drivers, said many gig economy workers were hit harder than other workers, having no employer-provided health insurance and being on average in a more precarious financial situation because of the nature of their work.[43]

A similar situation is playing out in consumer markets. For decades, groups such as Consumer International and its various national affiliates have played a key role in defending consumer rights in disputes with retail chains, consumer good companies, and government services. To do so, they could count on an enthusiastic base of members, who paid a membership fee each year and in return benefited from the class action the organization took on their behalf. But these groups too in recent years were faced with multiple challenges. On the one hand, fewer consumers became or remained members, giving the group less means and bargaining power. On the other hand, large Internet companies appeared as new sellers, with often new business models and less of a physical presence. As many of these Internet platforms offered free services to their users, the action radius of consumer groups needed to change, from advising on product quality and the best places to buy, to scrutinizing the practices of the platform companies instead.

But to alleviate these emerging new inequalities and insecurities, new civil society groups are needed. Companies and governments alone cannot provide the solutions workers and consumers need. What are some examples of organizations that are newly created or reinvented themselves in this era?

---

[42]"Uber and Lyft Drivers Guild Wins Historic Pay Rules," Independent Drivers Guild, December 2018, https://drivingguild.org/uber-and-lyft-drivers-guild-wins-historic-pay-rules/.

[43]"I'm a New York City Uber Driver. The Pandemic Shows That My Industry Needs Fundamental Change or Drivers Will Never Recover," Aziz Bah, Business Insider, July 2020, https://www.businessinsider.com/uber-lyft-drivers-covid-19-pandemic-virus-economy-right-bargain-2020-7?r=US&IR=T.

Consumer Rights Groups

Humanity Forward is one example of a modern consumer rights group. It's a nonprofit founded by former US presidential candidate Andrew Yang. Aware of the fundamental changes brought about by the Fourth Industrial Revolution in American society, the organization puts forward solutions such as universal basic income (UBI) and data as a property right.[44] Conceived as a monthly check for $1,000 written to every American adult, Humanity Forward believes UBI can serve as a safety cushion for workers already operating in the gig economy or those faced with a life or work situation that requires a basic safety net. Seen from our perspective, such a check may not be the panacea it is made out to be. But it does engrain some of the fundamental perspectives of both the stakeholder model—in which everyone should receive equal opportunities—and the Fourth Industrial Revolution, which will continue to disrupt the labor market for decades to come. It therefore deserves further scrutiny and debate.

Yang's initiative to enshrine "data as a property right" provides a truly interesting example of how individuals can coalesce in a modern stakeholder way around their rights. Yang argues that "data generated by each individual needs to be owned by them, with certain rights conveyed that will allow them to know how it's used and protect it," rather than the current Internet platform practices where "data is owned by the people who collect it" (i.e., the Internet platforms).[45] Humanity Forward wants to bring consumers together and use their common power to force regulators and companies to respect their ownership rights and ensure they get remunerated when they are shared. To do so, consumers can sign up for the Data Dividend Project.[46] As tech media The Verge reported, "the project is betting on collective action as a means of changing the law and extending data property rights to users across the country." Whether initiatives like these succeed will crucially depend on the support they receive from citizens in their society. But they show that also in today's tech-enabled

[44]Humanity Forward, https://movehumanityforward.com/.

[45]Data as a Property Right, Humanity Forward, https://movehumanityforward.com/data-property-right.

[46]"Andrew Yang Is Pushing Big Tech to Pay Users for Data," The Verge, June 2020, https://www.theverge.com/2020/6/22/21298919/andrew-yang-big-tech-data-dividend-project-facebook-google-ubi.

economy, individuals can gather and stand up for what they believe to be right. It is through these kinds of civil society actions that societies will evolve for the better.

Modern Unions

In the workspace, too, there should be room for modern unions, as previously argued by academics such as Jeffrey Hirsch and Joseph Seiner in their paper "A Modern Union for the Modern Economy."[47] But how can we get there? We already saw how in some countries, such as Denmark, union membership remains high, and constructive attitudes lead to more competitive companies and salaries there, as well as a workforce that is constantly reskilled. That is the power of unions at their best. But equally, we've seen how in countries such as the UK or the US, unions have lost a lot of membership and power over the past few decades, coinciding with lower wages and fewer investments in employee training. To the extent that this decline in union adherence and power is the result of anti-union policies, the right answer is to end such practices. At the same time, there is another factor at work: work in the gig economy globally has been on the rise, but traditional unions have so far largely been unable to provide adequate answers to its challenges.

For gig workers, forming a modern union may be most important. Already, in the US, an estimated 57 million workers are freelancing,[48] meaning that they work without a traditional employee contract. As a sign of how much this trend represents the future of work, more than half of the Generation Z—those born in the 1990s and early 2000s—are starting their careers by freelancing, with many seeing it as a long-term career path. Similar trends are playing out in countries such as Serbia, Ukraine, Pakistan, India, or Indonesia, home to Puty Puar, the successful designer from Chapter 5. In these countries, many young workers start their careers on e-working platforms such as Upwork and often work for employers based in the US and other affluent economies, rather than

[47] "A Modern Union for the Modern Economy," Jeffrey M. Hirsch and Joseph A. Seiner, *Fordham Law Review*, Volume 86, Issue 4, 2018, https://ir.lawnet.fordham.edu/cgi/viewcontent.cgi?article=5483&context=flr.

[48] "Sixth Annual 'Freelancing in America' Study Finds That More People Than Ever See Freelancing as a Long-Term Career Path," Upwork, October 2019, https://www.upwork.com/press/2019/10/03/freelancing-in-america-2019/.

their own. There are certainly benefits to this situation, as it helps prevent a "brain drain" away from these countries, ensures that dollars or other, stable foreign currencies flow into these economies, and strengthens the local economy through the additional purchasing power of these tele-workers. But there may be significant downsides too. As one media report showed, such graduates end up dreaming of earning $2,000 a month or more telecommuting.[49] But they may not immediately realize they're in a more vulnerable position than salaried workers, as they don't have long-term contracts, benefits, or legal protection, including against unemployment.

This shouldn't lead though to despair but rather to a new form of unionizing workers and international collaboration. A good place to start is probably with those gig workers who work exclusively for one platform or in one industry, such as drivers. It is what the Independent Drivers Guild in New York and Gig Workers Rising in California do. Both groups gather drivers who work primarily for Uber, Lyft, and other similar platforms and advocate for "better wages, working conditions, and respect."[50] It has led to some structural changes in the status and treatments of such drivers. In August 2020, a California court ordered ride-hailing and delivery apps such as Uber and Lyft to treat their drivers as employees.[51] It would require these companies to provide a minimum wage, health insurance, and overtime pay and paid sick leave, media reported.[52] However, the court battles on this legislation continued into the Fall, and as we saw earlier, voters rejected Proposition 22 in November 2020, overturning much of the previous legislation on the matter, making Uber, Lyft, and other drivers contract workers once more.[53] (At the time of writing, it continues to be battled in court by the platforms in question.) In New York, as we saw above, the Independent Drivers Guild managed to force

---

[49]"The New Balkan Dream Is a $2,000 Per Month Telecommute," Sandra Maksimovic, Deutsche Welle, August 2018, https://www.dw.com/en/the-new-balkan-dream-is-a-2000-per-month-telecommute/a-45258826.

[50]"About Us, Gig Workers Rising," https://gigworkersrising.org/get-informed.

[51]"Court Orders Uber, Lyft to Reclassify Drivers as Employees in California," Sara Ashley O'Brien, CNN, August 2020, https://edition.cnn.com/2020/08/10/tech/uber-lyft-california-preliminary-injunction/index.html.

[52]Ibidem.

[53]"Human Capital: The gig economy in a post-Prop 22 world", Megan Rose Dickey, TechCrunch, November 2020, https://techcrunch.com/2020/11/07/human-capital-the-gig-economy-in-a-post-prop-22-world/.

progress on pay, securing a minimum pay after expenses of more than $15 per hour, the state minimum.

From a stakeholder perspective, the so-called contractors are right to unionize in this way and advocate for decent pay and benefits. And it should be common sense for governments to grant them similar rights as other workers. As Alex Wood of Oxford Internet Institute in the UK argued, in an interview with *Wired* magazine:[54] "If you are dependent on that platform for your livelihood, there aren't rival platforms you could work for, if they control your data, and if the reputation system locks you into the platform—then that's when you need labour protections and that's why we have labour laws." From their side, the companies in question would do well to take into account their demands and set up a consultative body with these organizations, rather than fight them in court.

Freelancers who work in other industries, such as communication, IT, or creative design, would do well to form professional interest groups and push for better protections as well. The fact that the market for such e-work is often virtual and/or international should not mean that labor standards must be an unstoppable race to the bottom. It should be possible, for example, to require that contract work in specific states or countries respects the same minimum hourly pay, whether for "online" or "offline" workers. And when virtual contracts are performed across borders, new bilateral or multilateral agreements could be made, with governments establishing under which conditions it is possible to virtually commute between them. It is in workers' best interest to advocate for rules that guarantee them such appropriate remuneration.

Here, the journey ahead is a long one. To our knowledge, there is no fully adequate freelance legislation anywhere, and few if any effective freelance unions exist.

In New York, one of the largest organizations for freelancers is Freelancers Union,[55] an organization founded by Sara Horowitz, a lawyer and daughter of union representatives. Freelancers Union mostly distinguishes itself by offering discounted health insurance, skills training, and a co-working space. It was also an early and vocal advocate for

---

[54] "The Government's Good Work Plan Leaves the Gig Economy Behind," Sanjana Varghese, *Wired Magazine UK*, December 2018, https://www.wired.co.uk/article/good-work-plan-uk-gig-economy.

[55] "This New Program Aims to Train the Growing Freelance Workforce," Yuki Noguchi, NPR, January 2019, https://www.npr.org/2019/01/04/681807327/this-new-program-aims-to-train-the-growing-freelance-workforce?t=1597649731065.

The Freelance Isn't Free Law, which it says "protects freelancers from non-payment" and "serves as a blueprint for other cities and states."[56] But it has so far shied away from advocating for minimum pay and benefits for the freelancers it represents, making it less a union and more a member-based organization offering membership benefits. That's also the main criticism it has received from the left: "the Freelancers Union treats workers like consumers of the services they provide. It doesn't deserve to be called a union," the socialist publication *Jacobin Magazine* wrote in an early critique of the organization.[57]

Moreover, much of the gig regulation has narrowly focused on the equivalent of taxi and delivery drivers and much less on workers with less dependent work relations or workers making virtual commutes. The European Parliament in April 2019, for example, adopted "new rules introducing minimum rights for all employees,"[58] including a right to receive compensation in case of late cancellation and free mandatory training, as well as a ban on exclusivity clauses. Those rules were supposed to help all workers on zero-hours contracts, as well as domestic workers and on-demand drivers or couriers.[59] But as labor economists such as Valerio Di Stefano of the University of Leuven pointed out,[60] they fell short in providing similar rights and benefits to others freelancers, such as the IT workers from countries such as Ukraine, Serbia, Pakistan, or India I described earlier.

Advocacy Groups

A final segment of civil society whose concerns should be heard in the stakeholder model are the newly formed advocacy groups and other movements asking for social justice.

Whether it concerns Black Lives Matter, LGBTQ rights groups, men and women advocating the equal treatment of genders on the work

[56]"The Freelance Isn't Free Law," Freelancers Union, https://www.freelancersunion.org/get-involved/freelance-isnt-free/.

[57]"A Union of One," Ari Paul, *Jacobin Magazine*, October 2014.

[58]"Gig Economy: EU Law to Improve Workers' Rights," European Parliament, April 2019, https://www.europarl.europa.eu/news/en/headlines/society/20190404STO35070/gig-economy-eu-law-to-improve-workers-rights-infographic.

[59]Ibidem.

[60]"Gig Economy Protections: Did the EU Get It Right?" Knowledge at Wharton, May 2019, https://knowledge.wharton.upenn.edu/article/eu-gig-economy-law/.

floor, or any other group asking not to be left behind, everyone in a leading position should seek to converse with these newly emerging civil society groups. They are often led by new generations of citizens and workers, whose concerns will only grow over time and whose pulse is, therefore, closer to the future direction of any society.

Getting such conversations right is not easy, and neither is solving the issues that are put on the table. Some problems of discrimination have been around for decades, if not centuries. The causes of issues such as race- or gender-based discrimination are usually systemic in nature, implying a single stakeholder will find it hard to do away with them entirely. And, while some demands need to be addressed with haste and urgency, striking a balance between progress and stability, or the contradicting demands of one group versus another, is a long-term exercise and very difficult to get right in one go. Finally, while many established stakeholders mostly have a clearly identified spokesperson or negotiator, some of the most successful new advocacy groups prefer not to have a formal leader. (And they shouldn't be forced to have one either, in our opinion.)

All of this makes it hard to take into account the concerns of these civil society groups and find the right answers. But none of these considerations can be an excuse not to seek the dialogue, to invite representatives of these advocacy groups or minorities to the table, and to take concrete action toward social justice. A society can only advance if everyone is on board, and it is no longer acceptable to leave anyone behind. In response to these demands for social, economic, and climate justice, company management and boards should first of all subscribe to the notion of stakeholder responsibility and make it an agenda point on their quarterly and annual meetings. Second, they should be explicit about the targets they have in domains such as diversity and inclusion, pay equality, and wage levels and indicate which groups they are seeking engagement with. (In recent years, some US companies, from FirstEnergy[61] to Starbucks,[62] have started to tie executive pay to diversity hiring and promotions.) Finally, they should report every year

---

[61] "Want More Diversity? Some Experts Say Reward C.E.O.s for It," Peter Eavis, *The New York Times*, July 2020, https://www.nytimes.com/2020/07/14/business/economy/corporate-diversity-pay-compensation.html.

[62] "Starbucks Ties Executive Pay to 2025 Diversity Targets," Heather Haddon, *The Wall Street Journal*, October 2020, https://www.wsj.com/articles/starbucks-ties-executive-pay-to-2025-diversity-targets-11602680401.

on the progress they have made on their chosen metrics and targets and be accountable to their stakeholders on their progress.

On a more practical level, to see how social justice can be achieved, it may be worthwhile to look at some examples from unexpected places. Take, for instance, the situation of the Sheedi population in Pakistan,[63] a group I became acquainted with through the World Economic Forum's Global Shapers, a network of young people from around the world. (The Forum created the community of Global Shapers to ensure that the next generation—people between age 20 and 30, roughly—would be empowered to help shape our common future, by informing each other about the local and global challenges they see and addressing them together. It is active in more than 400 cities all around the world, from Atlanta to Accra, and from Zurich to Zagreb.[64]) The Sheedi are South Asia's largest African minority, numbering several hundreds of thousands, and "the descendants of the African slaves, sailors, and soldiers who made South Asia their home in centuries past."[65] For decades, this group was marginalized, "battling both prejudice and wider socioeconomic ills."

But in 2018, the situation started to change, as Tanzeela Qambrani, then a 39-year-old Sheedi mother of three, was the first Sheedi to be elected to parliament in Sindh, the country's province with the largest African-Pakistani population. As the Shapers pointed out, "the groundbreaking election was marred by dissent, including the resignation of a fellow party member," but Qambrani has been "vocally outspoken on the discrimination against Sheedi people in Pakistan" ever since and received support from her party leader, Bilawal Bhutto (the son of murdered former prime minister Bhenazir Bhutto). Indeed, "in March 2019 she pushed through a resolution that penalized educators who displayed racist behaviour towards Sheedi students," the Shapers wrote,[66] and "she is also leading a protest resolution in the provincial assembly against anti-Black racism in the US, in the wake of the killing of George Floyd."

[63]"Black Lives Matter—for Pakistan's Sheedi Community Too," Zahra Bhaiwala, Neekta Hamidi, Sikander Bizenjo, World Economic Forum Agenda, August 2020, https://www.weforum.org/agenda/2020/08/black-lives-matter-for-pakistans-sheedi-community-too/.

[64]Global Shapers Community, World Economic Forum, https://www.globalshapers.org/.

[65]"Meet the First African-Pakistani Lawmaker," The Diplomat, September 2018, https://thediplomat.com/2018/09/meet-the-first-african-pakistani-lawmaker/.

[66]"Black Lives Matter—for Pakistan's Sheedi Community Too," Zahra Bhaiwala, Neekta Hamidi, Sikander Bizenjo, World Economic Forum Agenda, August 2020, https://www.weforum.org/agenda/2020/08/black-lives-matter-for-pakistans-sheedi-community-too/.

It seems quite obvious that Qambrani's fight against Sheedi discrimination, together with various grassroots movements will be a long one, with ups and downs, given the systemic nature of the discrimination they face. But one important lesson is that hers and other struggles for social justice are accelerated when minorities or other advocacy groups get a seat at the table. Representatives can help point to the issues minorities or other groups face and help establish credibility in their fight for justice. Reuters, the international press agency, for example, in June 2020 reported on the protest resolution Qambrani submitted in the Sindh parliament against a "wave of racism" after the killing of African American George Floyd in the US. Similarly, our Shapers wrote an article for the World Economic Forum's Internet Agenda, again hailing Qambrani as a community leader and drawing parallels between the Black Lives Matter fight for social justice in the US and that of the Sheedi in Pakistan. In both cases, Qambrani's status as MP helped establish the credibility of the article and with it, the cause it was about.

■ ■ ■

The lesson of Mærsk, New Zealand, and the civil society groups we just discussed is that success of organizations and individuals cannot be achieved in following traditional patterns. History is a process with evolving beliefs, practices, and doctrines. The time where an organization has only its own interests in mind and pursues them without taking into account the interests of its stakeholders is over. In a society that is so interconnected and where the success of each actor depends on great connectivity and interaction with many other actors, decisions can only be taken if there is a positive outcome for the whole system. For companies, this means specifically, that the winds of history will blow into the face of those who stick to the concept of shareholder primacy. But it will provide tailwinds to those who have recognized the signs and practice stakeholder capitalism.

Conclusion
The Road to Stakeholder Capitalism

In the immediate months that followed the outbreak of the COVID-19 pandemic, the world as we knew it was turned upside down. Like most people, I was constrained to observing the situation from inside my home and our empty offices, and I relied on video calls to know how others were doing. In Geneva, as in so many other cities around the world, the eerie silence on the streets, devoid of cars, commerce, and the hustle and bustle of people, was only equaled in intensity by the stir in hospitals, where entire wards were hastily transformed in to makeshift COVID facilities.

In those moments of crisis, it was hard to be optimistic about the prospect of a brighter global future. Several million people lost their lives or were severely ill. Tens, perhaps hundreds of millions of people lost their livelihoods. And probably well over a billion children and elderly people were cut off from the outside world, unable to learn or see their loved ones for months. The only upside, perhaps, was the temporary drop in greenhouse gas emissions, which brought a slight relief to the planet's atmosphere. It shouldn't have come as a surprise, then, that many started to wonder: Will governments, businesses, and other influential stakeholders truly change their ways for the better after this, or will we go back to business as usual? Can we, in other words, make the turn to stakeholder capitalism, or are we doomed to revert to more short-term and selfish reflexes of a rawer kind of capitalism?

After reading the first half of this book, you may have been inclined to give a pessimistic answer. As we saw in the first chapters, we are facing enormous economic, environmental, social, and political challenges. With every passing year, these issues, as many people have experienced directly, seem to get worse, not better. That is true for income and wealth inequality in almost every country of the world. It is true for climate

247

change, which affects us all. And it is true for social and political division, which is on the rise across continents from America to Asia. We seem to be living in a vicious global economic system, in which possibility of progress is engulfed by the much darker road toward decline.

Part II of this book demonstrates that, despite society's progress, there are no easy ways out of this vicious cycle, even though the mechanisms to do so lie at our fingertips. Every day, we invent new technologies that could make our lives and the planet's health better. Free markets, trade, and competition create so much wealth, that in theory they could make everyone better off if there was the will to do so. But that is not the reality we're living in today.

Technological advances often take place in a monopolized economy and are used to prioritize one company's profits over societal progress. The same economic system that created so much prosperity in the golden age of American capitalism in the 1950s and 1960s is now creating inequality and climate change. And the same political system that enabled our global progress and democracy after World War II now contributes to societal discord and discontent. Each of those policies were well intended but had unintended negative consequences.

Yet we should not lose our optimism. There are reasons to believe a more inclusive and virtuous economic system is possible—and it could be just around the corner. As the initial shock of the COVID crisis receded, we saw a glimpse of what is possible, when all stakeholders act for the public good and the well-being of all people, instead of just a few. Mere months after the pandemic began, work was started on more than 200 potential SARS-CoV-2 vaccines, and by December 2020, the first vaccinations were planned in various countries, including the US, Germany and the UK[1]. Many of them resulted from multinational collaboration involving both the public and the private sectors. Companies approached the World Economic Forum's COVID Taskforce with offers of hygiene products, ventilators, containers, funding to help the emergency health response. There was also a strong desire for cooperation between governments and business, to secure the funds needed for vaccine development and distribution. To me, these initiatives showed that we can improve our global economic system if we set our mind to it

---

[1]"US, Germany and UK could start Covid vaccinations as early as December", Helen Sullivan, The Guardian, November 2020, https://www.theguardian.com/world/2020/nov/23/us-germany-and-uk-could-start-covid-vaccinations-as-early-as-december.

and that this crisis could also bring out the best in all of us, as we work to overcome the pandemic.

In Part III of this book, I've tried to show how such virtuous instincts can become a feature of our economic systems, rather than a rare exception. I have shown how companies, governments, international organizations, and civil society can reinvent themselves. Rather than chasing short-term profits or narrow self-interest, they could pursue the well-being of all people and the entire planet. This does not require a 180-degree turn; companies do not have to stop pursuing profits for their shareholders, and governments do not have to stop putting the well-being of their citizens first.

All it takes is that they shift to a long-term perspective, looking beyond the next quarter or fiscal year, to the next decade and the next generation, and that they take the concerns of others into account. That is what companies such as Mærsk have done, while remaining profitable and competitive. And it is what countries such as New Zealand and Singapore are doing, creating prosperity for all their citizens and businesses, while respecting others and the planet.

We should all follow these trailblazers' example. We should think deeply about the future and change our own business model or mission statement to clarify how we can contribute to the broader well-being of people and the planet, while pursuing other, more short-term goals. Building such a virtuous economic system is not a utopian ideal. Most people, including business leaders, investors, and community leaders, have a similar attitude about their role in the world and the lives of others. Most people want to do good. But what's been missing in recent decades is a clear compass to guide those in leading positions in our society and economy.

For the last 30 to 50 years, the neoliberalist ideology has increasingly prevailed in large parts of the world. This approach centers on the notion that the market knows best, that the "business of business is business," and that government should refrain from setting constraining rules for the functioning of markets. Those dogmatic beliefs have proven wrong. But fortunately, we are not destined to follow them.

As I mentioned several times earlier in this book, in September 2020, my belief that a more virtuous capitalist system is possible was reaffirmed by the "Stakeholder Capitalism Metrics" initiative of the Forum's International Business Council led by Brian Moynihan of Bank of America. These are non-financial metrics and disclosures that will be added (on a voluntary basis) to companies' annual reporting in the next two to three years, making it possible to measure their progress over time.

Doing so will allow us to answer questions such as: What is the gender pay gap in company X? How many people of diverse backgrounds were hired and promoted? What progress has the company made toward reducing its greenhouse gas emissions? How much did the company pay in taxes globally and per jurisdiction? And what did the company do to hire and train employees?

But why did this project come to fruition now? At the World Economic Forum, we had been advocating the idea that companies should try and optimize for more than just short-term profits for decades. But around 2016 a handful of business leaders emerged who wanted the private sector to play a concrete role in achieving the United Nations Sustainable Development Goals (SDGs). Individuals such as Brian Moynihan and also Frans van Houten of Philips and Indra Nooyi, then at PepsiCo, subscribed to this notion and enlisted many of their peers to sign a compact confirming their commitment.

In the following years, pressure from social and climate justice movements such as Fridays for Future (inspired by Greta Thunberg), #MeToo, and Black Lives Matter added to the sense of urgency. Business needed to do more than make a well-intentioned but vague pledge. By the summer of 2019, Brian and others put forth the idea of creating a tool to measure themselves, to replace the "alphabet soup of metrics"[2] that existed until then. By the fall, the work was underway, and the "Big Four" consulting firms—Deloitte, EY, KPMG, and PwC—signed on to define the metrics.

By January 2020, a first consultation draft of the metrics was ready and was enthusiastically received. Then, the COVID-19 disaster struck. It turned out to be a real litmus test. Would the project survive this global crisis? And, more broadly, would the whole idea of stakeholder capitalism die a premature death in the COVID crisis? The concept had been embraced by the US Business Roundtable—a major lobby group of US firms in Washington—just months earlier. Now, it was feared, that nascent commitment to stakeholder capitalism could make way for a more realistic, *sauve qui peut* approach in companies: save what you can, even if it means laying off employees or cutting off suppliers.

But if anything, the enthusiasm of the companies working on the project increased. "There was a sense that this was really important, especially in the crisis," Maha Eltobgy, who headed the initiative for the

---

[2] "World Economic Forum Aims to Make ESG Reporting Mainstream", Amanda Iacone, Bloomberg Tax, September 2020, https://news.bloombergtax.com/financial-accounting/world-economic-forum-aims-to-make-esg-reporting-mainstream.

World Economic Forum, told us. Thus, when a physical meeting was cancelled in the spring, all leading project sponsors—myself included— dialed in to a virtual meeting. It was the spark that was needed to complete the project. And so, in the fall of 2020, the Metrics were finalized and publicly released, after many more workshops, interviews, and other meetings were conducted in the middle of the worst global public health crisis in a century. It is these kinds of developments that give me hope that stakeholder capitalism isn't a fad but a feature of our future system.

Of course, we remain far from our goal of achieving a better global economic system for all. The Stakeholder Capitalism Metrics are just one of many initiatives that are needed to get to such an outcome—and time is quickly running out. But in a world where pessimism is increasingly the order of the day, and narrow and short-term self-interest is still alluring, initiatives like these demonstrate that a more inclusive and sustainable model is possible.

After the devastation of World War II, I was lucky enough to grow in a town and a society that embraced the stakeholder mindset in all that it did. I saw it at work at my father's factory, where everyone, from the shop floor to the corner office, had the same drive to make the company and its products a long-term success, and everyone shared in the fruits of it when it arrived. I saw it in Friedrichshafen and Ravensburg after the war, as all citizens, as well as the entire local government, came together to rebuild what had been destroyed. And I have been advocating for it ever since, whether in business or in government, and going from Swabia to Singapore.

I hope that you too, after reading this book, are convinced of the stakeholder model. I hope that you concluded—as have I—that the state of the world isn't a given but that we can improve it if we are all committed to a better world. And I hope that all of us—together—will now build the more resilient, inclusive, and sustainable economy we need, in the post-COVID world. That is the essence of stakeholder capitalism: a global economy that works for progress, people, and planet.

Acknowledgments

This book is the result of a true team effort; it results from the education I got from my parents, the community and society I grew up in, the collaborators I have at the institution I founded, and the constituents from all over the world who are part of the World Economic Forum. In this way too, it is for me the embodiment of stakeholder collaboration, and I would need another chapter to thank all of those who—knowingly or unknowingly—contributed to it. Allow me to thank here those who were very actively involved.

First and foremost, I wish to thank Peter Vanham, my head of communications and trusted aide in writing this book. As part of this project, Peter traveled the world, searched the Internet libraries, and spoke to many of my contacts over the course of two years. As we moved to writing the book, his contributions ranged from drafting the various sections of the manuscript to reflecting on the blueprint of the 21st century stakeholder model. Having written a first book on the stakeholder principle 50 years ago, I am glad to see that a new generation of global-minded citizens like Peter are embracing this idea today and helping define it for the world of tomorrow.

As executive chairman, I would also like to thank the president of the World Economic Forum, Børge Brende, with whom I have formed over the years a great working relationship—we are a true "tandem." Børge has taken over much of the daily management of our institution, and he performs this role in an excellent way. Over the past months, that allowed me in turn to spend sufficient time on *Stakeholder Capitalism*, despite the challenges posed by the COVID crisis.

Other close collaborators including, Adrian Monck, Mel Rogers, Kelly Ommundsen, and Susanne Grassmeier, equally played crucial roles in the realization of this book. Adrian, our head of public engagement, was the first to champion this book project internally. He served as a first editor to the manuscript and an adviser on the writing style. If you enjoy the "firsthand" reporting in this book, it is thanks to Adrian's style, which we opted for. Mel was an important strategic advisor and motivated all involved to persevere, even in the midst of the COVID crisis. And Kelly and Susanne enabled many of the interviews on which this book is based. All participated in the internal brainstorms we had on the content, title, and cover of the book.

Many other of our close contacts, whether family, co-workers, or outside collaborators, also contributed to the final manuscript. A special thanks goes out to my wife, Hilde, who made a number of valuable remarks during our discussions of the book and who acted as a critical reader at various occasions. Other "second readers" I wish to thank are Thierry Malleret, who co-authored with me *COVID-19: The Great Reset*, Paul Smyke, our head of North America, Alan Fleishmann, a valued sounding board of mine in Washington, DC, and Valeria Suppini, Peter's wife. At various stages in writing the book, they provided critical feedback, support, and suggested edits.

At Wiley, I wish to thank Chairman Jesse Wiley, Executive Editor Bill Falloon, Managing Editor Purvi Patel, Development Editor Christina Verigan, and the team of copy editors and graphic designers who made this book what it is. Jesse and Bill were the first to believe in this book, meeting me in December 2018 in New York and offering their commitment. Bill and Purvi later guided us through the editing and publishing process with a unique combination of patience and diligence so that it could find its way to the bookstores in time for our January 2021 Davos Agenda Week. And Christina Verigan masterfully edited the book, providing both content and stylistic feedback that made the book what it is as you read it.

In identifying and defining the stakeholder model, I received help from constituents of the World Economic Forum from all over the world. Our Beijing office, including Pengcheng Qu, Muzi Li, and Chief Representative Officer David Aikman, helped set up meetings with various Chinese interviewees. In our New York office, Maha Eltobgy played a pivotal role in bringing together the leaders of the International Business Council (IBC), and the Big Four accounting firms, Deloitte, EY, KPMG, and PwC, to create the Stakeholder Capitalism Metrics. The IBC's chairman, Brian Moynihan, deserves special praise: it is thanks to his leadership and vision, that companies that are committed to the stakeholder principle can now "walk the talk" because of the metrics.

I would like to also thank all academics, journalists, business leaders, global shapers, heads of international organizations, ministers, and other "stakeholders" who agreed to grant interviews for this book. From Richard Baldwin, the professor of international economics at the Graduate Institute of International and Development Studies in Geneva, to Annisa Wibi and Winston Utomo, our Global Shapers from Indonesia, all of you allowed us to broaden our view on the global economy and realize the crucial building blocks for a better future going forward. I thank all of you in a separate interview acknowledgments section.

And finally, and most importantly, I would like to thank my late parents, Eugen Wilhelm and Erika, who, despite living in extremely difficult circumstances during the war and in its aftermath, provided me with all the possibilities to become an international citizen. Through my parents, I got to meet people from other countries, to travel, and to study abroad. My father was also a role model in another way. He inspired me in his own role as company leader but also in his role of assuming many functions in the public life in post-war Germany, to embrace the stakeholder model. He demonstrated that business leaders should bring their experience and capabilities also to public functions and that we should all try and build a better world together.

For this, and for all you have done for me, I am eternally grateful.

Klaus Schwab

■ ■ ■

I also wish to acknowledge everyone who gave an interview for this book. Thank you for your time, your insights, and your contributions. (Names are listed alphabetically by first name)

Ahadu Wubshet, Founder and General Manager, Moyee Coffee, Addis Ababa, Ethiopia

Adi Reza Nugroho, Co-founder and Chief Executive Officer, MYCL, Bandung, Indonesia

Angel Gurria, Secretary-General, OECD, Paris, France

Araleh Daher, Sales Executive, APL, Djibouti City, Republic of Djibouti

Annisa Wibi Ismarlanti, Co-founder and Chief Financial Officer, MYCL, Bandung, Indonesia

Arekha Bentangan Lazuar, Co-founder and Chief Technology Officer, MYCL, Bandung, Indonesia

Asrat Begashaw, Manager, Public Relations, Ethiopian Airlines, Addis Ababa, Ethiopia

Carl Benedikt Frey, Director, Future of Work, Oxford Martin School, Oxford University, Oxford, UK

Chong'En Bai, Professor in Economics, Tsinghua University, Beijing, China

Claus Jensen, Forbundsformand, Dansk Metal, Copenhagen, Denmark

Daniel Moss, Opinion Columnist covering Asian economies, Bloomberg, Singapore

David Autor, Professor in Economics, MIT, Cambridge, Massachusetts, US

David Lin, Chief Science Officer, Global Footprint Network, Oakland, California, US

David M. Rubenstein, Co-founder and Co-executive Chairman, Carlyle Group, New York, US

Diane Coyle, Director, Bennett Institute for Public Policy, Cambridge University, Cambridge, UK

Dominic Waughray, Managing Director, Centre for Global Public Goods, World Economic Forum, Geneva, Switzerland

Fabiola Gianotti, Director-General, CERN, Geneva, Switzerland

Geert Noels, Chief Executive Officer, Econopolis, Antwerp, Belgium

Gideon Lichfield, Editor-in-Chief, *MIT Technology Review*, Cambridge, Massachusetts, US

Guohong Liu, Deputy Director, China Development Institute, Shenzhen, China

Greg Ip, Chief Economics Commentator, *The Wall Street Journal*, Washington, DC, US

Heather Long, Economics Correspondent, *The Washington Post*, Washington, DC, US

Heinrich Huentelmann, Head of Global Public Relations, Ravensburger, Ravensburg, Germany

James Crabtree, Associate Professor of Practice, Lee Kuan Yew School of Public Policy, Singapore

Jim Hagemann Snabe, Chairman, Siemens; Chairman, A.P. Moller Maersk, Copenhagen, Denmark

Joseph Stiglitz, University Professor, Economics, Columbia University, New York, US

Josh Bivens, Director of Research, Economic Policy Institute, Washington DC, US

Kai-Fu Lee, Chairman and Chief Executive Officer, Sinovation Ventures, Beijing, China

Laurence D. Fink, Chairman and Chief Executive Officer, BlackRock, New York, US

Lina Khan, Associate Professor of Law, Columbia University, New York, US

Liwei Wang, Senior Writer, Caixin Media, Beijing, China

Maha Eltobgy, Head of Shaping the Future of Investing, World Economic Forum, New York, US

Michelle Bachelet, High Commissioner for Human Rights, United Nations, Geneva, Switzerland

Min Zhu, Chairman, National Institute of Financial Research, Beijing, China

Nicholas Thompson, Editor-in-Chief, *Wired* magazine, New York, US

Nicholas Stern, Chair, Research Institute on Climate Change and the Environment, UCL, London, UK

Puty Puar, Illustrator and Content Creator, West Java, Indonesia

Richard Baldwin, Professor of International Economics, Graduate Institute, Geneva, Switzerland

Richard Samans, Director of Research, International Labour Organization, Geneva, Switzerland

Robert Atkinson, President, Information Technology and Innovation Foundation, Washington, DC, US

Robin Løffmann, Tillidsrepræsentant, MAN Energy Solutions, Copenhagen, Denmark

Roland Duchatelet, Founder, Melexis, Sint-Truiden, Belgium

Saadia Zahidi, Managing Director, Centre for the New Economy and Society, World Economic Forum, Geneva, Switzerland

Sean Cleary, Executive Chair, FutureWorld Foundation, Cape Town, South Africa

Seniat Sorsa, Local General Manager, Domestic Affairs, Everest, Awasa, Ethiopia

Susan Lund, Partner, McKinsey Global Institute, Washington, DC, US

Tharman Shanmugaratnam, Senior Minister, Government of Singapore, Singapore

Thomas Søby, Chief Economist, Dansk Metal, Copenhagen, Denmark

Tilahun Sarka, Director-General, Ethio-Djibouti Railways, Addis Ababa, Ethiopia

Tim Wu, Professor of Law, Science and Technology, Columbia Law School, New York, US

Tristan Schwennsen, Lead Archivist, Ravensburger, Ravensburg, Germany

Wei Tian, Host, World Insight with Tian Wei, CGTN, Beijing, China

William Utomo, Founder, IDN Media, Jakarta, Indonesia

Winston Utomo, Founder, IDN Media, Jakarta Indonesia

Yu Liu, Senior Research Fellow, Low-Carbon Economy, China Development Institute, Shenzhen, China

Zia Qureshi, Visiting Fellow, Global Economy and Development, Brookings Institution, Washington, DC, US

Index

Page references followed by *fig* indicates an illustration.